# Gains and Losses

Recent Titles in

# Gains and Losses

## *How Protestors Win and Lose*

JAMES M. JASPER, LUKE ELLIOTT-NEGRI,
ISAAC JABOLA-CAROLUS, MARC KAGAN,
JESSICA MAHLBACHER, MANÈS WEISSKIRCHER,
AND ANNA ZHELNINA

OXFORD
UNIVERSITY PRESS

# OXFORD
UNIVERSITY PRESS

Oxford University Press is a department of the University of Oxford. It furthers
the University's objective of excellence in research, scholarship, and education
by publishing worldwide. Oxford is a registered trade mark of Oxford University
Press in the UK and certain other countries.

Published in the United States of America by Oxford University Press
198 Madison Avenue, New York, NY 10016, United States of America.

CIP data is on file at the Library of Congress

ISBN 978-0-19-762326-8 (pbk.)
ISBN 978-0-19-762325-1 (hbk.)

DOI: 10.1093/oso/9780197623251.001.0001

1 3 5 7 9 8 6 4 2

Paperback printed by Marquis, Canada
Hardback printed by Bridgeport National Bindery, Inc., United States of America

*For Francesca Polletta, Christine Elliott-Negri,*
*Leeann Marie Graham, Gerhard Weisskircher, and Carine Clément*

# Contents

# Preface

On our high school football team, I played in the middle of the front line on the kickoff return team. My task was to block the kicker, whose job in turn was to linger around midfield in case our runner broke through. He was the other team's last line of defense. Our opponents scored often, allowing them to kick off, so I was in this position a lot. It was absurd: I was supposed to knock down a kid who was nowhere near the play (our runners never got to midfield).

In one game, at Sidwell Friends School in Washington, their kicker and I worked out a tacit understanding to take advantage of this silliness. After his first kick, as I ran toward him trying to look as menacing as possible, he pushed his hands toward the ground, in a gesture implying, "Cool it." On each succeeding kick I would run up close to him but not hit him, and he would not try to run around me. I felt I had found someone who took the game as unseriously as I did. (Those nonviolent Friends!)

Our little farce worked well until, as our kickoff return team took the field for the fourth or fifth time, Spence Leavitt, our hulking captain, shouted to me, "Knock somebody down, Jasp!" Had he noticed our charade? Had the coach noticed? I felt a wave of shame. Given our little agreement, it would have been easy to actually knock down the kicker this time, as he stood there unawares, and perhaps to give our side a boost of badly needed pride. But how could I do this to a well-meaning stranger? How could I break our separate peace?

Our arrangement worked fine in this game. But had our runner by some miracle broken through, the kicker and I would have suddenly been in the spotlight. We would have had to engage: he would have tried to tackle our runner, while I tried to stop him. He would have had an advantage, as he could see downfield whereas I was facing away from the rest of the action. He would have made a tackle; I would have been chewed out on the sideline.

In strategic engagements there are always games within games: in this example, offense, defense, kickoff team, return team; the frontline and the backfield; and at any given moment up to eleven pairs of players trying to overpower or trick each other. Some of the pairs remain the same, like the kicker and me, while others change depending on the play and over the course of a play. In the pros, individual players also think about their salaries and statistics; coaches worry about their jobs; the referees contemplate their aching knees. Not to mention boosters who bribe referees or give automobiles to amateur college players. Beyond who wins, each of these outcomes has repercussions—some more significant than others—on future action.

And while sports are an entertaining metaphor for strategic action, they are all quite simple compared to the players and arenas involved in political engagements.

The scholarly literature on social movements has focused on big outcomes like public policies or voting rights, ignoring the hundreds of smaller gains and losses that lead toward or away from these big achievements—or toward entirely unforeseen results. The traditional approach, correlating initial conditions and eventual outcomes, is a bit like looking for a connection between who wins the coin toss and who wins the match. Too much happens in between to allow much of a correlation. Recently, more outcomes have been studied, but in a rather random way—public opinion here, individual biographies there. We hope that by looking at a variety of players across diverse arenas, through long sequences of interaction, we can better understand the patterns of gains and losses they achieve.

Many debates in social science pit those who feel comfortable seeing structures in the world, frozen moments with related parts and some stability over time, against those who prefer to see fluidity and process, with all the parts moving at once. The study of social movements has shifted from structural to more fluid approaches in recent years, with one exception: the study of movement outcomes. Here we still tend to think of the rise of a movement, its work, then its impact, usually on a political system. Revolutions used to be the definitive model. This book adopts a different view, breaking down movements and political systems into smaller pieces. Then, we can see ongoing interactions, along with a constant flow of gains and losses, many of which are invisible in the structural perspective. The structural view is useful in many ways, but my hunch is that we are going to understand more about the consequences of protest if we adopt the fluid approach for a while.

In some ways this is a tragic or at least complex view of human life as full of tradeoffs, dilemmas, compromises, and losses that accompany any gains. It contrasts with the structural tradition in political thought, a progressive, Whiggish vision in which political structures eventually improve, incorporating the excluded, giving more rights to citizens, avoiding wars rather than seeking them. The structures are designed to exclude various groups, but eventually the barriers will fall. In a world of species extinctions and climate change, a world of Victor Orban, Recep Tayyip Erdogan, and Donald J. Trump, we must be sensitive to history's tragic setbacks as well as its occasional progress. Social movements make small gains, suffer backlashes, and are simply stymied by the rules of arenas built to contain and control them.

Our interactive approach is deeply cultural. We attempt to get inside players' heads as they assess situations, feel the weight of tradeoffs, make decisions, and build bonds with others, as they invent new players, arenas, and paths of action. Players watch and interpret each other's actions. Our tools exist at the intersection of culture and psychology, of tradition and innovation, of calculation and feelings. The point of view of players matters, even as they encounter the constraints of traditions, laws, resource distributions, and the traps and blockages imposed by other players. The Oxford Studies in Culture and Politics seems a good home for this book.

Compared to many studies of protest, in this book the reader will encounter many individuals, who feel, think, and make decisions that actually matter for interactions and outcomes. Far from being colorful illustrations of a point, they embody and grapple with the feelings, thoughts, tradeoffs, dilemmas, and decisions that propel our stories. They are the core of strategic interactions at a microlevel.

Since 1987 I have taught Ph.D. seminars on social movements at NYU, Princeton, the New School, and the CUNY Graduate Center. The students I had at the Grad Center in the fall of 2014 were the best group ever, and I could not resist asking several of them to work on a joint project, which became this book. One of them, Gabriele Cappelletti, dropped out early on, but we soon replaced him with a brilliant student from the European University Institute, Manès Weisskircher. Although each of my coauthors worked up one of the case studies, we jointly discussed the literature, worked out our theoretical framework, and wrote and edited the text.

We would like to thank Guya Accornero, Sean Ahern, Ed Amenta, Andrew Beane, Paul Bigman, Lorenzo Bosi, Alex Caring-Lobel, Candice Chau, Sarah Cherin, Arnold Cherry, Edward Chin, Karine Clement, Michael Davis, Donnatella della Porta, Bob Donegan, Steve Downs, Kevin Edberg, Paul Filson, David Freiboth, Joyce Gelb, Adam Glickman, Arthur Goldberg, Sarah Goldstein, Marty Goodman, Leeann Graham, Sonny Hall, Sterling

Harders, Ron Hayduk, Ksenia Isakova, Pramila Jayapal, Alexa Kasdan, David Katzman, Eddie Kay, Nicole Keenan-Lai, Ramy Khalil, Daria Khlevnyuk, Brayden G King, Anna Klepikova, Michael Koncewicz, Tatiana Kosinova, Maureen Lamar, Irving Lee, Mary Clare Lennon, Josh Lerner, Nick Licata, Erin Markman, George McAnanama, John McCarthy, Ruth Milkman, John Mollenkopf, Sejal Parikh, JP Patafio, Frances Fox Piven, Calvin Priest, Dieter Reinisch, Norman Resnick, Julia Rone, Jonathan Rosenblum, Alan Saly, Suzanne Sateline, Kshama Sawant, Tim Schermerhorn, Shoshana Seid-Green, Nienke, Kurt, and Katrina Schuler, Arthur Schwartz, Mike Scott, Leonard Smith, Russ Smith, Celina Su, Lynn Thompson, Ekaterina Trefilova, Anna Veduta, Joshua Welter, Sage Wilson, Howard Wright, Ming Xia, and an anonymous reviewer.

We also appreciate the aid and feedback provided by participants at the 2015 Collective Behavior and Social Movements Mini-Conference in Chicago, NYU's Tamiment Labor Library, PBNYC Staff and Steering Committee Members, the Public Opinion Programme at the University of Hong Kong, and the Scuola Normale Superiore in Florence. And of course we could not have produced this book without the many interviewees involved in the six cases.

Andy Andrews wrote a brilliant, generous review for the press. Also at OUP, James Cook shepherded the book for many years, backed up by the industrious Emily Mackenzie, awesome copy editor Lori Jacobs, and indexer Shoshana Seid-Green.

The wise and wonderful members of the Politics and Protest Workshop at the Graduate Center weighed in on two of these chapters, and we thank them for their suggestions. After presenting one of those chapters at the workshop, we went to a local Szechuan restaurant for dinner. My fortune cookie advised: "Failure is the tuition you pay for success." Defeats set processes in motion that can lead to later victories. This is only one of the many packages of gains and losses that we'll discover in the pages that follow.

James M. Jasper

# Acronym list

| | |
|---|---|
| CDP | Community Development Project |
| CE | Chief Executive |
| CFDT | Confédération Française Démocratique du Travail |
| CGT | Confédération Générale du Travail |
| CHRF | Civil Human Rights Front |
| CORE | Congress of Racial Equality |
| CUNY | City University of New York |
| CVH | Community Voices Heard |
| DDOS | Distributed denial of service |
| DPNI | Movement Against Illegal Immigration |
| HKFS | Hong Kong Federation of Students |
| HKPOP | Public Opinion Programme, University of Hong Kong |
| HKSAR | Hong Kong Special Administrative Region |
| HoW | *Hell on Wheels* |
| IIAC | Income Inequality Advisory Committee |
| KKK | Ku Klux Klan |
| KPÖ | Communist Party of Austria |
| LegCo | Legislative Council |
| MABSTOA | Manhattan and Bronx Surface Operating Authority |
| MSA | Main Street Alliance |
| NAACP | National Association for the Advancement of Colored People |
| ND | New Directions |
| NGO | Nongovernmental organization |
| NPCSC | National People's Congress Standing Committee |
| NYCT | New York City Transit |
| OA | *see* MABSTOA |
| OECD | Organisation for Economic Co-operation and Development |
| OHKLP | Occupy Hong Kong with Love and Peace |
| PB | Participatory budgeting |
| PBNYC | Participatory Budgeting in New York City |
| PBP | Participatory Budgeting Project |
| PCF | French Communist Party |
| PEGIDA | Patriotic Europeans Against the Islamization of the Occident |

# Introduction

## The Long Game

Every advantage is temporary.

—Katerina Stoykova Klemer

In warfare there are no constant conditions.

—Sun Tzu

Let's begin where so many theories of protest have started, with the US civil rights movement. In 1961, SNCC (the Student Nonviolent Coordinating Committee) was running a voter registration drive in one of the nation's most racially backward places, the hill country of Southwest Mississippi. They began with Freedom Schools, to help local Black residents learn enough about the state constitution to pass a test interpreting it. Organizer Bob Moses then took six of the students to the courthouse in McComb, where they passed the test. Several others were allowed to fill out registration forms. Local Black citizens were excited and impressed, and support for the young SNCC organizers grew.

Powerful local whites did not at first grasp what a registration drive was, or where it might lead. But "as local authorities came to understand that something was going on more systematic than a few individuals trying to register, things got tougher" (Payne 1995: 115–116). Moses was arrested, then badly beaten. The handful of completed registration forms mysteriously disappeared. Harassing crowds appeared in front of the registrar's counter. Local African Americans persisted, but the costs facing them increased. All the initial gains disappeared.

But other gains replaced them. SNCC was blocked at the registrar's office but impressed potential supporters and participants. The beatings they took gained them credibility. Besides, setbacks can be learning experiences.

*Gains and Losses.* James M. Jasper, Luke Elliott-Negri, Isaac Jabola-Carolus, Marc Kagan, Jessica Mahlbacher, Manès Weisskircher, and Anna Zhelnina, Oxford University Press. © Oxford University Press 2022.
DOI: 10.1093/oso/9780197623251.003.0001

"McComb is always remembered as a defeat for SNCC, which is true in a narrow sense, but it overlooks the fact that SNCC learned in McComb that merely the process of trying to organize a town would attract young people" (Payne 1995: 119). The blocked registration efforts won admiration, recruits, and lessons that could be applied elsewhere. Modest short-run gains led opponents to mobilize to eliminate those gains, but the movement in turn used that setback to strengthen itself for the longer run. *Gains and losses come in complex combinations.* Some are unpredictable bundles, but others are familiar packages that we can anticipate in advance to the extent that we understand strategic dilemmas and linkages between arenas.

Social movements are a key source of change in the modern world, so it matters to all of us what helps them win and what makes them lose. Along with corporations and states, protest groups and their close cousins, nongovernmental organizations (NGOs), struggle to shape history. They battle over cultural understandings, public policies and laws, the rules that govern strategic arenas, and much more. These struggles may rage for years and decades, even as the players and arenas change. We need to understand when and how protestors win or lose, but also *what* they win and lose.

Theories of protest and social movements have turned toward strategy in recent years, as intellectual fashions shifted from structures to action and agency. Political opportunity structures have been replaced or at least joined by political processes and mediation. We now appreciate that protestors interact with a variety of other strategic players and targets, in a number of structured arenas, and that they do not simply face a static "environment." Players on all sides encounter strategic tradeoffs, grapple with dilemmas, respond to other players, and make decisions. As a result of this paradigm shift, fine-grained microlevel histories have increasingly replaced broad structural hypotheses and correlations in empirical studies. Scholars trace processes through detailed sequences of mechanisms.

Chapter 1 presents our heuristic language of players and arenas, gains and losses, and bundles and packages in more detail. The players-and-arenas terminology is intended to highlight the many types of human interactions. Players take many forms, including individuals, informal groups, formal organizations, and factions within groups and organizations, all the way up to nation-states. The ways they engage each other are almost infinite. Sometimes they do so in well-organized and familiar arenas purposefully designed to generate decisions, but also in backstages, such as living rooms, that are meant to affect formal arenas only indirectly. Players and arenas suggest an interpretative, strategic, and mostly microlevel approach to explanation.[1]

The new dynamic and strategic models allow us to rethink an old issue, the success and the consequences of protest. The dominant structural approach saw success when challengers managed to conquer barriers to participation, in order to join a polity, and when they gained new laws and policies that favored their constituents. But many structurally oriented scholars were uneasy talking about success at all, as this might hinge on the subjective point of view of participants. Most of these scholars began to talk instead about the outcomes and consequences of movements, allowing for the possibility of negative outcomes as well as positive or neutral ones, unintended as well as intended ones. But as they tried to avoid the goals of players, they sometimes lost any sense of the emotional and cognitive dynamics that accompany *feelings* of failure or success.

A strategic outlook suggests a combination of the two concerns: there are a variety of outcomes, some of them related to goals and others not, and a few of which are big successes or failures. But mostly there are small gains and losses, which may or may not ever add up to ultimate success. In a (US) football match, we speak of a gain or a loss (of yards) on each play. These may or may not add up to points on the board before the other team takes possession of the ball, yet the resulting position on the field or time of possession may indeed affect later outcomes—depending on how ensuing interactions unfold. It is also possible for a team to advance the ball all the way down the field in one overwhelming play, to score a touchdown.

Politics is more complex than games, with many types of gains and losses. Each player and subplayer has its own intentions, gains, and losses for each relevant arena. As Jon Elster (1989: 42) puts it, "It is often useful to think of an action as generating an indefinite *stream* of (intended or expected) outcomes or consequences." (We would add unintended, unexpected outcomes to the stream as well.) The language of gains and losses implies an alternative to both success/failure and consequences models, combining the strengths of each but also going beyond them to the causal mechanisms beneath them.

---

[1] For more on this players-and-arenas framework, also dubbed the strategic-interaction paradigm, see Accornero (2021), Duyvendak and Jasper (2015), Jasper (2021), Jasper and Duyvendak (2015), Jones et al. (2018), Stoddart et al. (2021), and Verhoeven and Duyvendak (2017). Field theory contains some similar intuitions: Fligstein and McAdam (2012). Elsewhere, Jasper describes the shift from structure to strategy (2012b) and from macro to micro (2010, 2012a) in more detail. Also see Jasper and King (2020).

Most strategic engagements are long wars of position (fought in the trenches, if you prefer that metaphor). There is no single battle that decides everything, no final court decision or vote, after which all the strategic players pack up and go home. Yes, some decisions are more sweeping than others, and some lead to the mobilization or demobilization of players. But these decisive moments are the exception, not the rule. Almost always the players or subsets of players regroup or reform, or turn their attention to other goals and arenas. *Politics is a game of gains and losses, of various sizes, in many arenas, over long periods of time.* Players have more short-run tactical goals than long-run strategic goals, and the unintended outcomes usually outnumber the intended.[2]

A strategic perspective encourages attention to different players in different arenas. This again contrasts with the structural view, which tended to simplify the world into insiders and outsiders, usually a state versus a movement. That dichotomized view of conflict, with two primary sides pitted against one another, lends itself to a zero-sum view of decisive outcomes, in which one player loses when the other wins. The challenger gains entry to the polity; a social movement wins a law that benefits its members. If, instead, we acknowledge a number of different compound players (and subplayers within each), in shifting alliances and with many things at stake, we can more easily recognize the multiple gains and losses in wars of position. It may not be useful to talk about the success or impact of a "social movement" at all.

What we call social movements rise and fall, or at least it seems that way due to media labels and coverage. *But the players that comprise movements continue, sometimes under new labels.* Individuals and organizations regroup, take a break, rethink their goals, and adopt new causes or tactics. This kind of activity is hard to trace using a structural model of a polity and its challengers. One reason that it is difficult to define "the impact" of a social movement is that a social movement itself is hard to identify. Scholars often resort to linking prospective movements to demographic categories such as class, race, or sexual orientation: the women's movement, gay rights, the labor movement.

The question of when movements "emerge" is just as misleading as that of their consequences. It is rare for an entirely new movement to appear;

[2] Our critique of outcomes resonates with social theory more generally. Abbott (2007: 4; also 2005) questions the very concept of "outcomes" for individuals in nonstrategic as well as strategic settings. "People move endlessly through the life course. They become different people and strangely enough, they now often live so long . . . that they have outlived old regimes of inequality, only to inhabit new ones." Like compound players, individuals change, partly in relation to the arenas they enter.

instead, new issues are taken up by remnants of older movements, by the same individuals, networks, and formal organizations that have participated in other causes. Even the issues are not entirely new, but they typically are related to existing ideologies and sensibilities. In many cases, factions of an existing movement apply their vision to new areas. The US Civil Rights movement did not spring to life in 1954 or 1955 but stretches back to Reconstruction, and before that to Abolition and enslaved people's revolts.

By taking seriously the points of view of players, a strategic approach confronts the numerous tradeoffs and dilemmas that players face. (We define *tradeoffs* as preexisting, always lurking there; they become *dilemmas* when players recognize and grapple with them.) They are the reason that decision-making is difficult. Every option comes with benefits, costs, and risks, some of them relatively certain (the cost of supplies, for instance) and some of them very uncertain (the likelihood of police violence or a dictator's overthrow). Many moves result in gains *at the same time* as losses. Jasper (2006) has highlighted dozens of these tradeoffs, and in this book we will encounter many of them in the course of accounting for gains and losses. Table I.1 lists some common ones.

These tradeoffs often combine gains and losses into recurrent, familiar packages. A package begins with a strategy, that is, a set of decisions in response to several related dilemmas. The choices reflect the hopes and goals of a strategic player but also contain risks; each strategy involves a flow of uncertain gains and losses. Once players embark on strategic paths, they may not be able to manage the results as well as they would like; they end up with a package of results. The chapters to follow highlight a number of prominent packages, notably arena creation, institutionalization, an electoral package, issue ownership, radicalism, and the charismatic personality.

Another way that we incorporate the perspectives of strategic players in this book is by examining their emotions, evident especially in talk of hope and disappointment and victory and defeat. The language of success or failure makes for moving stories, which is why activists and recruiters talk that way. We are inspired by success, by the idea that we can change history. And we are angered, outraged, and saddened by failure, sometimes encouraging and sometimes discouraging further action. *Perceptions* of success and failure are crucial to a theory of action, even if structural theories avoid them.

Just as wars consist of many battles on many fronts, social movements pursue many objectives across a variety of arenas. Chapter 1 reviews the trajectory by which specialists went from strategy to structure and then back to strategy over the last fifty years. It also lays out our own approach to the

**Table I.1**  Some Common Strategic Dilemmas

---

**Being There:** Players select what arenas they will operate in. They may decide to boycott an arena, hoping to discredit or cripple it. But in absenting themselves they give up considerable control over what happens there.

**Engagement Dilemma:** Players open interactions or enter arenas with the hope of favorable outcomes. But even the most powerful player can never fully control what happens in an arena. Every new engagement entails some risk.

**Extension Dilemma:** Most players try to expand, by making alliances or recruiting individuals, but expansion brings greater difficulties in coordination and agreement.

**False-Arenas Dilemma:** A player may enter a new arena only to discover that the arena's influence is curtailed in order to limit the player's power. But if it refuses to participate, it may look stubborn or duplicitous.

**Janus Dilemma:** Players devote some time and attention to its own members, and some to outsiders such as opponents. They need the former to survive, the latter to have an impact. The balance between the two varies enormously.

**Naughty-or-Nice Dilemma:** Players that are more disruptive, aggressive, and willing to break the rules of an arena sometimes get what they want that way, but they typically lose some popularity and admiration in doing so. Plus, aggressive players may arouse repression by the authorities.

**Powerful-Allies Dilemma:** A player may get more of what it wants by having allies that are more powerful than it is, but those allies may use that player for their own purposes rather than in pursuit of its goals.

**Pyramid Dilemma:** Players may be more centralized and hierarchic, or less. There are advantages to each structure.

---

*Sources:* Jasper (2004, 2006).

gains and losses that strategic players experience as they try to advance. The following chapters present six empirical cases that helped us develop the language and themes that chapter 1 presents.

Chapter 2 traces the process by which Seattle became the first US city to adopt a $15-an-hour minimum wage. It highlights engagement dilemmas, when players face choices about which arenas would give them the most gains. We also see that players who control positions and resources can design new arenas to get what they want. Mayor Ed Murray formed not one but two small arenas before he accomplished his goals. The *creation of an arena* brings a package of potential risks and outcomes.

Chapter 3 moves to New York City, tracing the development of participatory budgeting (PB), a reform won by activists in 2011 that gives residents a direct voice in selected city budget decisions. The city council's gradual expansion of PB exemplifies a common *institutionalization package*: in exchange for stability and resources (especially paid staff time), proponents of

PB lost control over the program's direction. Protest groups that manage to attain some policy influence almost always face something like this institutionalization package and the strategic dilemmas that it entails.

In chapter 4 we observe a fifteen-year insurgent movement inside New York's Transport Workers Union. Beginning as an effort to encourage workplace job actions, the organization evolved into an electoral vehicle that ultimately won control of the union. Gains and losses along the way led to changes in its membership, leadership, perspectives, and priorities, all part of an *electoral package*. The "successful" outcome in union elections was muddied by the in-fighting necessary to achieve it.

Graz, Austria's second largest city, is the setting for chapter 5, which scrutinizes the local communist party's persistent electoral support in the face of communists' decline almost everywhere else in Austria—and the world. The chapter underlines the importance of multiple arenas for this radical left player, beyond the legislature and the government, the arenas that political parties are usually associated with. Politics of direct help on the one hand, and mobilization through awareness-raising, direct-democracy campaigns, and street protests on the other hand, produced a boomerang effect that brought gains in the arenas of parliament and government. The communists managed to bolster their reputations across arenas by coming to *own the issue* of housing.

Chapter 6 looks at the beginning of Hong Kong's Umbrella Movement, a seventy-nine-day occupation of government and commercial areas. The organization Occupy Hong Kong with Love and Peace (OHKLP) advocated mass civil disobedience to pressure the Chinese government to grant the region universal suffrage. Yet in the end, the organization neither initiated nor controlled the occupation. Internal struggles within the pan-democracy movement influenced the gains and losses that OHKLP experienced. Moreover, the actions of the government, which as a compound player also contained internal discord, empowered more radical players within the pan-democratic camp, helping them kindle the Umbrella Movement. *Radical strategies* such as occupations offer a package of great publicity along with decentralization of control, risking public disapproval via the naughty-or-nice tradeoff.

We travel to Moscow in chapter 7, where electoral reformers faced an intransigent regime. Opposition politician Alexei Navalny and his team tried to transfer the gains they had made in street politics in the course of the "Winter Revolution" of 2011–2012 into electoral arenas, most notably in

Moscow's mayoral elections in 2013. Their efforts to turn the false arenas of authoritarian elections into open-ended arenas where gains could be made had mixed results: on the one hand, the new players, Alexei Navalny and his team, developed and established a broad reputation; on the other, their impressive effort inspired more government repression. A number of individuals advanced their own careers while the broader movement dissipated. With this case we discuss the *personality package*, in which both symbolic and strategic power are vested heavily in a single person.

In all these cases, we dig beneath the headline outcomes to see a complexity of gains and losses. Many of these extend to other arenas, and to other players. Individuals, for example, are often relevant players who take their lessons and reputations with them to new movements and new arenas. Most of the arenas we examine are city-level, which may offer greater access to grassroots groups, but we believe that the same interactive dynamics operate in arenas of wider scope and with different rules.

Our cases are not a random or representative sample of protest efforts. They reflect our own experiences and interests. We tried to find instances in which there was some significant headline gain, in order to see what other losses and gains there were behind the headlines. Those acknowledged gains include elections (chapters 4, 5, and 7), policy advances (chapters 2, 3, and 5), and dramatic mobilizations (chapters 2, 6, and 7). But our unit of analysis is not a "movement" and its "impact" but smaller things like strategic choices, losses, and gains, so we have plenty of observations from which to draw conclusions. We just cannot generalize about "the" outcome of a movement, since we view both of those terms as a bit fictional.

In the conclusion, we address how to build from the local, microlevel of interaction back up to the big things that have interested so many political analysts: revolutions, capitalism, social change, and so on. Some interactions have decisive consequences, such as the storming of St. Petersburg's Winter Palace (at least as portrayed in later Soviet mythmaking). In other cases, a number of different interactions add up to something big. In all cases, we need to trace long chains of interactions, with gains and losses along the way, to assess the real outcomes of politics. The actions of SNCC and the civil rights movement are still reverberating through American politics today, faintly for a while but with renewed energy recently in the form of Black Lives Matter. All politics is local, but the most local events can have broad consequences.

# 1

# Theories of Strategic Outcomes

> Politics is a strong and slow boring of hard boards. It takes both pas-
> sion and perspective.
>
> —Max Weber

Inspired by the social movements that scholars saw around them in the
late 1960s, they began to study those movements as a rational political process distinct from crowds and fads, naturally asking what caused those
movements to succeed or fail. According to the new view, movements (and
especially the organizations that comprise them) articulate goals and promote policies as strategic players with ends and means, and so their progress can be evaluated in light of their goals. In contrast to their predecessors,
who feared the crowds they studied, the new generation of researchers cared
about the success of protestors for political as well as intellectual reasons.
They wanted to help (most of) them win.

Yet their strategic concerns were soon swamped by more structural
models, inspired by Charles Tilly's long historical studies and by cross-national comparisons such as Theda Skocpol's study of revolutions. This research had little interest in cognitive and emotional processes, including
strategic decision-making. In the 1990s, the pendulum began to swing back,
toward culture and meaning, agency and strategy, and even emotions. Today,
strategic models acknowledge constraints in the surrounding environment
but seek to grasp how they are internalized in the perspectives of the players
facing them. In different ways, they integrate structure, strategy, and culture.
Theories of structure and theories of action have begun to blend.

*Gains and Losses.* James M. Jasper, Luke Elliott-Negri, Isaac Jabola-Carolus, Marc Kagan, Jessica
Mahlbacher, Manès Weisskircher, and Anna Zhelnina, Oxford University Press. © Oxford University Press 2022.
DOI: 10.1093/oso/9780197623251.003.0002

## From Strategies to Structures

When do protestors win and when do they lose? Frances Fox Piven and Richard Cloward (1977) famously argued that disruptive protest is more likely to succeed, at least for poor people, but as organizations become more formal and bureaucratic, they tend to discourage just this kind of disruption. Some groups have more "disruptive power" than others, positioned so that they can shut down processes that their opponents value, through tactics like sit-down strikes in factories or boycotts and lunch-counter sit-ins for civil rights (Luders 2010; Piven 2006).

In our gains-and-losses framework, we can reformulate Piven and Cloward's work as highlighting two strategic dilemmas. Disruption, whether peaceful or violent, poses the naughty-or-nice dilemma: it is sometimes possible to intimidate your opponents into quick concessions, but breaking the rules frequently damages your reputation as a morally admirable player (Jasper 2006: 106). In the long run you may lose allies and public support. The aggressive option usually makes sense if the public already dislikes you, or if the potential gains are substantial and cannot easily be reversed later on.

Piven and Cloward view formal organizations as undermining a group's chances for success. The founding of new organizations creates new goals for protestors, namely, the maintenance and growth of those organizations themselves—institutional well-being—that divert attention from external engagement. Other scholars counter that organizations can sometimes advance their members' goals. The debate reflects a tradeoff and the organization dilemma (Jasper 2004): there are some tactics that bureaucracies do well and some they do poorly. They may be better at regular activities, such as accumulating resources and building organizational infrastructure (Andrews 2004), than at short-term massive resistance like general strikes. They give up short-run disruptive potential in exchange for longevity as players.[1]

The naughty-or-nice and organization dilemmas are linked in Piven and Cloward's model: planning for the long-run survival of the organization prevents protestors from taking advantage of short-run anger and outrage, which offer their only real chance to mobilize large numbers and pressure

---

[1] Another way to analyze these organizations is that they provide benefits primarily for those leaders and staff employed by them, splitting a player into two subplayers with conflicting interests (also Ahlquist and Levi 2013). Thanks to Fran Piven for this observation.

elites. This is especially true of the poor people's movements that Piven and Cloward studied. As often occurs, resolving one dilemma affects what happens with others. What kind of player you are is always linked to what you will do, and short-run versus long-run tradeoffs are ubiquitous in the world of strategic interaction.

Identifying strategic tradeoffs and dilemmas helps us make sense of the mixed empirical results found for disruption. Most researchers analyze one outcome at a time, and whether violence or disruption works may depend on which impact a scholar chooses to measure. Every short-run gain or loss affects the movement or organization's future development in subtle and dynamic ways. We disaggregate success and failure into assorted gains and losses, examining how they are related, what determines the balance, and what this means for future engagements.[2]

In contrast to Piven and Cloward's contempt for formal organizations, William Gamson (1975) counted organizational stability and recognition as a form of success. He distinguished two kinds of success: recognition of the group as a legitimate representative of some population and benefits for that population. The former consists of a group's right to enter new arenas; the latter is whether they can get what they want in those arenas. As we will see in chapter 3, institutionalization carries a familiar package of gains in resources, stability, and longevity, combined with losses in control and often a shift in goals (which many protestors scorn as a watering down).[3]

Like Piven and Cloward, Gamson was especially interested in the role of violence and disruption in movement success.[4] By looking at a wide sample

[2] Some authors find that violent strikes are more successful than peaceful ones (Shorter and Tilly 1971), while others find the opposite (Snyder and Kelly 1976). Of course, strikes are already disruptive; violence is much *more* disruptive but also more *frightening* to bystanders and other players. Emotional reactions differ according to the threats. We need to dig beneath these broad correlations to get at the packages of gains and losses at work; violent and nonviolent disruption may differ enormously in how they unfold. Chenoweth and Schock (2015) found what the naughty-or-nice dilemma would predict: violence produces more benefits in the short run than in the long run. Nonviolence helps build a broader, more diverse superplayer to promote change, and during the transition, arenas are created that foster nonviolent means (Chenoweth and Stephan 2011).

[3] Gamson's concern with the institutionalization of a movement had parallels in research in political science on the formation of parties. Herbert Kitschelt (1989) examined the ecology movement and the parties it created, as if that kind of institutionalization were the ultimate fate or goal of successful movements. Other scholars saw this as the cooptation and demobilization of movements (Alvarez and Escobar 1992; Wallerstein 2002). Structural approaches leave little room for the complex tradeoffs involved in processes such as institutionalization. (But see Combes 2015, who views parties through a players-and-arenas lens.)

[4] Although Gamson (1975: 74) refers to them as "unruly," he examines violence ("deliberate physical injury to property or persons"); Piven and Cloward (1977: 18) view mass violence as one form of defiance and disruption among others.

of cases, Gamson had to ignore a great deal of contextual nuance in order to isolate a broad correlation between aggression and success, based in turn on a dichotomized view of the players: *challengers* face *elites* who want to keep them out or exploit them. Only by threatening and embarrassing elites, by dividing them, or by taking away their profits or legitimacy can protestors gain concessions. Piven and Cloward examined how poor people's movements won, but they too operated with dichotomized models of challenger-authority and success–failure. Protestors have to select the right strategic key to open the gates of political arenas.

Because Gamson and Piven and Cloward were active in the movements of the 1960s, they focused on what protestors could and should *do*. Another great scholar of the time, Charles Tilly, taking a long historical view, saw protestors as highly constrained by available repertoires of action and thus lacking meaningful strategic choices. Instead, their success in both mobilizing and gaining concessions depends on the state's ability to fight back. Because he saw states partly as bands of economic and military thugs, he did not expect them to give up power or include newcomers unless forced to, perhaps when the state elites are themselves badly divided or when a war has devastated their coercive capacities. When states weaken, challengers can occasionally push their way in. Insurgents have little control over the conditions that matter to their success; institutional arenas tend to be solid.[5]

The ultimate model of preexisting conditions was political opportunity structure theory in the 1980s, derived from Tilly's state-centric viewpoint. Political opportunity structures explained both the mobilization and the success of movements; all of a movement's gains are tightly correlated, because they all take advantage of the same political openings. Not all insurgents take advantage of the opportunities, but those who do are likely to mobilize, enter an arena, and succeed there. Key openings include the fiscal collapse of the state, defeat of its armies in war, and deep splits in political–economic elites (McAdam 1982; Skocpol 1979). Revolutions were often the model of success.[6]

---

[5] Tilly (1978: 222) primarily addressed the problem of success or impacts in the form of revolutionary outcomes, which, he said, are too complicated and normatively charged to allow scholars to explain much beyond "facile generalizations." This makes sense to us, in that successful revolutions involve results in many different arenas. His respect for historical complexity generally prevented Tilly from looking for simple correlations between preexisting conditions and later outcomes.

[6] Reflecting the spirit but not yet the language of political-opportunity theory, Jack Goldstone (1980) reanalyzed Gamson's data to find that organizational and tactical factors made little difference to success. What did matter was some sort of state crisis, especially external crises such as wars, which

Political-opportunity models primarily addressed the timing of a movement and its success: why did it emerge *now* rather than earlier or later? A submerged assumption, common among historical–structural theories, was that groups like African Americans, the working class, or women eventually *had* to be incorporated into the polity. History was on their side; the civil sphere tends toward inclusion (Alexander 2006). The question was when, not if.[7]

This focus on oppressed groups demanding citizenship led political-opportunity theorists to explain both mobilization and success in the same way. If a citizenship movement simply grew large enough, it could almost inevitably force its way into the polity—sooner or later. The problematic relationship between mobilization and success was not yet obvious. With Tilly and Doug McAdam, structure eclipsed Piven and Cloward and Gamson's concern with strategy in theories of protestors' success or failure.

## From Outcomes to Interactions

In the late 1990s, most scholars shifted altogether from explaining success or failure to a language of consequences, outcomes (Giugni, McAdam, and Tilly 1999), and impacts (Amenta and Young 1999). This makes sense from a structural perspective because it abandons the messy perceptions, feelings, and choices of the players. These scholars followed McAdam and Tilly more than Gamson and Piven and Cloward—but they soon worked their way back to strategic models.[8]

One scholar of this move, Marco Giugni (1999: xx–xxi), offers three reasons for the shift to outcomes.[9] First, "success or failure tends to be attributed to an

allowed groups to gain inclusion. Goldstone interpreted this more as a need to rally around the flag, but it could also be attributed to the weakness of the state.

[7] The Whiggish view of history as progress was never well tested outside the European and American contexts, and even there it seems questionable in the face of fascism's rise a century ago but also the recent authoritarian turn of countries such as Hungary, Poland, Russia, Turkey, and Donald Trump's America.

[8] Even McAdam, Tarrow, and Tilly (2001) shifted from a structural toward a more strategic perspective, although their proliferation of terms confused many readers. Our mechanisms are more consistently social–psychological than theirs, but our packages are roughly parallel to their "processes" ("frequently recurring causal chains, sequences, and combinations of mechanisms": 27). Similar too is their relative (and newfound) lack of interest in big outcomes. "Revolutions," they say (226), "are not A Single Thing."

[9] We selected Giugni to represent arguments in favor of the shift from success to outcomes because of the influence of *How Social Movements Matter* and because they are also articulated more fully in Kriesi et al. 1995. Interestingly, when Kriesi et al. (1995: 212) list fourteen types of impacts

entire movement." This is a problem for many questions in the social movements literature, not just the issue of success. Movements are never sufficiently unified to be a well-defined player—although (for their own rhetorical purposes) their members often claim to be. An interactionist framework avoids this problem by insisting on clarity about the players and typically rejecting "social movements" as the relevant players. Instead, we look for players or subplayers who share clear goals and work together, usually organizations with mission statements but also factions and ultimately individuals. If success and failure tend to be attributed to social movements, gains and losses can be linked more easily to subplayers of those movements.

Second, Giugni—reflecting his structuralist roots in political-opportunity theory—rejects success as overly subjective: "Movement participants and external observers may have different perceptions of the success of a given action." Even within a movement, different factions and individuals may have different definitions of success (a way of saying that they have different goals). Again, this actually helps us to distinguish different subplayers (not only different organizations but different parts of an organization, like its leaders and staff versus its rank-and-file members), whose expectations and reactions matter. They have different emotions if they believe they have won or lost, with an impact on their subsequent actions. Analyzing players' beliefs about success and failure does not prevent a scholar from adding her own assessment of what a player has gained or lost, especially if we recognize the multiplicity of gains and losses.

Third, success is a problematic explanandum, according to Giugni, because "it overemphasizes the intention of movement participants in producing certain changes (xxi)." But attention to intended outcomes does not preclude additional acknowledgement of unintended consequences, a staple of the sociological tradition. Once we put aside a simple dichotomized outcome (success or failure) and look at a range of consequences, we can easily see both intended and unintended ones, sometimes in familiar combinations. Intended outcomes in one arena are frequently linked to unintended outcomes in another.

that movements can have, eight have to do with changes in players, four with changes in arenas, and only two with outcomes *in* arenas. In *How Social Movements Matter,* Amenta and Young (1999) argue for the term "impacts" because it moves even further from success and failure; they look instead for collective benefits for a movement's constituents. They remain close to the outcomes paradigm in focusing on relationships to the state, changes in arenas as the highest benefits, a concern with "important" results (22), and rejection of group affirmation as a collective benefit (35). Amenta would move further from the outcomes paradigm in later work, as we see below.

Because an interactionist gains–losses approach insists that we incorporate the intentions of *all* players, we quickly see the obvious: the intentions of a protest group interact (sometimes clashing, sometimes overlapping) with those of its opponents and other players. Complex interactions among *all* players' intentions and actions, along with the rules and conditions of the arenas, and a fair amount of contingency during the engagements, all lead to complicated results. Success and failure remain useful factors, joined with many other results. We use a player's intentions to explain its actions, and these actions in turn help to account for outcomes; intentions only indirectly and sometimes remotely affect outcomes. In fact, Giugni (1999: xxiv) recognizes this, embracing a more interactive view, in which we should gather evidence not only about "a given movement and its alleged outcomes but also about the actions of other actors."[10]

The central architect of the reintegration of strategy and structure, Edwin Amenta (2014: 27), captures this shift in perspective toward symmetric attention to multiple players: "The transformation of movements from something to be explained, to an explanation of political phenomena, means starting from politics and working back to movements, without losing sight of them. After all, these are not 'movement outcomes' as the literature often claims, but political outcomes that may sometimes be influenced by movements." We need to look at what happens in arenas, where protestors but also many other players operate.

The "outcomes" literature usefully pushed beyond the explicit goals of social movements, but perhaps not far enough. Most research in this tradition continues to focus on the kinds of impacts that protestors explicitly seek, especially policy decisions and voting rights. Because these are usually complex outcomes that have gone through many arenas, scholars have had a hard time isolating cases of clear movement influence. But the long game includes many more gains and losses, such as shifts in alliances, the stabilization and

---

[10] A recent volume on movement impacts, *The Consequences of Social Movements*, still operates within the outcomes paradigm (Bosi, Giugni, and Uba 2016), but in attempting to fill some of that paradigm's "silences," it brings attention to alternatives. One third of the book is devoted to the biographical consequences of activism, suggesting that if we break players down into their component parts—from movements to organizations, then to factions within organizations, moderate versus radical flanks, down to subfactions, then we eventually arrive at individuals, who may pursue their own goals distinct from the group's goals. *The Consequences of Social Movements*, in its title, accepts social movements as players, but the book also nods to new arenas (specifically markets) and players (corporations). These are certainly important in today's world, but they are just the beginning of the kind of catalogue of players and arenas that would move us beyond the outcomes paradigm (McAdam and Boudet 2012; Uba and Romanos 2016).

positioning of formal organizations, cultural impacts on players and publics, the careers and reputations of individuals, and (often grudging) acceptance into new arenas. *Players and arenas are both transformed along the way to the more obvious outcomes.*

Taking into account multiple players and arenas also allows us to see strategic decision-making more clearly. Amenta shows that different strategies are appropriate to different situations, pushing beyond simple correlations between strategies and success. Amenta (2006: 26–28) suggests that assertive strategies are the best option for challengers when politicians and bureaucrats are unsympathetic. In such cases, assertive strategies such as ballot initiatives or new political parties are necessary. When regimes are more sympathetic, educational and informational campaigns may suffice. Giugni (2007) offered a similar "joint effects" model: movement actions must appear alongside favorable institutional conditions in order to succeed (also Halfmann 2010).

We need to distinguish arenas as well as strategies: each arena offers both moderate and aggressive or transgressive strategies. Assertion involves both the choice of arenas and the choice of tactics within them. (In Amenta's example, creating a new party and conducting an educational campaign are actions in different arenas and are not mutually exclusive.) Even then, the strategic choice is not a simple one between naughty or nice but depends on specific circumstances and timing in each arena. At a general level, we cannot do much better than observing, "For the most radical results, challengers have to do everything in their power and be fairly lucky" (Amenta 2006: 29).[11] Because we will never find simple correlations between initial conditions or choices and external outcomes, we must dig beneath the level of broad correlations to the mechanisms beneath.

Amenta's assertive strategies return us to the naughty-or-nice dilemma. Whether aggression works depends on how other players respond. A targeted politician, acting rationally, could go either way: bow to the intense pressure or react sharply in rejecting it. Any human being, capable of emotions such as anger, may be more likely to reject pressure tactics, perhaps even in the face of calculations that recommend doing the opposite. We may need to know more about those individuals: their sense of honor; their outrage or bitterness; do they feel betrayed or desperate? What personal relationships

---

[11] General strategic observations—and advice—are always abstract, thanks to what Jasper calls the hollow core of strategy, the fact that there is so often a real dilemma and a choice to be made that cannot be calculated in advance but reflects the myriad nuances of the moment (see Jasper 2006: 181–184, on the abstract—and not very helpful—quality of most strategic advice).

do they have with allies and foes? Biography is often a central piece of the explanatory puzzle.

Major laws and policies may seem like simple decisions, because (in most political systems) they ultimately face a vote in a legislature and are signed by an executive. In fact, they have passed through many arenas on the way to this final passage. Legislation results from many small gains and losses. We cannot simply add those up, however, as some are more influential than others; a loss in one arena, such as a key parliamentary committee, can be fatal to a plan (but not to a movement). We cannot understand the final outcomes without following engagements in all those arenas. Even new legislation is rarely a full endpoint. Many laws are simply "stepping stones" to later ones (Evans 2015), and implementation is a notorious arena of its own, or set of arenas (Andrews 2001; Pressman and Wildavsky 1973).[12]

Amenta (2006: 28) distinguishes different phases of the policy process: agenda setting, content, passage, and implementation. (Burstein, Einwohner, and Hollander (1995) and other authors have similar lists.) We can flesh out these categories by seeing them as distinct arenas, which Amenta suggests operate in a fixed sequence but which can also operate simultaneously. We can look at media coverage, legislative committees, courtrooms, and administrative bureaucracies for the interactions and outcomes that occur there. Protest groups may have more influence in agenda-setting arenas (King, Bentele, and Soule 2007; King, Cornwall, and Dahlin 2005; Soule and King 2006) and in implementation arenas (Kitschelt 1986).

The reader will realize that there is not a unified "movement" operating in each of these arenas but distinct subplayers usually corresponding to formal organizations. To cite the civil rights movement again, the National Association for the Advancement of Colored People (NAACP) pursued civil rights through the courts; the Southern Christian Leadership Conference (SCLC) through mass meetings and marches; the Student Nonviolent Coordinating Committee (SNCC) through direct action such as sit-ins; and the Congress of Racial Equality (CORE) directed the Freedom Rides. (Even SNCC nearly split in two in 1961 when one faction wanted to pursue voter

---

[12] Research on outcomes in other arenas also tends to concentrate on a single ultimate reward. In US labor research, the most studied outcome is probably union certification elections, a big prize. When they are the dependent variable, it is easy to overlook the decisions and processes that brought the union to that moment, such as which workers will be included in the bargaining unit, as well as the subsequent arenas in which actual bargaining occurs (or, often, fails to occur) even after the union is certified.

registration instead of direct action.)[13] These organizations pursued different objectives in different arenas, and only at the vague level of "civil rights" did they share a goal sufficiently broad to be perceived as a homogeneous player, the civil rights movement, which was really "'a movement of movements' with competing goals, purposes, strategies, organizations, and leaders" (Andrews and Gaby 2020: 125).

## The Search for Mechanisms

Recently the outcomes and interactionist approaches have both searched for the mechanisms beneath the broad correlations that earlier scholars had observed between strategies or state structures on the one hand and successes or outcomes on the other. Even the political-opportunities tradition has moved toward a fine-grained study of interactions, more dynamic and contingent than originally portrayed (Trevizo 2006). Joshua Bloom (2015) discusses "leveraged opportunities" but really describes the interaction between civil rights leaders and Harry Truman in 1946, centering on strategic calculations on both sides. By distinguishing subplayers within the civil rights movement, he discerns Truman's reaction to each, getting beneath the macrostructural shifts of traditional political-opportunity theory: "the crucial macro-structural processes—namely the Cold War—had no discernible direct effect on insurgent influence." The effect operates through meso- and then, more precisely, through microprocesses; there is no such thing as a single political opportunity structure (Luders 2016).

Felix Kolb (2007) replaced the term "political opportunities" with "mechanisms," each of which consists of a player's ability to influence an arena. Plaintiffs can gain standing and win lawsuits in courts (the "judicial mechanism"), although he points out that the influence of court decisions depends on other arenas. Disruptive protest and public opinion can each influence legislative arenas, Kolb says, although typically when combined with player access such as lobbying and voting rights. His "political access mechanism" involves both player access to a legislative arena and successful maneuvering within it; his "international politics mechanism" brings

---

[13] Voter registration drives *turned out* to be a form of direct action, as whites reacted violently and considered them disruptive. Ella Baker kept SNCC together by suggesting that it think of itself as having two wings, or two subplayers (Payne 1995: 111). See Biggs and Andrews (2015) on the creation of a new arena, lunch counters, which brought new players, private businesses, into the conflict.

foreign governments into play by pressuring legislatures and (especially in the United States) executives. Kolb is most interested in big gains such as changing the rules of arenas and gaining new laws and policies, but his list of mechanisms suggests the utility of crossing players and arenas in a matrix of potential outcomes.

Edwin Amenta's institutional mediation model represents the return of strategy more fully and influentially. The term "mediation" is meant to capture the circuitous route from player intentions and strategies to a variety of outcomes, by way of a range of institutional arenas. Amenta used the term "political mediation" when those arenas were primarily elections, legislatures, and courts, but he adopted the more general term "institutional mediation" when his work turned to news organizations. (And see King 2008 for the model's application to corporations.)

We have seen that Amenta's interest in explaining important outcomes leads to models in which movement actions are one contributing variable among others, and often only making a minor contribution if any. He suggests (Amenta and Shortt 2020: 155; also Amenta et al. 2010) that scholars should "begin by addressing how institutions work and examine closely the causal literature surrounding them. From there, they should theorize about how movements might engage or intervene in the workings of institutions' usual determinants." In explaining nuclear energy policies, Jasper (1990) found antinuclear movements to have minor effects even when they were large and vociferous. And many or most laws and policies reflect no input from movements whatsoever, as there is no real public opinion or interest in them (Burstein 2014, 2020).

In contrast, our interest in accounting for a variety of local outcomes, many of them internal to movements, allows us to continue to focus on movement decisions, reactions, interactions, and emotions. Yet nothing in our interactionist framework precludes institutional processes of the kind that Amenta highlights, and many appear in the pages in this book. Another difference is that Amenta is trying to explain prominent institutional events or outputs while we are attempting to develop a heuristic toolkit of mechanisms to understand a range of political action. In our lists of gains and losses, we include large ultimate outcomes such as new policies, but if we focused on them, we might overlook the byways, dead ends, player construction, arena building, and other processes that represent most of politics.

Kenneth Andrews has developed a similar dynamic approach that follows players across arenas, focusing on the classic civil rights movement. For instance, court orders for school desegregation led to a proliferation of private academies and shifted civil rights efforts into new arenas (Andrews 2002). He highlights the "movement infrastructure" that allows flexible adaptation across arenas (Andrews 2001), while also observing that dramatic protests do not necessarily help organizations develop and expand (Biggs and Andrews 2010).

In *Freedom Is a Constant Struggle*, Andrews (2004) urges researchers to "move beyond a success/failure dichotomy because movements often have conflicting, multiple, and changing goals" (17). He recommends identifying various arenas and the multiple outcomes possible in each, as well as tracing interactions over long periods, so that we can ask, for instance, "Are movement gains in one arena undermined by losses in another arena?" (19). If Amenta focuses slightly more on arenas, Andrews highlights players in what he labels his "movement infrastructure model." He focuses on "the interaction of three factors: the movement's infrastructure and strategies, the forms of resistance and repression by movement opponents, and the structure and activities of [political] actors—including courts, government agencies, and law enforcement" (13). Because many government units are both players and arenas, Andrews can incorporate institutional rules and resources under this third rubric. In the cases that follow, we will try hard to distinguish players with goals from the arenas in which they interact (including cases when players present themselves as arenas).

By distinguishing carefully between players and arenas, we aim to refine Kolb's idea of mechanisms. Unlike his use of the term to refer to arenas, the mechanisms we use are more granular, such as strategic dilemmas, choice points, evocative emotions, player identities, and entry or exit from arenas. In fact, with this more refined toolkit at our disposal, we rarely need to use the overall term "mechanisms" in the chapters to follow. But they permeate our interactive analysis.

## Players

To push beyond the simplified language of "social movements," their "environment," and their "outcomes," we use a language of players and arenas. Strategic players are individuals or groupings of individuals who share some sense of themselves as a team with goals they pursue in strategic arenas. Many of them, such as corporations or other formal organizations, are stabilized by laws, legal names, and internal rules. But compound players (as opposed to simple players, namely, individuals) are never fully unified, and we can break them down into their subplayers when that is useful. We can keep subdividing them, all the way down to individuals, if we find it helpful. Players are never stable but are constantly redefining membership, changing goal priorities, and presenting themselves in new ways.

Although in some cases it can be difficult to identify a player, the terminology helps us avoid theological definitions over what is and is not a social movement (or a state, or any other label that promises more unity than it can deliver).[14] Our language of strategic interaction should apply to any player, including political parties, which are also central in any theory of political outcomes. Paul Burstein (1999) shows the difficulties of distinguishing social movement organizations, interest groups, and political parties. By acknowledging a range of players, we do not need to care so much about those abstract labels, instead watching concrete players as they move among arenas. A typology of players is not of much interest in the players-and-arenas framework. Instead of asking, "Is this a social movement?," we can remain agnostic about what to call the players, or at least we can acknowledge their heterogeneity and fluidity. We care more about the actions they accomplish.

Players work hard to craft identities, which perform both internal and external functions for them. Internally, individuals take pride in their identification with larger groups, and their interactions with other group members give them a variety of direct pleasures. Players can use the same collective identities to make demands on outsiders, especially recognition and benefits from state agencies, corporations, and other powerful players. Of course, there is often conflict between the identities most satisfying to members and those most appealing to outsiders. Groups tailor their identities to the arenas they enter, although they face dilemmas and risks in crafting identities for different arenas (Bernstein 1997).

As summed up in the idea of an identity dilemma, collective identities often represent a package of losses and gains (McGarry and Jasper 2015). Internal gains include pride, solidarity, and strengthened networks, while internal losses may include individuals who feel excluded from the identity formulation, or who compromise their individual goals and values. External gains include a projection of power, the ability to formulate demands on

---

[14] The label "social movement" is usually a rhetorical claim by a network of individuals and organizations that wish to project more unity of purpose and strategy than they actually share, or greater strength and national (or even international) breadth.

behalf of a group, and an aura of strategic inevitability, while potential external losses include the strains of incorporating new identities, highlighting a group's stigma, struggles recruiting new individuals, and increased power for those leaders who are seen as representative of the group (Jasper and McGarry 2015: 3).

Shared tastes in tactics help define a player, as disagreements over what to do are likely to pull it apart. Tactics are never entirely neutral means but also partly morally charged ends. A protest group may be devoted to nonviolence or to participatory democracy, for instance. Its members have precommitted themselves to one side of a strategic dilemma, nice instead of naughty in the case of nonviolence versus violence. The strategic choice of nonviolence, like all attempts to resolve dilemmas, will give them certain gains, for example, an improved reputation among bystanders and the media, as well as some losses, such as predictability or a decreased ability to disrupt things.

Building coalitions with other groups is usually seen as a gain, although it brings with it the extension dilemma: larger players tend to control more resources, knowledge, and sheer numbers of participants, but at the cost of more disagreements over means and ends as well as sheer coordination and communication costs. For instance, many supporters of social movement unionism see coalitions between unions and community organizations as the key to union revitalization and success, but the largest coalitions are not always the most effective ones (Tattersall 2013). The broader the coalition, in addition, the greater its identity dilemmas.[15]

Table 1.1 lists some of the gains or losses that involve changes in players. They can get larger or smaller. They can gain—or lose—control over resources. They can change internally, in their emotions, beliefs, or goal priorities. They can gain or lose the attention of other players, such as the media.

Even if a player does not flourish in an arena, its very existence may provide some gains. It symbolizes a particular point of view, grievance, or social problem. And it can promote alternative perspectives, counterideologies, even when it can do little to institutionalize them. It is available to journalists looking for a statement from "the other side." And when conditions change, it may be able to take a more active role with greater alacrity (Voss 1993). But participating in an arena always brings risks from the being-there and engagement dilemmas.

---

[15] Edward Walker and Lina Stepick (2013) review the literature on the extension dilemma, finding the kind of mixed results from coalitions that the dilemma would predict.

**Table 1.1**  Gains and Losses Involving Players

| |
|---|
| A player forms or dissolves |
| A player expands or shrinks |
| A player gains or loses resources or capabilities |
| Alliances change |
| An existing player gains (positive or negative) attention |
| Internal structures of a player change |
| Players' attitudes, expectations, and emotions change |
| Players are physically threatened or coerced |
| Players change their positions or reprioritize their goals |
| A player gains a new position within an arena |

As we differentiate players into smaller groupings and factions, we ultimately arrive at individuals and the "biographical" factors in protest (Jasper 1997). The biographical consequences of political participation are one of the best-documented outcomes of social movements.[16] Participants tend to remain active after leaving a movement, thanks to factors such as activist identities, social bonds with other individuals, or a feeling of empowerment (both individual and collective). They also come away with specific organizing skills that they take pleasure in deploying later in life (Van Dyke and Dixon 2013). Even those in a losing cause are likely to return if they feel they were at least treated fairly (Helander 2016).

In addition to lifelong propensities like these, individuals can get more immediate rewards from politics. Olivier Fillieule (2010: 4) has pioneered research on how individuals craft activist careers in and out of organizations and movements, observing that engagement is "long-lasting social activity articulated by phases of joining, commitment, and defection." To our long list of potential gains and losses in political actions, we must add gains and losses for individuals: an activist ends up with a government position, two activists get married, or someone finds a paying job in a movement after years of volunteering. After both revolutions and peaceful transitions of power, many outsiders become insiders. There are also losses: someone may be blackballed from a desired position because of her radical past.

---

[16] Recent contributions to the massive literature on biographical consequences include Fillieule et al. (2018) and Pagis (2018).

Some of these outcomes are intended and others not. For our purposes, individuals may experience dilemmas and dynamics similar to those of compound players, but individuals have a unity—or at least an ontological reality—that the latter can never achieve. In some cases, individuals can pursue their own goals independently of shared goals; more often they pursue personal goals *at the same time* that they pursue group goals. There are forever tensions over different subplayers' goals.

Only individuals have emotions, which provide a wide range of mechanisms that not only define gains and losses but, even more, explain the impact of gains and losses on future action (Jasper 2018b). (The fact that individuals alone can have emotions does not prevent both individuals and their emotions from being deeply social.) Anger, outrage, and shock help draw recruits into a movement but also help to keep them there. Fear, disgust, and shame may prevent them from joining or help them defect.

Moods, a category of emotions that give people more or less energy for activity, are easily influenced by gains and losses. A sense of momentum, optimism, and confidence can arise from small wins as well as from ideological apparatuses (such as an historical narrative that predicts future victory). Losses can destroy these useful moods, replacing them with resignation, depression, cynicism, and despair. (On the other hand, gains sometimes demobilize and relax players, and losses can pump them up.) Such emotions arise from social and political interactions, especially membership in a group, but they operate through the central nervous systems of individuals.

Here we find a good example of the limits of the structural-outcomes paradigm. Karen Beckwith (2016) usefully points to how participants learn things during long protests—in her case, strikes—whether they "win" or they "lose" in the short run. They develop collective identities, confidence, and a lot of know-how that can come in handy for future rounds of activity. But her notion of political learning contains no emotions: none of the frustrations, the pride of continuing for long periods, the solidarity with one's group, the sense of desperation that can often motivate radical acts, or the fatigue and fear that sometimes force individuals to withdraw. Structural paradigms have little room for such dynamics, but we cannot understand players—or how they learn—without them. Almost all action, even when it results in severe losses, can stimulate learning.

Protestors are not the only players in politics. Opponents, various subplayers of the state, the media, corporations, and bystanders all populate the arenas that protestors enter. All these players face parallel challenges of cohesion and identity, coordination, and strategic tradeoffs. By looking at arenas, we insist on symmetry among players, at least at the theoretical level: all can play a role. This does not mean that they have equal power in those arenas (in many cases protestors are impotent or excluded altogether), or that we need to give them equal attention in our research. It only means that we should not ignore them. For instance, we should look for *rivalries*, pairs of players who are attuned to each other and adopt the goal of punishing each other when possible.

Most arenas contain bystanders who primarily watch the action but who can also intervene if they wish, so that influencing their opinions, feelings, and activities is typically a gain or a loss. Han and Strolovitch (2015) call them "proto-players." Public opinion is the usual conceptualization of bystanders, and movements almost always hope to influence it: as a means to influence policy, a way to recruit new members, or an end in itself. This goes beyond getting attention and placing an issue on the political agenda; it involves the substance of cultural views. Through media attention, large protest events influence both agendas and views (Banaszak and Ondercin 2016).

## Arenas

Arenas are places where players engage each other, make decisions, and produce outcomes. They range from actual physical settings, such as meeting rooms, legislatures, and courtrooms, along with all the decorations, props, archives, and pageantry that these include, to more metaphorical places such as online discussion forums or the construction of public opinion. Even these metaphorical places are grounded in the physical: server farms enable online interaction; participants sit at computers and other devices. Some arenas are constructed purposely for the making of decisions, others are more casual and ad hoc. The rules and customs of an arena are usually clear, although players may ignore, reinterpret, change, or even break them.[17]

There are other places where strategic action unfolds: backstage spaces where important action occurs in advance of—usually as preparation

[17] In the literature on players and arenas, some authors prefer a narrow definition of arenas as physical places and their virtual extensions (Jasper 2021), while others are satisfied with a looser definition that includes outcomes such as media products, culture, and attitudes, which are not always developed through clearly defined decision-making processes (Duyvendak and Fillieule 2015). In this book, we adopt the broader definition.

for—engagements in arenas ("adjacent rooms," Fran Piven likes to call them). Just as a sports team has weight rooms and training fields, so political players hold fundraisers, commemorations, private pep talks, and celebrations intended to influence their own team. This might involve mobilizing resources, sharing ideas, or reinforcing collective identities—internal advances that should pay off with gains during external engagements. Backstage interactions are sometimes less conflictual, but no player is ever completely unified and free of conflict. Subplayers vie for influence and positions. Backstage, people relax, talk, tell jokes, bond as players, and generate emotional energy, but they also squabble, calculate, deliberate, and prepare.

Compound players become arenas when they must debate and make decisions. Their internal arenas may be quite formal, as with board meetings and congresses. Or they can be quite loose, emerging unexpectedly from backstage settings. Any group, even the most informal crowd, can "decide" to do something: start running, throw some bricks through windows, or go home because of the rain. Only in the loosest sense would we say that they become arenas just because players have acted in a new way, even if there is some discussion and a decision. They were not created as an arena, nor was the event advertised as being about making decisions.

Some strategic moves directly affect decisions within arenas: a vote, or the refusal to vote; a speech at a meeting. Other moves are indirect: educating voters; a blockade or occupation that shuts an arena down; persuading, frightening, or bribing a legislator to vote a certain way; and training security guards to keep order. This used to be the definition of social movements versus other forms of participation: protestors were those who deploy indirect moves; members were those who rely on direct ("institutionalized") moves inside arenas.

Although some players are defined by their activity in a single arena, most face choices about which arenas to enter.[18] They must juggle their commitments, allocating time and attention to the most promising arenas.

---

[18] One limitation of field theory (Fligstein and McAdam 2012) is that it tends to see a player as existing in a single field, with no capacity to select fields. By being more precise and institutionally grounded, the concept of arenas suggests the work that goes into selecting venues for action. In some ways, field theory is compatible with our approach, as it allows for a constant struggle, with small gains and losses as individuals change their position relative to others in the same field, with no final endpoint. The limitation of field theory is that players and fields mutually define each other, so there is little room to allow players the autonomy to move to new fields, as they can to new arenas. Martin (2011) complains that most field theorists "either bastardize the idea of a field to a mere heuristic typology, or confound it with a field of contestation completely reducible to the summation of individual actions" (269). Further, he says, "Because fields are known only by their effects, it is tempting to proliferate invisible fields that 'explain' whatever is in question. Such an explanation may simply be a restatement of the problem, with the word *field* inserted somewhere" (280). See Duyvendak and

When blocked in one, they may seek another arena in which to continue their projects. But their choice of arenas can be constrained, sometimes severely. On occasion, they lack the resources to enter an arena. In other cases, the arena's rules formally exclude them. Their opponents vigilantly block their entry.

The influence or scope of an arena is always subject to change as a result of strategic action. For example, a player may not want to enter the trap of a "false arena": a setting whose decisions can be made moot or at least less influential once the new player enters it (Jasper 2006: 169). Blue-ribbon commissions are often an example: an outsider may feel flattered to be invited, but politicians can easily ignore the subsequent findings and suggestions of the commission, especially if public attention has turned elsewhere by the time the commission finally completes its work. At various times in labor history, radicals have rejected grievance procedures and even collective bargaining as forms of cooptation, distracting union attention from more influential political arenas.[19]

But no arena is entirely false, with no possibility of any impact. If nothing else, a player may be able to use its participation to shape its reputation: telling its members that they are being taken seriously, because they are meeting with the mayor or the CEO. A new player may also be able to enlarge the arena, by asking questions, gathering additional resources, and going to the press with statements. These processes are true for all arenas: the stakes change both qualitatively and quantitatively. A powerful arena can be starved of resources and capacities to make an impact; a new or small one can grow more important. Just as new arenas can be created and flourish, old ones can shrivel and disappear.

Some players have the capacity to create new arenas, a powerful advantage of holding offices. In chapter 2, we will encounter a mayor who created an arena to promote minimum wage legislation; when he did not get the outcome he wanted, he created another, smaller arena that came through for him. In this case, as in many others, the creation of a new arena was a response to pressure from a social movement—whether or not the arena eventually

---

Fillieule (2015) and Jasper (2015, 2021) on similarities and differences between fields and arenas, including an attempt to reconcile the two concepts.

[19] "Cooptation" is a normative term often used to imply that an arena is false: protestors who are coopted must moderate their goals or give them up entirely. It represents the kind of either–or thinking (either they have succeeded in gaining entry to an arena, or they have been coopted) that we are trying to move beyond, in favor of nuanced attention to tradeoffs.

yielded the outcome the movement desired. All players face dilemmas about whether to enter arenas, but only a few have the option to create new ones.

The creation or choice of arenas is fraught with dilemmas. Foremost is the engagement dilemma: you enter an arena where you think you can do well, but all arenas have contingencies that are hard to anticipate (Jasper 2006: 26). Even powerful, confident players can be tripped up. (In fact the Titan's hubris dilemma suggests they are often *too* confident to assess an arena's hazards accurately: Jasper 2006: 112.) As we will see in chapters 2 and 3, players create new arenas that they expect to control—but they rarely do so completely. All engagements harbor risks.

Refusing to enter an arena carries its own risks, as it is usually harder to influence an arena from the outside: the being-there dilemma. The refusal must transform, discredit, or destroy the arena. Boycotting elections is the classic example: you must be able to render the results illegitimate, hoping to force new elections or to move the action into a different arena such as armed struggle. Most of the time, players enter an arena whenever their opponents do, in the hopes of either making gains or at least avoiding losses (Meyer and Staggenborg 1996). Tina Fetner (2008) observes that dueling movements often mimic each other's tactics because they must enter the same arenas (also Bob 2012). Ira Katznelson (1981: 135) calls this a "mimetic response," citing Arno Mayer's idea that every revolution has a corresponding counter-revolution, which "borrows its central ideas, objectives, styles and methods from the revolution."

There are other ways that players influence each other, especially those in direct conflict or rivalries. They strengthen the boundaries they see separating them, which increases internal solidarity and external demonization. Their interaction also has its dynamics, especially a kind of emotional seesaw, as each one acts in a way that the other feels to be threatening or outrageous. They respond in turn, continuing the cycle.

The intricate dance between protestors and their targets can also produce accommodation. In a study of corporations frequently targeted by activists, McDonnell, King, and Soule (2015) found that their receptivity to protest increased over time, as they learned to anticipate challenges and defend against them. This was partly public relations work to bolster their moral reputations, but it also included independent monitors and better behavior. Research into prolonged interactions can uncover these dynamics, as players change in response.

Table 1.2 Gains and Losses in Arenas

---

A new arena is formed to make decisions about an issue

A new arena is formed that *could* be used to make relevant decisions

Formal rules and informal expectations of an existing arena change

An arena is opened (or closed) to a player

An arena is shut down

A player enters an arena

An audience in an arena changes: different people, or different opinions and feelings.

A decision is made in an arena

---

Players may enter arenas where they are not comfortable or expected. Corporations and states may enter "grassroots" arenas, either to counter the protest groups that are at home there or to pretend to be grassroots movements themselves. American corporations targeted by environmentalists helped to create the misleadingly self-proclaimed "wise-use movement" at the end of the 1980s to protect logging, mining, and other extractive industries and occupations. When anti-Putin protestors took advantage of social media— a much-remarked venue for recent social movements—his administration created its own bloggers to counter the ones who had attacked him.

Just as gains and losses can pertain to players, they also take the form of changes and outcomes in the arenas where those players operate (see table 1.2). The rules, audiences, and expectations in arenas change, including rules that exclude or include players. New arenas are created; old ones are shut down. And, of course, arenas generate decisions through their normal procedures: the kind of laws and policies that are the focus of outcomes theories.

## Toward the Local

In the older structural paradigm, movements succeed when they move "from mobilization to revolution" (Tilly 1978). The kind of success that counts most, for normative as well as theoretical reasons, is an overhaul of the state, overthrowing an old elite and its regime in favor of a new one, supposedly (this is the normative part) with a broader franchise and greater accountability. All arenas are expected to change at once. Not all revolutions have worked out so well, of course, and the dismal history of the great revolutions led to a political rethinking of movement goals.

After 1968, great revolutionary projects fell from favor. In France, the central "old social movement" at the time was not labor but the French Communist Party (PCF), whose stated mission still included the overthrow of the state. The PCF's Louis Althusser provided a structuralist theory which purported to justify his party's program, especially the supposed contrast between the humanistic, immature Marx (favored by students) and the later, "scientific" Marx (favored by the PCF). But theorists of 1968, especially Alain Touraine and Michel Foucault, pushed back in an effort to decapitate not only the sovereign but also those who wished to replace him with a new central power, the Party. Touraine's "new social movements" were self-limiting; instead of seeking to seize the state, they hoped to establish alternative institutions and to influence policies from the outside—a key aspect of the so-called new social movements that is often overlooked (Touraine et al. 1983).[20] According to the new view, politics can take many small forms (Goldfarb 2006) and is not restricted to headlong assaults on the state— the kinds of big transformations that interested Tilly, Skocpol, and other structuralists.

Foucault was explicit in theorizing power as operating through microinteractions among individuals in a capillary image rather than as radiating out from a center (or down from the top): drill sergeants training new recruits, mothers anxiously observing their children, teachers indoctrinating their pupils, policemen arresting juvenile delinquents, and psychoanalysts probing the dreams and jokes of patients in their care. Resistance to these disciplinary practices must take many local forms, instead of lodging in a grand revolutionary organization that would replace one powerful sovereign with another. Foucault at the end of his life was seeking a microinteractive, strategic perspective without quite breaking entirely with structural imagery.

Laclau and Mouffe (1985) drew on Foucault's ideas in their powerful critique of Marxist theories that saw class as the basis for all revolutionary struggles. Instead of arising from a particular structural position, any number of identities can form and, through discourse and interaction, become the basis for progressive politics. Through cultural work, local players

---

[20] Touraine's image of the new social movements was closely tied to the politics of the Confédération Française Démocratique du Travail (CFDT) trade union, with a Christian-socialist heritage and often dominated by "new class" technical workers, as opposed to the Confédération générale du travail (CGT), more closely tied to the communists and popular with factory workers.

can emerge and align in ways that are hard to predict a priori. "There is no subject—nor, further, any 'necessity'—which is absolutely radical and irrecuperable by the dominant order, and which constitutes an absolutely guaranteed point of departure for a total transformation" (169). Following Foucault, they criticized Marxist theories that "imply that every form of domination is incarnated in the state. It is clear that civil society is also the seat of numerous relations of oppression, and, in consequence, of antagonisms and struggles" (170). We can never predict in advance what new political players will emerge. And if those players ever merge into one, Laclau and Mouffe argued, it will be because they have decided to align themselves, not because of some underlying structural unity to a "class" or to "society."

Intellectual trends like these have slowly come to the study of social movements, bringing attention to specific players and arenas rather than offering grand models of society or history. Once we identify the relevant players, we are ready to observe their ongoing interactions. They react to one another, anticipate moves, assess weak spots, and try to get inside each other's heads. They are agents, not passive "carriers" of history.

The term "social movement" tends to imply a national or perhaps international entity more than the term "player" does, a holdover from structural models of each successive movement facing "a state." Although national political systems differ, they all contain fewer national-level arenas than local arenas. All the cases in our book involve mostly city-level arenas, partly because so much politics occurs at these local levels. Most social movements are loose alliances of very local groups, mainly found in urban areas. Cities are dense, able to foster critical masses of those interested in a new issue, and with plentiful backstage spaces or "scenes" in which politics can emerge: the local bookstore, coffee shop, or pub (Creasap 2022). They provide an opportunity for us to bore down to all sorts of hopes, risks, gains, losses, and interactions.

## Interactions

For decades, scholars have recognized that political outcomes emerge from interactions between protestors and their opponents, but the agency of opponents was largely made into a structural factor that changed through no influence by protestors. Many political opportunities were exogenous events such as a state's defeat in war or its fiscal collapse (Skocpol 1979). Others had to do with relatively permanent features of state structures (Kitschelt 1986; Kriesi et al. 1995). Protestors' main activity was to find the right key to open the state's structural lock. There was little acknowledgement that both sides are continually changing their locks as well as their keys as part of their strategic engagements, often in anticipation of what the other will try (Jasper and King 2020; McCammon 2012).

Instead of conceptualizing patterns of interactions *as interactions*, older views tended to structuralize opponents' power and position into an independent variable. In her wonderful study of the Knights of Labor, for example, Kim Voss (1993) uses "employer association" (specifically whether there was one or not) as a variable in her statistical analysis, but then tells a much richer story about what employer associations actually did to break unions and to unify small and large employers, in a seesaw between strikes and lockouts. She shows how important it is to treat employers as strategic players, facing mobilizing challenges and tactical tradeoffs parallel to those that employees face (albeit with different solutions).

We need to view targets of protest as players who fight back (Jasper and Poulsen 1993). And because corporations, state agencies, organized religions, and other targets tend to have greater resources and credibility than protestors, their actions usually matter even more. Sometimes they are sympathetic to change, or contain factions who are, but more often they resist. To complicate matters, most controversies contain more than two players, and each side tries to recruit allies, persuade others, or at least neutralize potential allies of their adversaries. For instance, protest groups often enlist government players to pressure corporations, but in other cases they use corporations to help them change government agencies (Young and Schwartz 2014). Gains and losses emerge from the interactions among all these players (e.g., Amenta and Shortt 2020; Burstein et al. 1995; Markoff 1997). In some cases, that interaction can be viewed as the imposition of different kinds of costs on other players—and presumably benefits as well (Luders 2010).

To understand interactions, we must usually plumb the depths of the microsocial. For example, Rick Fantasia (1988) observes how a handful of workers (he was one of them) shut down a small manufacturing plant, detailing the body language, clustering, words, and motion that eventually united the workforce in a common action.

Microinteractions depend heavily on emotional dynamics, an integral part of all action but easily overlooked in macrostructural images (Jasper

2018a). Fantasia (1988: 137) describes union supporters in the early stages of organizing as building bonds "by expressing their frustration, anxiety, and hope . . . with emotions serving as a common denominator of experience." Emotions are the core of all consciousness raising, vital to early gains as players congeal. As Summers-Effler (2010: 199) notes, "The lesser the distance between an observer and the processes being observed, the more emotional and cultural motivations will be apparent." For instance, we might see riots, typically analyzed as a naughty tactic of coercion of targets, as a thrill with the capacity to commit participants to further action (Case 2021; Thompson 2010).

Just as most gains are modest tactical victories in a larger strategic campaign, so a lot of losses are petty frustrations and disappointments, annoyances that eat away at us, demoralize us, and poison our relationships. These can add up to huge costs. Occasionally, especially long after movements have faded, memoirs by and about protest leaders show the costs to the individuals and their families: some are fired from jobs, get divorced, are estranged from their children, move away, start abusing alcohol, or suffer from depression. Just as movement scholars focus on success rather than failure, they typically overlook the human sacrifice that moral causes usually demand.[21]

Even a big victory needs to be followed by further engagement, usually in new arenas, if it is to remain a gain. Fantasia tells a story of union organizing that is sadly familiar. A group of nurses and technical workers in a Vermont hospital voted narrowly for union representation, an apparent "beachhead" that is the kind of major success scholars hope to explain. The pro-union side demobilized after their victory. Six years later, Fantasia reports (1988: 168), "It now seems that the first union contract with management will not be negotiated. The union has never been recognized by management." Many of the nurses involved in the union drive have moved away, and "contact with the union waned considerably after the organizing drive," angering many of the workers. They were demoralized by the long wait, with little to do and no further signs of success. Implementation failed.

Occasionally there are crises in which no player has very good moves to advance its goals—a stalemate. In our language, either one or several arenas have lost their ability to generate outcomes. New players must arrive to break

---

[21] For a touching memoir that is honest about the personal costs of activism, see Wiwa (2000), a memoir by the son of slain Nigerian activist Ken Saro-Wiwa. Most whistleblowers, another kind of protestor, suffer heavy retaliation and personal costs (Alford 2001).

the stalemate, or the rules of the arena(s) must be changed—although the same players that are preventing decisions can usually also block changes meant to allow decisions to flow again. Sometimes a *frozen arena* must be abandoned, or at least it comes to be dominated by another arena. Some players may benefit from a frozen arena, just as some players are better able to switch to new ones.[22]

Some arenas are intentionally frozen, or better put, powerful players try to freeze out new players from the arenas they dominate. This was the essence of structural theories, which nonetheless lacked much attention to how the structures had become rigid and how they remained that way, the work that successful players had put into protecting their positions. Structures were too often taken for granted. A players-and-arenas approach demands attention to the strategic work of powerful players, even when that work is not directly interacting with less powerful players. The powerful construct their fortresses with newcomers in mind even before the newcomers show up.

Because strategies unfold as interactive processes, we need to uncover the mechanisms that link hopelessly broad variables such as "violence" and "success." As Marshall Ganz (2000: 1041) puts it, "Since strategy is interactive, getting it 'right' in a big way is likely to be evidence of having learned how to 'get it right' in numerous small ways—and doing it time after time." "Success" consists of many little successes, but most often there are losses as well as gains. They transform players, arenas, and much else along the way. Our main task is to trace these and to see how they are related. Ultimately the challenge will be to follow these local outcomes as they link together in chains to form broader results at the level of the corporation, industry, public opinion, and legislatures.

## Perceptions

When anti-Israel organizers in 2011 drew a crowd of several hundred in front of Israel's embassy in Amman, Jordan, they declared victory when they caused the staff to evacuate (Schwedler 2018: 66). *Perceptions* of success or

---

[22] An obvious question is who benefits from crises? Those who can switch their activities to different arenas? Who have multipurpose resources such as money that allow them to switch? Those who can imagine new moves in frozen arenas? Dobry (1986) inspired extensive French theory about the fluidity of crises. Wagner-Pacifici (2000) similarly discusses standoffs.

failure are themselves important gains and losses. For emotional reasons, big victories often demobilize the victors; small gains can keep them going, through a sense of momentum and confidence. There is frequent tension between the confidence that small gains bring and the indignation that losses arouse. Alinskyites formulate the best sequence of interspersed gains and losses as FWFWFLFH: Fight, Win, Fight, Win, Fight, Lose, Fight Harder (Beckwith n.d.). They recognize that progress is a series of small gains and also sometimes losses, not one big win or loss.

A perception of success affects multiple audiences, including an organization's own members and those it claims to represent. As Michael Schwartz (1976: 173) once put it, "On the one hand, it looks out to a possible membership which must be convinced of the efficacy of the organization in winning the changes they wish. . . . On the other hand, those already inside the organization must be constantly reinforced in their belief that the organization is succeeding." Keep hope alive. The perception of momentum affects other players as well, including one's opponents and the media, who also make judgments about momentum.[23]

In situations in which no likely outcome is a gain for a player, its objective becomes to minimize losses. Players that do this may actually feel some relief and proclaim a kind of victory—just as armies are proud of "successful" organized retreats (such as Allied soldiers at Dunkirk). Our expectations shape what we claim as a gain or a loss: if we do better than expected, we can claim a victory. In many cases, all players claim victory from the same engagement.

The pace of interactions, with momentum changing hands repeatedly, results from perceptions. One side wins, but not by much, and the other is outraged and redoubles its efforts. This kind of interaction has an impact on moods, which influence energy levels, the key to mobilization.

To view a modest gain as a success is more than a way to instill confidence and hope in supporters. It is to construct a view of the world as a place in which reforms happen little by little, but still a place in which they do happen—a world open to the influence of protest movements. In this Whiggish view of inevitable change and progress, one small gain is the beginning, not the end. The implications go beyond this effort, this movement, this arena; they involve the whole world of social movements and their impacts.

---

[23] Pride and confidence that come from success, but also the anger and outrage that come from failure, can motivate further collective action (Tausch and Becker 2012).

It is a vision cherished by those whose professional careers are devoted to this kind of work (Baillot 2017: 632). Perceptions of success or failure can influence broad appetites for engagement.

For that reason, the final arena for most interactions is the writing of the history of the interaction: how to understand what went right and what went wrong. Such interpretations are often controversial. At stake are positive feelings about one's own participation, but also lessons about future political action. Meyer (2006) suggests that players can bundle these thoughts and feelings into useful narratives:

> A fortifying myth extends the historical scope of a story line, allowing activists to recognize past efforts as a foundation for organizing in the present and future. Such a myth identifies a reasonably permanent collective actor, for example organized labor, drawing a boundary between it and authorities. The clear boundary line encourages all concerned to see each victory or defeat in a social movement episode to be part of a larger story, one whose origins and eventual outcomes extend beyond the boundaries of a single campaign—or even life. (214)

Activists package gains and losses into a narrative, whether or not there are causal connections among them. Those stories identify villains, victims, and heroes, suggesting appropriate feelings and actions toward each (Jasper, Young, and Zuern 2018, 2020).

## Packages of Gains and Losses

Tables 1.1 through 1.3 aim to categorize gains and losses in order to recognize and distinguish them: some gains or losses change the players, others the arenas; some create new players or arenas. We also aim to look for patterns and linkages among them. Typically, a change in an arena reconfigures players; the assemblage of a player tends to carry decisions about strategies, and so on. One important type of gain, decisions made in arenas, is the kind most often studied, the paradigm of outcomes. But it is only one kind of change among many others.

Charles Tilly (1999) offered a list of unintended outcomes, in addition to the explicit goals of movements:

Movements also leave political by-products that lie outside their programs and sometimes even contradict them: new police personnel and practices; the generation of rival movements and organizations; alterations in laws of assembly, association, and publicity; cooptation of activists and their organizations by governments or political parties; transformation of social movement organizations into pressure groups; the creation of legal precedents for subsequent challenges by other social movements. (268)

In this list, we see two examples of new players (police and rivals), two changes in arenas (laws and precedents), and two changes in existing players (cooptation and transformation into pressure groups).

This small sample suggests the multiple outcomes that spell decline or progress for strategic players. US civil right activist Bob Zellner

once compared organizing to a juggling act—how many plates can you keep spinning at once? Organizers had to be morale boosters, teachers, welfare agents, transportation coordinators, canvassers, public speakers, negotiators, lawyers, all while communicating with people ranging from illiterate sharecroppers to well-off professionals and while enduring harassment from the agents of the law and listening with one ear for the threats of violence. Exciting days and major victories are rare. Progress is a few dollars raised, a few more people coming to pay poll tax. (Payne 1995: 246)

Every one of those activities involves a possible gain or loss, through interactions with individuals in arenas and backstage areas; money, attention, and information spread in ways that shape future interactions.

Because strategic interactions are continual, so are the gains and losses that accompany them. But they are not necessarily random. In writing about strategic interactions, Jasper (2006) identified dozens of implicit tradeoffs, which become explicit dilemmas when acknowledged by the players facing them. These translate into combinations of gains and losses: they are dilemmas because a gain is typically accompanied by a corresponding loss. A short-run win undermines long-run prospects; an alliance with one player prevents an alliance with another; investment in certain means and techniques make some actions easier but others harder. Some of these combinations come in predictable, familiar packages; others remain contingent bundles (Bosi 2016). This book aims to identify several common packages.

Packages begin to form in a cluster of decisions made in the face of several strategic dilemmas. A player coalesces around those choices and the actions it pursues. Sometimes those pathways harden as other players react. Lines are drawn, characteristic ways of interacting emerge, and feelings are labeled. In many cases the actions, reactions, and outcomes begin to take recognizable form, emerging as a package of actions, gains, and losses. In other cases, the array of decisions and actions may take a new form, a bundle in which the gains and losses are connected in new ways. Although we appreciate the contingency of bundles, we hope to identify packages that are familiar in other settings, generalizable from our case studies.

Jasper (2006: 172–173) groups strategic dilemmas into several major categories. Some have to do with their scope or extension: across time, across space, or across social groupings. Whose goals take priority? How are short- and long-run tradeoffs managed? How much attention do leaders give to other players versus to their own team members? A second group have to do with hierarchy: what kinds of leaders do we cultivate? How much formal organization, and how hierarchical is it? Do we seek powerful potential allies? A third set of dilemmas involve speed and change: How fast can we innovate without losing support? Can we train our teams in new techniques? Other dilemmas are about playing it safe or taking risks. Many dilemmas, finally, have to do with form and content, or means and ends: Do we get our hands dirty with immoral means? How aggressive should we be? Do we follow the rules or break them?

These gains and losses have impacts far beyond strategic players in strategic arenas. Ultimately, players hope to influence other humans or the material world such as the environment. Strategic arenas have something at stake for those not in the arenas, just as legislation does not apply only to the lawmakers. Players hope to change the hearts, the minds, and the actions of strangers, of nonplayers (see table 1.3). These are important outcomes, which we cannot understand without grasping the complicated paths along the way.

Table 1.3  Changes outside the Strategic Interactions

Incentive structures (legal, financial, normative) are changed for individual nonplayers
Nonplayers change attitudes, feelings, and actions
Objects (such as technologies) are changed

We turn now to three basic types of linkages between various gains or losses: over time, across arenas, and across players.

## Over Time

Because all interactions unfold over time, as players react to each other, time sequences must be one of our basic building blocks, alongside ongoing structural conditions (Jabola-Carolus et al. 2020). In some cases, gains lead to other gains; in other cases they contribute to later losses. Likewise with initial losses: some lead to gains and others to further losses. In addition, we need to distinguish cases in which outcomes at one point contribute to other outcomes, from cases in which they are merely followed by other outcomes without necessarily helping to cause them.[24]

Through their formal rules and informal traditions, arenas impose a certain pace on interactions, such as turn-taking, time limits, schedules, pauses, and holidays. Interactions vary enormously even within those structural constraints, partly because of strategic decisions and partly because of the flow of emotions. We can discern different packages of outcomes as a result.

We have seen that a gain today can generate emotional confidence and a sense of momentum for a player, leading to gains tomorrow by encouraging further action and mobilization. Social psychologists have studied the mechanism behind this link, a feeling of empowerment. Although individuals may feel empowered, the effect seems to be strongest when people associate it with a group identity: just as outrage is stronger when it is a group that has been insulted or oppressed, so fighting back feels more effective when it is a group that fights back (Drury and Reicher 2005; Drury et al. 2005).

Players' gains may have ripple effects, far into the future, which they might welcome but could not have foreseen, especially through impacts on players and arenas. The KKK's mobilization of voters in the American South during the 1960s was still influencing voting in 2000, increasing Republican identification among white voters partly through social networks the KKK had established (McVeigh, Cunningham, and Farrell 2014).

---

[24] Devashree Gupta (2009) also discusses patterns of small gains and losses, identifying bandwagon effects (gains increase the size of the compound player), satiety effects (gains deflate the player), and friend-in-need effects (which combine the two other effects, in the kind of tradeoff we analyze).

Likewise, one loss easily leads to others, as opponents attack, reputations shrink, moods sour, and participants quit. In situations of direct conflict, growing momentum on one side usually implies shrinking momentum on the other, although perceptions differ from realities so that leaders on both sides may claim momentum, encouraging feelings of confidence and hope among their members.

In contrast to these positively correlated chains, a gain by one side may lead to its own demobilization and to even greater mobilization by opponents, and thus to losses in the future. Jasper and Poulsen (1993) identify this early gains/later losses pattern in the antinuclear and animal rights movements, while Voss (1993: 226) observes, "the Knights [of Labor] failed because their rapid growth and early successes resulted in the mobilization of powerful employers' associations." Although Jasper and Poulsen refer to "early gains," this implies that we can know the full trajectory of a movement, indeed that we can identify a unified movement capable of having a trajectory—views that we would reject. One player's gain at any time can lead opponents to react.

Bernstein (2003) finds a similar pattern for US gay and lesbian rights in comparing the intervals 1961–1977 and 1986–1991; a strong homophobic backlash movement formed in between, curtailing gains in the later period. This was part of a much broader set of backlash movements against the social justice advances of the 1960s (Faludi 1991). In such cases, the stakes are perceived as growing larger, partly for symbolic reasons but also because of the increasing scope of the contest in broader arenas (Yamasaki 2009). Opposed players feel threatened. In some cases, a gain encourages a player to push too far. As always, outcomes depend on how players respond to each other's moves.

The reverse may also happen, when a loss leads to later gains. Although most groups collapse in the face of adversity, some manage to regroup and rebuild. Cristina Flesher Fominaya (2010) found groups that turned inward in the face of failure but then used participatory processes to form collective identities that later proved helpful. In this case, a player used the shock of a loss to rebuild itself as a stronger player (also Beckwith 2016). Organizational and individual learning is more likely to follow from losses than from gains.

A pattern in which external losses are followed by internal gains suggests the Janus dilemma: there is a tradeoff between devoting time and resources to interacting with other players versus dedicating them to one's own team.

Turning inward is often a way to make the best of a bad situation, and to preserve one's team as a player despite demoralizing losses. At the extreme, a group can go into abeyance, or survival mode, for a long period, consolidating internal affective bonds with little external impact (Taylor 1989). A more concentrated network or organization can survive intact, preserving ideas and leaders for a resurgence years later. But most movements in abeyance never revive, and to understand why some do, we need a detailed catalogue of different kinds of gains.

The causal flow may work the other way, too: internal failures may lead to an external focus as a deflection, much as politicians sometimes go to war to unite their nation behind them. (It is easier to see how internal gains can lead to external gains, or vice versa, as players strengthen with each gain or weaken with a succession of losses.) The mechanism here has to do with switching to new arenas, which can happen after either a defeat or a gain.

In the face of state repression—clearly a loss—protestors can react in different ways, either retreating from public engagement or redoubling their efforts and turning out in even greater numbers. Brockett (2005) dubs this the "paradox of repression," in that repression often backfires. Attention to emotions can usually resolve the paradox. Fear can paralyze, but increased indignation can renew protestors' courage (Ellefsen 2021). Additional participants may be drawn in by the new grievance of police violence. Lauren Young (2016) suggests that while fear generally has a demobilizing effect, this is mediated by individual propensities to feel fear and assess risks. Repression may have its intended effect in some arenas but stimulate backlash in others. With civil rights, for example, Andrews (2004: 75, 113) finds an energetic backlash against white repression in the short run but a longer-run deterioration in movement infrastructure.

There is a more general interactive dynamic at work here: one side gains a victory, but the other is so outraged that it redoubles its own efforts, resulting in spirals of aggression. The paradox of repression reflects this: states often find themselves facing more protestors after clumsy efforts to scare them away. In many cases, we can understand spirals of aggression better by looking inside the broad players, for example, seeing radical flanks within movements or aggressive arms of the state that drag their allies along with them.

There are at least two time dynamics—of short versus long run—behind Piven and Cloward's classic work on disruption. The naughty-or-nice dilemma links short-run gains and long-run losses. There are immediate concessions, often by a panicked or desperate opponent or authorities, but in the long run, a tarnished reputation can undermine a player's position in various arenas. A naughty player hopes that its short-run gains outweigh the long-run losses.

In Piven and Cloward's work, we can also see the organization dilemma as a tradeoff between the short run and the long run: organization-builders are willing to give up some immediate gains in order to invest in the future, while critics of formal organizations believe immediate gains should be pursued. Scholars (such as Ganz 2000) have analyzed the tradeoff by distinguishing different types of organizations. "Strong movement infrastructures," observes Andrews (2004: 25), "have diverse leaders and a complex leadership structure, multiple organizations, informal ties that cross geographic and social boundaries, and a resource base that draws substantially on contributions from their members for both labor and funds." Of course, each of these factors harbors its own tradeoffs and dilemmas.

The institutionalization of a player, its practices, or its demands represents a familiar package of gains and losses (see chapter 3; Jabola-Carolus et al. 2020). Protestors lose considerable control when a government agency recognizes and takes over their problem area. Their goals are often moderated, and radicals in a movement will complain of cooptation or selling out, but there are new resources to stabilize attention and solutions over time. Institutionalization is a form of the powerful-allies dilemma: you lose control over events even as you gain the strength of your new ally, who has more power to shape impressions and outcomes than you do. All movements hope to leave some type of *institutional trace* behind, whether new laws, new organizations, court precedents, or artworks; not all of them manage to do so.

We have pointed to a number of dynamics over time. Tradeoffs between short- and long-run outcomes pose perhaps the most basic of strategic dilemmas, as all interactions unfold over time. But short- and long-run patterns are merely correlations that stand in for other mechanisms that we need to understand in more detail, from organization-building and institutionalization to aggressive intimidation and sharp responses by other players. Most of these mechanisms have to do with changes in players or arenas, as well as tradeoffs among different players or different arenas. *What actually happens between the short term and the long term?*

## Across Arenas

Although tradeoffs necessarily occur over time, to burrow down to the mechanisms driving them we need to link them to more specific changes in players and in arenas. Arenas can be related to each other in various ways: in a formal hierarchy as with appeals courts; through territories that aggregate into other territorial units; or simply because the same players appear in different arenas and bring understandings, feelings, resources, and reputations with them.

General capacities, such as resources like money, can often be transferred from one arena to another. Players who can generate money in one setting such as taxing, markets, or donations can use it to advance their interests in other arenas. We do not always approve of these transfers, as when the rich hire better lawyers and get "better" justice, but there is little that can be done to stop the pollution of many spheres by money (Walzer 1983). For individuals, personal charm is a capability that they can employ in many arenas. Confidence is another: this is one reason why victory and momentum in one arena often aid the player in additional arenas.

Most countries have some form of federalism, which can be understood as a hierarchy of arenas by territories, from the very local, to the regional, up to the national. The United States grants an unusual degree of autonomy to the lower levels in its federal system; states especially have well-defined protections from the central government. Cities have fewer protections from the states, and this has become an issue in recent years as Republicans have gained control over most state legislatures but few big-city governments. Arizona passed draconian anti-immigration laws, while Phoenix prohibited its police from turning in undocumented residents. After Birmingham raised the minimum wage to $10.10 an hour, Alabama prohibited cities from setting wage standards. The broader territorial arena usually trumps smaller arenas within its borders.

Even when they are not tightly coupled, significant gains or losses in one arena can affect morale, tactics, and resources in other arenas. The civil rights movement again provides an example. "It is frequently said that the movement's loss of energy and direction in the post-1965 period came because the movement had achieved its goals. 'Civil rights' had been achieved, more or less. From the viewpoint of local people in Greenwood." Payne (1995: 361–362) observes, "that makes little sense. It puts too much emphasis on legal changes, which, while welcomed, were only part of what local people wanted. For local people, the movement was about freedom, not just civil rights. At the very least, their conception of freedom would have included decent jobs, housing, and education." Many goals were yet to be accomplished, and the Civil and Voting Rights Acts "whetted their appetite for further change." What's more, "participation had been made relatively safe, for one thing, and potentially worthwhile in terms of economic rewards, prestige, or political influence." A gain in one arena, the capacity to vote, allowed gains in others, such as jobs. Civil rights activism had not lost energy but moved to new arenas.

A player's attitude toward an arena can change over time. For example, its goals can change. Antipathies toward a competing player may develop, so that the goal is no longer to get whatever rewards are available in the arena but to punish that other player. A rivalry between two players takes center stage. (Divorce courts are familiar with this kind of transformation.) More often, a player is blocked in one arena and seeks more promising ones; how they are blocked (for instance, fairly or unfairly) may affect what they do in the next arena. Or they may simply seek arenas where their capabilities are more effective.

A player also faces a choice about how many arenas to enter at the same time. Jasper (2006: 146) describes this basket dilemma: concentrate all your attention on one arena, possibly setting up an all-or-nothing outcome, or spread the risk so that no single defeat is too harmful (but no gain is enormous either). Some players lack the resources to operate in many arenas simultaneously. Others gain synergies from operating in multiple arenas, with positive "interrelated effects" (Bosi 2016; see chapter 5).

In both the Janus tradeoff and cases of survival mode, we have seen players that were pushed out of (or withdrew from) official public arenas and tended to private relationships. Combes and Fillieule (2011: 12) try to find gains within such losses: "what initially appears as the end of protest is sometimes actually the result of organizational networks going on standby, temporarily renouncing open protest and instead favoring more discreet or less visible forms of action." (Also see Melucci 1989 on submerged networks.) They criticize correlational studies and call for attention to strategic interactions to grasp how these outcomes arise.

Strategic interaction unfolds in arenas, so the packages we identify in the chapters to follow necessarily entail changes in and of arenas. The electoral package (in chapters 4 and 7) forces players to concentrate their attention on elections, often to the neglect of other arenas, but in chapter 5 we observe a political party that managed to use nonelectoral arenas as a kind of boomerang to enhance their success in elections. Chapter 2 explores the perils of creating new arenas, while chapter 3 looks at the institutionalization of a movement's demands through new arenas, the control of which was up for grabs. These strategic packages reflect clusters of tradeoffs and dilemmas, but they issue in a set of gains and losses that will be familiar in other cases.

## Across Players

In addition to changes in and changes of arenas, changes in players are among the most common form of gains and losses. Obviously, a gain for one side in a conflict is usually a loss for its opponents, but there are tradeoffs like this even for players on the same side. A compound player's gains and losses are never equally distributed: some individuals and factions get more of what they want than other members of the same team. A gain for moderates in a movement may come at the expense of its radical flank; unity and survival may require expulsion of some members.

The identity dilemma reflects this kind of package: every collective identity favors some members and downgrades others (McGarry and Jasper 2015). Those who control the construction of identities usually craft them in their own image, so that they become the ideal types for the group. Those with alternative visions of the group may defect, or they may simply lose enthusiasm. The US women's movement, trying to gain respectability in the late 1960s, notoriously tried to hide or exclude its lesbian members, who soon formed their own movement.

One of the most common packages involves gains for a compound player and losses for individual members, who may be martyred for the cause. Even if they do not literally lose their lives, they often pay high costs for the collective effort. Other life satisfactions—careers, leisure, raising children, enjoying partners—may suffer from their political commitments. Perhaps just as often, individual players may gain even while their movement suffers losses. A protest leader becomes famous and can pursue various career options whatever happens to the movement (Gitlin 1980).

On the other hand, individual and collective gains can be positively correlated: revolutionaries succeed and then win elections as politicians or jobs as local officials. Or more realistically, some revolutionaries have careers in the new regime while others do not (Viterna 2013). Losses can also be correlated: a celebrity or politician who aligns with a movement may go down with it, soiling her reputation in an unpopular cause. Think of Charles Lindbergh's embrace of the isolationist America First Committee.

Discussions of the biographical consequences of activism usually focus on gains, finding that former participants tend to remain politically active in similar causes. (Family failures and mental health problems are less often studied as outcomes.) Even movements that fail in their public goals may leave behind a large number of gains through their empowering impact on individuals.

There are some familiar cleavages in how gains and losses are distributed across a compound player: women versus men, radicals versus moderates, celebrated leaders versus anonymous foot soldiers, young versus old. Almost all our case studies find these differences, especially prominent individuals who managed to capitalize on their movement's losses as well as on their gains.

Among the packages we highlight in the following chapters, two especially involve players and their internal dynamics. In the personality package, which we observe in chapters 4 and 7, a player organizes itself around a key individual who both makes important decisions and represents the player symbolically to internal and external audiences. The personality package is a frequent part of the electoral package. The radical package (chapter 6) emerges when a player chooses more aggressive, disruptive tactics, taking a large risk that sometimes results in visible gains but more often erodes the reputation and solidarity of the player. Packages that are mostly about players also involve arenas, just as packages that are mostly about arenas also involve players.

## The Logic of Inquiry

The kind of interactionist approach we have laid out suggests a nonstandard approach to causal analysis. Success or failure and other dichotomized dependent variables lend themselves to correlations: are violent tactics or bureaucratic organizational structures correlated with success? Initial conditions or strategic choices are correlated with eventual outcomes, an approach common to many quantitative techniques as well as most comparative sociology.[25]

---

[25] Comparative and historical sociology were lumped together awkwardly in the 1980s but have since gone their separate ways. Historical approaches are capable of the kind of fine-grained tracing we aspire to, while cross-national comparisons (which always have more variables than cases) are not (Jasper 2018a).

A detailed description of interactions, in contrast, is more likely to benefit from interpretation, intentional explanations, and narrative accounts. "Historical arguments," said Robert Alford (1998: 102), "focus on events in time and place and on concrete actors, although they use theoretical concepts drawn from substantive theories of many kinds." They depict events "as processes that happen simultaneously and converge at given historical moments. The convergence of separate processes is contingent, and not predictable, but each process is potentially explainable by itself" (46). (He contrasted historical arguments with multivariate and cultural approaches, although he favored a combination of all three.)

The standard method for pushing beyond broad correlations is to find the causal mechanisms that link the two factors (Alford's "processes"). This is what we are proposing with the players-and-arenas framework and with gains and losses. In some cases, mechanisms are used as simply middle-range theories (McAdam et al. 2001), but we prefer to see them as dropping down to a different level of reality: from the macro to the micro, and frequently from the institutional to the individual and the interactive (Stinchcombe 1991). We can then add psychological and social–psychological factors (Elster 1998). We adduce a variety of causal mechanisms, such as familiar dilemmas, but the backbone of the explanation is the detailed narrative of interactions.

"Process tracing" is the awkward term for this kind of analysis. These processes are the stuff of social life, the bits and pieces of actions and interactions. We can usually present them in a narrative sequence, as long as we are clear about what is driving that sequence causally at each stage. Instead of "Faced with the mob, the king fled the palace," we would prefer, "Faced with the armed mob, the king feared for his life and for his family, and fled"—in other words inserting plausible psychological mechanisms. Process tracing thus works best in case studies, and it is perhaps better for theory invention than testing (but see Beach and Pedersen 2013). If traditional positivist theory equated explanation and prediction, process tracing tends to view a thorough description as a sufficient explanation, especially when it lands at obvious human motivations and reactions, such as fearing for one's life.

To understand the rapid turns of interactions, we need to grasp the perspectives of many players at the same time, and various social–psychological mechanisms are crucial tools. Decision-making and emotions must be front and center. Feeling-thinking processes come in combinations, unfold in sequences, and affect all action (Jasper 2018b). They hold compound players together or tear them apart; they embolden or frighten us as we react to other players; they help us start paths of action and tell us when to stop. They are not easy to describe in their full complexity, but they must be central to any interactive account. In what follows we try hard to remain sensitive to them.

Revolutions offer a good example of the superiority of process tracing over a correlational method; they are long, complicated series of gains and losses, some of which lead to a new regime, most of which do not. Players act in several existing arenas but also try to establish new arenas at the same time. Weighing established theories of revolution against the Iranian case, Charles Kurzman (2004) rejects all of them. They all propose to explain revolutions by correlating them with initial conditions: economic, organizational, cultural, and military. None of the initial factors, even in combination, can account for the success of the Iranian revolution of 1979. How, instead, did revolutionaries create their own conditions for success? We hope that our approach does something to help answer this "Kurzman challenge" (Jasper 2018a; Volpi and Clark 2019; Volpi and Jasper 2017). The intentions of players, whether or not they are realized, play a key role, as do emotional dynamics.

One limitation of our approach is that it is impossible for researchers to observe what happens in some arenas, since many players have an interest in keeping those arenas secret, or at least closed to outsiders. This is a methodological challenge, but we should not change our theory to accommodate our lack of perfect information. There are some ways around our blindness; we do not have to accept players—especially elite players—as black boxes, even though they have considerable power to exclude us from their deliberations.

The study of social movements has been plagued by the problem of small numbers and the limitations of case studies. If we dualistically envision a social movement facing off against a state, it is natural to ask, who wins and why? The number of successful cases—revolutions, union recognition, movements that win the laws they want, groups that gain entry to the polity—is small. An interactionist approach alleviates these challenges by proliferating observations within each movement. If we examine the interactions of many players—including breaking the state and the movement into their component subplayers—and if we look for all sorts of gains and losses, then we vastly expand the cases we have in front of us. Instead of dozens of successes, we have thousands of gains (not to mention losses). In this book we examine six empirical cases, but it is not a comparison of those cases, as the old correlational method would have favored.

Even qualitative research—such as Piven and Cloward's—often retains a kind of multivariate explanatory strategy, so that factors that contribute to success are presented as if they were preexisting variables. Upon consideration, they are no such thing. Almost all of them are actions that players take during long engagements: they strengthen collective identities, find powerful allies, recruit people, monitor public opinion and subtle changes in arenas, mobilize resources, craft resonant frames and stories, attract media attention, help their participants enjoy the marches and rallies. Do most of these things and you are more likely to win. These are the mechanisms and the processes. *Where you start does not entirely determine where you end up.*

On the one hand, lists like these are frustrating because they offer no magic formulas. On the other hand, *of course* they don't offer magic formulas. They offer us a number of actions to watch during the unfolding of strategic engagements, so that after the fact we can describe and explain how they unfolded as they did. Eventually an accumulation of such studies will highlight causal mechanisms—especially dilemmas and packages of losses and gains—that we should look for. Strategic lists offer activists possible options to consider, especially tactics that have worked in the past, but activists understand that there are no magic formulas.

Many collective actions are both means and ends, something that traditional models of success or of big outcomes miss. If we concentrate on the humans involved instead of an imagined "challenger" or "movement," we see that it can be satisfying to join a big crowd, assert a proud collective identity, or riot (Case 2021). Protesting can itself be a deep joy, an end for many participants. But a satisfying rally in turn reinforces participants' identities and willingness to return, making the movement stronger and more able to make demands on other players. This kind of effect is amplified by positive media coverage. One small gain becomes an advantage in future engagements. Ends and means fuse into flows of action.

This suggests that many gains happen outside strategic arenas. For instance, traditions of "organizing" have their distinctive goals: helping people feel empowered, getting them interested in politics, and recruiting them to act in various arenas. Someone persuades a friend to go to a rally, or to stop eating meat. These gains are hard to observe because they mostly happen outside strategic arenas themselves. They occur in living rooms and bars, break rooms, and commuter trains; in the streets outside factories shut by strikes. Those gains—or, in the opposite case, losses—translate into new strategic interactions in arenas old and new. Scholars recognize the importance of these processes but rarely include them as movement outcomes or consequences.

Our approach combines strategic interaction with a local, microlevel focus to examine players as they interact in and around arenas. This framework allows us to see multiple gains and losses that are linked in a variety of ways, moving beyond questions about success or failure but also about big "consequences." Impacts differ for different subplayers even on the same team. The complexities can be daunting, but that's the nature of reality.

---

The chapters that follow try to make sense of these complexities by identifying packages of gains and losses associated with protestors' strategies. Chapter 2, about Seattle's battle over a $15-an-hour minimum wage, highlights the challenges of establishing a new arena. The player who creates an arena "owns" it in a way, so that it gains credit for its accomplishments there but is also blamed for its failures. Powerful players expect to control what happens in the new arena, but—as the engagement dilemma suggests—perfect control is impossible. We'll see Seattle's Mayor Ed Murray, who created not one but two new arenas to get the minimum wage passed, struggle with the "arena-creation" package that resulted from his strategy. He personally owned the main arenas that drafted Seattle's new minimum wage law.

# 2

# Creating Arenas

## $15 an Hour in Seattle

> For this major offensive victory to take place is huge, and it could
> easily not have taken place, and it could have been defeated at a
> number of points.
>
> —Activist from Socialist Alternative

On June 2, 2014, the Seattle City Council passed the first ever $15-per-hour
law in a major US city. As of 2021, every Seattle worker made the new minimum wage (most made it before then), and the wage will continue to grow
with inflation. The players who crafted the bill include an avowed socialist,
the owner of Seattle's iconic Space Needle tower, many representatives of the
city's labor movement, and Democratic Mayor Ed Murray. If the bill's content
was unusual, the agents of its construction were even more so.[1]

Since fast-food workers in New York City went on strike in 2012, demanding $15 an hour and a union, the $15 number has been discussed
across the country. Before Seattle, the demand seemed aspirational, but since
June 2014 many cities have followed suit, suggesting that Seattle inspired
movements, organizations, and elected officials elsewhere.

How did Seattle do it? Although Seattle has some legal–structural
features (nonpartisan local elections; city-level ballot initiatives) that helped
movement activists, such features are not unique to Seattle. The city wrestles
with homelessness and other types of material inequality, but again, no

---

[1] Primary data for this chapter come from twenty-one interviews that Luke Elliott-Negri
conducted in 2016: four elected politicians (Mayor Murray, Councilmember Sawant, then-
Councilmember Licata, and now Congressperson Jayapal), one journalist, nine labor leaders, three
members of Socialist Alternative (in addition to Sawant), two leaders in community-based (though
labor-funded) organizations, and two business leaders. Unless otherwise attributed, all quotes come
from these interviews. In addition, we used secondary sources to construct the timeline of events that
comprised the strategic interactions leading up to the passage of the law.

*Gains and Losses.* James M. Jasper, Luke Elliott-Negri, Isaac Jabola-Carolus, Marc Kagan, Jessica
Mahlbacher, Manès Weisskircher, and Anna Zhelnina, Oxford University Press. © Oxford University Press 2022.
DOI: 10.1093/oso/9780197623251.003.0003

more than other cities. Seattle is relatively white, but again it is not the only US city with a high level of racial homogeneity (such as Portland, just a few hours south).[2]

Ultimately we need a granular, microlevel description of the strategic interactions that produced gains and losses on the way to the new minimum wage law in order to explain this exceptional outcome. There is no mechanical relationship between preexisting conditions or political opportunities and the outcome in Seattle.

In this case, we see the risks that a player faces in creating, or coming to own, an arena. Players can craft a new arena to their advantage, but this does not guarantee their desired outcomes. And if things go wrong, they may be blamed, as they now "own" the arena. The engagement dilemma suggests that no outcome is ever assured, so that opening a new line of engagement (including a new arena) always carries risks, even for well-positioned players. In constructing a new arena, a player also faces the pyramid dilemma, over how centralized the arena should be, and the powerful-allies dilemma around whom to include. The eventual result is an *arena-creation package* of gains and losses (see table 2.1).

## The Origins of $15

Several previous rounds of strategic interaction were the relevant context in which political, labor union, community, and business players interacted to produce the $15 Seattle minimum wage in 2014. Since at least the 1980s, the network surrounding community organizer Jon Kest—formerly of ACORN (later rebranded as New York Communities for Change), and whose brother Steve was working for the Service Employees International Union (SEIU)— had proposed targeting fast-food workers for unionization. In the late aughts, the New York City-based Kest pitched to SEIU the idea of organizing fast-food workers around the demand for $15 and a union.

In 2011, a community-labor coalition in Seattle, comprised of many of the same players who would come together for the $15 fight, successfully passed paid sick leave legislation at the city level (covering private-sector and city employees), with little input from business leaders. "Paid sick leave came out of the blue, and it was passed before the Chamber [of Commerce] had a

---

[2] In 2010, Seattle was 66 percent non-Hispanic white, down from 85 percent in 1970.

Table 2.1  The Arena-Creation Package

| Dilemmas | Player's Goal | Likely Costs | Risks |
|---|---|---|---|
| Engagement | Make a substantive gain through a process that a player creates and controls | New arenas require time and attention to establish; other players have openings for maneuvering | Player increases its "responsibility" for outcome—or failure to produce outcome; creating enemies among players in existing arenas, which the player avoided in creating new arena |
| Pyramid | Produce outcome efficiently, with maximal control over process | Generate resentment among players excluded from arena | Players see the arena as false, or see the arena entrepreneur as both judge and player in a way that is unfair |
| Powerful allies | Admit players to the arena with the capacity to produce desired substantive gain | Reduced control over the arena, the details of the gain, or even the goal itself; once powerful players are in the arena, they can and do operate independently (like all players but more so) | Arena slips from creator's grasp |
| Solutions | Maintain positive relationships with players both in and out of the arena; explain to players from other arenas why there was a need for a new arena and that it does not undermine theirs; minimize the importance of the arena substantively or over time to excluded players. Manage the tradeoff between pyramid and powerful allies by exerting influence in the arena consistently but without being perceived as bullying. | | |

chance to react to it," said one Seattle owner. The paid sick leave project helped to build trust among various progressive players in Seattle, who learned to work together. This history—at once affective and practical—made the next round of strategic interaction in Seattle more doable for labor organizers. At the same time, business interests swore never to be caught flat-footed again.

As Occupy Seattle and encampments around the U.S. were fading in early 2012, a small left-wing organization called Socialist Alternative sought to redirect movement energy and attention into arenas other than public parks. They called for 200 Occupiers across the country to run for elective office.

Few took up the call, but in Seattle, Kshama Sawant ran for state representative, surprising herself and her organization by gaining nearly 30 percent of the vote as a socialist in a partisan general election. Socialist Alternative initially viewed electoral politics primarily as an opportunity to discuss socialism explicitly in public arenas. But the surprise showing gave the organization a boost of confidence: perhaps they could actually take office, not just educate.

Socialist Alternative strategist Philip Locker says, "The pithy answer [to how we came to run a serious campaign for elective office] is luck. The more politically correct answer, which I do believe, is that our run in 2012 really confirmed we had an analysis." A year later, Sawant won an at-large city council seat in a nonpartisan race, this time making a $15 minimum wage central to her campaign.

Meanwhile, two SEIU efforts—one national and one local—unfolded in parallel and then dovetailed. In New York, SEIU decided to fund Jon Kest's fast-food organizing, secretly at first, until it became a more obviously popular endeavor. These 2012 efforts spread across the United States over the coming year through SEIU's federated structure, notwithstanding Kest's death that year. In Seattle, several labor unions launched an effort to organize airport workers in the nearby town of SeaTac with funding from SEIU 775. When the coalition's efforts faced significant legal hurdles, the unions decided to run a $15-minimum wage ballot initiative, in part to build leverage against the main employer (the airport) but also influenced by the emerging national minimum wage fight. The initiative ultimately passed on the same day that Sawant was elected to the city council and Ed Murray was elected as mayor in Seattle. One business leader said explicitly that the SeaTac initiative was so potent and comprehensive that Seattle's business community was pushed to negotiate in earnest in order to prevent something similar. It also encouraged advocates to be assertive in their demands.

It is against this backdrop—a national push for $15 minimum wage from SEIU, a local one from Socialist Alternative, and two recent progressive victories—that strategic interactions unfolded toward the $15-minimum wage legislation. While the context is undoubtedly important, animating the strategy, emotions, and sense of possibility held by various players, the interactions that led to the legislation cannot be reduced to that context. Players responded actively to one another across a series of arenas—some created on the fly—with often contradictory or at least disparate goals, generating a series of gains and losses for all involved.

## $15 an Hour in Seattle

Sawant's surprising but ultimately failed 2012 race for state representative was a short-term loss bundled with important long-term gains: Socialist Alternative activists were surprised and inspired by their strong showing and felt empowered to return to the electoral arena, buoyed by emotions of confidence and excitement. Sawant gained attention from potential allies in the labor movement, an important news and culture blog in Seattle (*The Stranger*), and, of course, the broader urban public. Socialist Alternative refined their rhetoric (no more "End Capitalism!" on Sawant campaign posters), and Sawant ran for city council in 2013, another arena of electoral politics. At first, $15 was one of her three central policy proposals. But energized by the fast-food strikes, bolstered by the organizing in SeaTac, and with a sense that $15 was an economically reasonable number, Sawant's team put $15 at the center of its messages.

Numerous players in both the labor and business communities credited Sawant with making $15 "the issue" in the 2013 city elections. Although SEIU (and its partner, the nonprofit Working Washington) were organizing fast-food strikes in Seattle, they were initially more focused on organizing against employer wage theft than the $15 demand, according to Socialist Alternative members. "We were actually told by some of the organizers at the protests, 'Don't talk about 15. This is a wage theft campaign. We're going to have much more impact by talking about wage theft than we are about 15.'" But Sawant's strong showing in a first round of voting, along with several public opinion polls, demonstrated the resonance of the minimum wage issue.

Meanwhile, Ed Murray was running for mayor against a strong, progressive incumbent, who was portraying Murray as conservative. In September 2013, Murray and his team decided to come out in support of a $15 minimum wage, both in a public forum organized by SEIU and in a more detailed white paper. When interviewed later, Murray said, "Supporting $15 hampered my own campaign because it was a blow to relationships with business. . . . It was a risky move, but one I believed in." Sawant's focus on the issue mattered, and the SEIU helped convince Murray to adopt the position: two days after announcing his support for $15, SEIU 775 endorsed Murray, providing both money and "boots on the ground" for his campaign. Shortly after, the incumbent Mayor McGinn jumped on board, suggesting that he would even consider a $16 minimum wage. But by then, Murray had 775's support and was seen as a champion of the issue. Turning the mayor's race into a "can-you-top-this" minimum wage conversation was a clear-cut gain for the players—namely, Sawant/Socialist Alternative and SEIU—who had $15/hour legislation as their goal. A socialist organization and a labor union compelled two mayoral candidates to adopt that goal.

Election Day 2013 was pivotal in several ways. In SeaTac, the labor unions and community players won $15 at the ballot box. Strategic interaction doesn't end just because of a ballot victory: indeed, business-side players resisted the outcome in the courts for *years* after the victory, until the Washington State Supreme Court finally settled the matter in favor of labor in 2015. Still, the ballot win in SeaTac inspired movement players and frightened business players up the road in Seattle.

On the same day, both Sawant and Murray won their respective races for council and mayor, creating a sense in the business community that the $15 threat was real. Howard Wright—owner of Seattle's Space Needle—concluded that the legislation was coming one way or the other. This key business-side player now had a sense of its inevitability due to Sawant and Murray's electoral victories, as well as the SeaTac victory, contested though it was. Rather than oppose all legislation, he determined instead to engage in negotiations meant to weaken the final legislative product.

Sawant's election represented a gain for Socialist Alternative that is hard to overstate. Two years before, the organization had set the goal of transferring movement energy to electoral arenas. Sawant's first race achieved that in part by turning her into a serious contender and gaining the attention of some left-leaning segments of the labor movement, the media, and the public. But the second race cemented it. An administrative assistant in city hall described Sawant's new office as a kind of social work/social movement hub: telephone calls are as likely to come from tenants at risk of eviction as from constituents concerned about potholes. (We see a similar combination of electoral and practical housing efforts in chapter 5.) This electoral victory also came with another gain, money. Suddenly Sawant could employ several Socialist Alternative members as full-time paid staff.

An influx of cash and a mayor with a new $15/hour goal were both gains for "the movement," but they accrued to specific subplayers: Socialist Alternative/Sawant—not "the movement"—now had paid staff. Sawant's victory is an example of movement players not just influencing the state but actually becoming *part of it*. Rather than reading movements and states as homogeneous wholes, we find strategic interactions among players in various arenas that span diverse state and movement players, much like the new arenas for participatory budgeting we will see in the next chapter. Tracing these interactions gives us a clearer sense of the connection between a seemingly anarchic movement like "Occupy" and the $15 policy gain.

A month later, on a cold December 5, protesters walked from SeaTac to Seattle City Hall—dubbed the "15-mile march." The action gained media attention and sent a clear message to the business community: what happened in SeaTac was just round one. One SEIU staffer said about this trek in the freezing cold:

> I think after we won 15, I think a lot of people asked how did you do it, what's the formula? And I think that's one of the biggest mistakes in a question, right? Because I feel like a lot of what we did was react to things that were happening, and be proactive and push the dial, and my instructions when I got the fast-food campaign from my bosses at the time were like (a) create chaos, (b) experiment, and (c), I was specifically told that if we didn't make mistakes we were doing something wrong. So the idea that the 15-mile march wouldn't work wasn't that big of a deal, because worst case scenario, I'd have to go to the gym that night, right?

Despite the large literature critical of union bureaucracy, here we see union staffers given free rein to "experiment" and "create chaos." Occasionally, unions' deep pockets can be paired with social movement goals and tactics. At their best, labor unions can be both disruptive and well funded, allowing their allies to manage the powerful-allies dilemma.

At the same time, the SEIU staffer just quoted suggests what is so vital about a strategic-interaction approach to movement gains and losses: there are no universal formulas for victory.

## Mayor Murray Forms His First Arena

In mid-December 2013, after the march and after the victories of Sawant and Murray (but before they took office), strategic interaction around the $15 idea began in earnest. Murray is a career politician who had previously been a state legislator. However, for Sawant and Socialist Alternative, entering city politics meant something very different than it did for Murray. Sawant, as well as other members of Socialist Alternative, expressed in interviews her initial resistance to running for office, and her awareness of the risks of what we call the electoral package. Between her own orientation to the work and Socialist Alternative's explicit critique of careerism, Sawant was less bound by the political norms of the city council arena.

Mayor-elect Murray scheduled a press conference for December 19, at which he planned to announce the formation of a new arena: the Income Inequality Advisory Committee (IIAC), which would seek to craft legislation acceptable to all the key business, labor, and community players. We typically use the engagement dilemma to analyze benefits, costs, and risks when a player decides whether to *enter* an arena. But players confront similar tradeoffs when they decide to *create* new arenas, as the mayor-elect did here.

Despite a campaign focused on the number "15," there were no digits in the IIAC's name. Some gains can erode more easily than others. It is one thing for movement players to shift the mayor's goal priorities and yet another to maintain those priorities long enough to get a serious policy gain. The IIAC might have proved a false arena for pro-$15 activists, with the deck stacked hopelessly against them. Howard Wright hoped that $15 might not be in the final legislation at all, and the committee's name seemed to signal that was possible. "I really thought that we would be working toward a goal, $12.50, or . . . But very quickly it became clear we were going to $15."

On December 17, Sawant held her own press conference at city hall, two days before the mayor-elect's, promising to make good on her campaign commitment to $15 and upstaging her fellow victor. Representatives of SEIU 775 were present at *both* press conferences, and indeed Sawant was present at the mayor's as well. All three players had made the nominal commitment to a $15 minimum wage. Yet each player—Sawant, Murray, and SEIU 775—had multiple motivations and goals, as well as contrasting tastes in tactics. Among other things, Sawant wanted to build her organization, Socialist Alternative; Murray wanted to be seen as a successful new mayor; and SEIU 775 aimed to be the first local to win the minimum wage fight that their colleagues in New York had started.

In January 2014, Murray took office and officially formed what turned out to be a massive, unwieldy IIAC. The group was comprised of two dozen players representing various segments of the business community, the labor unions, and community organizations, as well as three members of the city council (which would ultimately have to pass any bill that emerged). The mayor faced tradeoffs associated with engaging powerful allies in the context of a new arena—admit too many players who were too powerful, and he might lose control, but restrict access too much and it might be seen as illegitimate, a false arena. The IIAC quickly bogged down. Proposals were neutralized through endless conversation, as Murray maintained a light touch in meetings. In interviews, players from both camps recounted long and generally fruitless gatherings.

In these early stages, it was hard to imagine labor, business, and individuals like Sawant finding a common ground. To maneuver in the new arena, labor and other sympathetic groups formed "$15 for Seattle," an ad hoc coalition to develop common strategy for the IIAC process, which included many players excluded from the IIAC itself. Meanwhile the business community formed "One Seattle" for similar reasons. At the start at least, the lines were clear: business versus labor and community, with Murray sidelined in ways he had not expected.

The decision to create an arena carries a package of expected gains and losses. Players who create arenas hope to increase their own influence, but to do this, they not only have to write the rules but also exert control over who is allowed into the arena. The excluded players, in turn, may make claims of illegitimacy, or seek other ways to influence the process—in this case through the two additional player/arenas. The IIAC did afford the mayor control, but perhaps not enough: the cumbersome interactions reflected the tension between control and exclusion that is typical of arena creation. In addition to the perils of the engagement dilemma, creating an arena normally leaves you owning it, with your reputation rising or falling with it.

## Players as Arenas—Dynamics within "the Movement"

For all the progressive groups except one, $15 for Seattle was not just a player but also the most important *arena* aside from the IIAC. Their plan was that decisions made inside the new group would then determine bargaining in the formal IIAC process. Socialist Alternative, however, had other ideas. In January 2014, Socialist Alternative announced the formation of yet another new player, 15NOW, which would build mass support for the legislative goal of $15 and agitate to make the law as strong as possible. One Socialist Alternative activist said, "For us it was a war, and the question was, how do we build the strongest possible army on our side? So that's what 15NOW was about, was building the strongest possible force on our side, in every way, both from making arguments publicly to people on the street making noise." 15NOW ultimately developed chapters across the city that met weekly and hosted monthly rallies that attracted hundreds.

This gain for Socialist Alternative was simultaneously a loss for the most powerful labor unions in the coalition. SEIU, the Central Labor Council, and others lost some control over the movement when Socialist Alternative created 15NOW. The name itself hit on a major point of contention, both within the labor coalition and between business and labor: if the $15 number seemed inevitable to some, the big question was *when?* From the outset, Socialist Alternative was publicly committed to $15 "now," meaning a $15 minimum wage for all workers in Seattle, the day after the law was passed. Others in the room were willing to be more flexible. A number of informants reported that some individuals in the coalition had their own personal agendas, making them less concerned with the details of the legislation, as long as it contained "15."

The Socialist Alternative path was particularly disconcerting for one co-alition partner, the Main Street Alliance (MSA), composed of politically progressive small business owners inclined to support pro-worker policies such as an increased minimum wage. MSA had been active in constructing and passing the paid sick days law in Seattle. "But nevertheless, I think it's fair to say that we [at MSA] were freaked out about the notion of 15 now and wanted to see it halfway toward yes," reported one organizer. MSA was certainly a labor ally, especially relative to some small business owners on the other side of the table who wanted 15 *never*. In any case, the "now" po-sition that Socialist Alternative took, while creating anxiety on the other side of the table, also created plenty on the labor side, highlighting potential disagreements in this compound player.

So even from the start, many tensions were at play. Inside the IIAC, busi-ness, and labor–community players were at odds. But inside the $15 for Seattle coalition, Socialist Alternative had, at least rhetorically, a core goal that varied significantly from the more flexible goals held by most others. As usual, the extension dilemma resulted in conflicts over tactics.

As soon as $15 for Seattle formed, it created a subcommittee to explore the possibility of a ballot measure, which lurked as a possibility if the final IIAC outcome failed to reach $15 an hour. Business players were apprehensive about the ballot: "We did three rounds of market research as the Chamber or as One Seattle, and the labor unions did at least one round that they shared with me. And that said, if this $15 issue goes to the ballot, it passes with between 68 and 73 percent of the vote." If the IIAC process failed, one or more players would take the project directly to the voters.

The labor unions in $15 for Seattle ultimately decided to hold back that tactic and remain committed to the IIAC process, at least rhetorically. In part, SEIU 775 and other unions did not want to threaten their relationship with the new mayor, who had staked his reputation on this committee. A failed IIAC would also mean a failed start in office for a new ally. But Socialist Alternative and Sawant had no such concerns. They felt that without the viable threat of a ballot measure—or ultimately a charter amendment, a similar tool but more difficult to overturn—business leaders would not negotiate with any sincerity in the IIAC arena.

## Activity outside the IIAC

In February, both business and labor players were active. Fast-food workers, again supported mostly by SEIU, staged a one-day citywide boycott of big burger chains. Throughout the day, protesters visited all twenty-five major chains, receiving extensive media attention. Such actions were part of SEIU's broader national fast-food worker organizing, but they also focused the local Seattle public conversation on the minimum wage. The protests did not directly target local business leaders who sat on the other side of the table in the IIAC.

"Big business" was active *within* the One Seattle coalition, hidden from the public in their resistance to a higher minimum wage. According to one informant, the business coalition "hired an African-American organizer to go around to all the Black small business owners and tell them it was going to be bad for businesses, and they got . . . some of the Asian businesses fired up." In February, the Chamber of Commerce conducted a poll of businesses, with many reporting that they would be forced to fire workers if there were extreme shifts in the minimum wage, a classic business tactic to scare residents and workers of the city.

The particular journalists who reported on these events were key. We tend to conceptualize "the media" and its response to "social movements" as if journalists were homogeneous players without agency. At the microlevel, where we observe simple players traversing intersecting sets of arenas, the line between media and social movements is more porous. Here we conceive of journalists as themselves strategic players. One interviewee noted: "[H]onestly the fact that it was Lynn Thompson of the *Seattle Times* covering it and not one of their more conservative reporters I think made a significant difference . . . [She spent] a lot of time talking to the right people and asking skeptical questions." The case of a second journalist is even more telling for the study of social movements. Anna Minard, from the *Stranger*, now works for SEIU-funded *Working Washington*. These two journalists were key allies for labor-side players in the media. They reported on the policy issue, not on the movement as disruptive outsiders (Amenta and Shortt 2020).

## The Radical-Flank Threat

With spring on the way, and after many weeks of slow negotiations at IIAC, Socialist Alternative filed the charter amendment initiative and began collecting signatures. Socialist Alternative stated publicly that they wanted the IIAC to work, but if business-side players would not negotiate with sincerity, they and 15NOW would run a massive ballot box campaign for a $15 minimum wage, to be implemented immediately upon its passage. There was finally an open fissure in $15 for Seattle. 15NOW hosted monthly public meetings attended by hundreds, who voted on the content of the amendment. Created by Socialist Alternative, 15NOW became another movement arena. Like Mayor Murray, Socialist Alternative faced the engagement dilemma in creating this new arena—they wanted broad participation but also to control the outcomes. The split was at once a loss and an opening for SEIU and top coalition leaders, generating a radical-flank effect. An ally was "out of control," but labor negotiators in the IIAC could now plausibly say to the business interests, in so many words, "You better back down or we don't know if we can control these folks." Labor players even attended the 15NOW meetings, suggesting to business-side players that Socialist Alternative might eventually convince them to support it.

The friction among movement players notwithstanding, to business leaders the ballot threat was compelling. Sawant and Socialist Alternative were the reason they were dealing with the minimum wage issue in the first place. "We knew from the election of council member Sawant . . . that this would be an issue that was dealt with. . . . It was too big an issue to be the first issue the mayor had to deal with. But I understand why he had to do it. Kshama put him in that position" (quoted in Feit 2014). Moreover, business leaders expressed in interviews a personal dislike for Sawant; they found her unpleasant to deal with. Her style and rhetoric, along with Social Alternative's tactics, made SEIU 775 president David Rolf and the other labor leaders seem more appealing.

Lynn Thompson, the journalist who reported on the IIAC process, said, "SEIU was all too happy to have this complete firebrand out front, who seemed even more radical. I mean, they kind of rode her momentum. So they would look conciliatory. 'This is what you're going to get if you don't work with us.'" In this telling, there was indeed a "movement" in which SIEU moderates worked comfortably and happily with the Socialist Alternative radicals. But a group interview with several labor leaders revealed more ambivalence. One said, "I think that that pressure from the left was not un-useful," but a second disagreed: "At the time, I don't think we saw it that way." And the third: "Nope, [we didn't]." Dilemmas create disagreements. Only in hindsight, after a victory, was SEIU "all too happy": flanks may create power, but they also rankle their nominal allies.

One elected official, Pramila Jayapal, captured the radical-flank dynamic as it unfolded not only between Socialist Alternative and SEIU but, in parallel, between Sawant and Murray:

> As much as Sawant and Murray did not like each other, I do think they needed each other, in a strange way, and that neither one of them would be successful without the other. Ed seems reasonable compared to Kshama, and he brings the business folks and everybody he needs to get in order to get the deal through, and Kshama pulls in the left edge and sets up a "bad guy" to rail against. They wouldn't admit it, but the two together are not a bad combination to get something done.

Left labor organizer Jonathan Rosenblum captures the radical-flank dilemma: "the question is, how do you use [tension] within the movement... to your advantage and not let it become something that weakens you and rather something that strengthens you?"

The tension between Socialist Alternative and the labor leaders was not the only one in the pro-$15 movement. Should unionized workplaces be exempt on the grounds that workers could bargain for what they wanted, such as other benefits in lieu of wages? Should tips be included, allowing employers to pay tipped workers a lower minimum wage? There were also demographic tensions: key labor leaders were white men, and the labor unions wielded more power than community organizations. These internal tensions reinforce a vital point: all compound players are, at times, also arenas. When facing business, $15 for Seattle was a player. But when determining goals and strategies, $15 for Seattle was an arena that one informant called "brutal."

Similar tensions and internal strategic interactions occurred in the business community, especially over whether small businesses should be allowed a lower minimum wage. Although it presented itself as a unified player inside the IIAC, One Seattle, like $15 for Seattle, was itself an arena where players battled over the ultimate goals of the larger player of which they were a part.

## Mayor Murray's Second Arena

The lines of antagonism in the IIAC were clear. The main issues the players faced were the length of the $15 phase-in period (if any), whether there would be an exemption for employers with tipped workers, and the definition of a small business. With IIAC negotiations dragging on, and facing the humiliating paralysis or collapse of his first arena, in March Mayor Murray formed a second arena that became known as the G8—an IIAC subgroup ultimately comprised of three labor leaders and three business leaders (two others dropped out). Murray again faced the tradeoffs associated with arena creation, specifically with respect to the pyramid dilemma, that is, how centralized to make the arena: he increased his control with the smaller arena, chairing meetings more aggressively (participants report his yelling at them on multiple occasions before storming out of the room), and the group made some progress. As the mayor himself reported, perhaps reflecting his growing confidence in office, "There seems to be something that people respond to when you're mayor, unlike when you're the chair of ways and means committee." He expected that the tighter group would make it easier for him to wield the charisma of office. But with increased control over a smaller number of players came a corresponding loss: decreased control over the excluded players, both those supportive of the legislation and those opposed.

The unions and business leaders who agreed to sit on the G8 also experienced various gains and losses. Business delay was no longer viable under Murray's watchful eye, a gain for labor, but Murray also wanted to make business happy. The new arena made these players more powerful than those who were left out, but less powerful relative to Murray. The opportunity to enter a new arena with a sympathetic but powerful "judge" presents a dilemma—the judge may sympathize with you more than with the opposition, but you also cede power to him. Any player who enters or creates an arena faces the engagement dilemma: the risks of starting a new line of interaction.

Outside the committee, 15NOW's charter amendment hovered. In order to make passage more likely, 15NOW felt they had to appease small businesses, to which many Seattle residents were sympathetic. Even Socialist Alternative committed itself to a three-year phase-in period for small businesses. For the labor negotiators, however, the three-year phase-in created a new and weaker baseline from which to negotiate inside the IIAC and G8. "If they were going to be involved," complained one, "they should have taken a hard line." Added another: "Kshama announced that they were going to introduce this compromise, without consulting with her [15 for Seattle] coalition partners, at a point where [Socialist Alternative had been] holding a very strong line. So . . . it was bad negotiating and premature compromise." Finally: "We wanted business to come forward with seven [year implementation] and we say no and land at three. Instead, we were saying, ok, three, so then they could say ten, and land at seven."

Of course, Sawant expressed her own perspective:

I would actually challenge—in a friendly way—challenge them [labor leaders] into thinking more deeply about this, because given that we knew we were not going to win 15 now, it's disingenuous to say, "We thought we were going for it all." No, we all knew there was going to be bargaining involved; let's be honest. It's a question of what terms you are willing to bargain on. I think that's the difference.

Another informant, affiliated with neither labor nor Socialist Alternative, suggested that, setting aside Socialist Alternative's calculations, labor negotiators could have gotten to five years, but they were not motivated to push hard at the end. Informants reported that simply having the number "15" in the legislation was more important for some than the many other details.

Socialist Alternative's distance from the $15 for Seattle coalition created a credible threat to which labor negotiators could refer, but not a flank over which they had meaningful control. There was no "movement" that experienced a conscious dilemma with explicit tradeoffs, but rather multiple players with disparate goals and means. Socialist Alternative's three-year rollout for small business made the amendment a credible threat but weakened—according to some—the bargaining position of the labor leaders in the G8. One player felt sure that a legitimate ballot or amendment threat was necessary to get the best possible outcome from the IIAC process, while others wanted Socialist Alternative to simply take a "hard line" and otherwise stay out of the negotiating details.

Business players took the ballot threat seriously, in their own version of the engagement dilemma. Despite their deep pockets, they could not be sure of turning public opinion around on the charter issue. Their loss in SeaTac was fresh in their minds, and they thought that labor might rejoin Socialist Alternative and Sawant in the charter campaign. Better, they decided, to make concessions in a familiar arena, the G8, than to enter a new and unpredictable arena, the charter ballot.

One key issue in negotiations—whether businesses offering health insurance or with tipped employees would be allowed to count this compensation against the wage—spilled into the public eye. In April, *The Stranger* blog received an email leak from One Seattle, the business-side coalition. It reported,

> [p]erhaps one of the most remarkable things discussed was a strategy to involve tipped workers themselves, the e-mail says. One bar owner reportedly said 20 bars and restaurants had a meeting with tipped employees to, according to the memo, **spread the idea that 15 Now wants to get rid of tips entirely.** They told the employees that if a $15 minimum wage is passed without a tip credit, **employees will no longer get tips at all.** (bold in original) (Holden 2014)

Business owners were meeting directly with workers to scare them into opposition. Socialist Alternative and 15NOW were quick to respond:

> [W]e started a counteroffensive. We made a giant banner that said, '15+ tips.' They were trying to organize a group of tipped workers.... We thought that that was ridiculous that they were trying to do that.... We bumped into a group of the tipped workers at ... an event at the council, and so one of our organizers spoke to one of the tipped workers there. And they talked for a few minutes, they set up a meeting, and so they met with some people from 15NOW and with Kshama, and all but one of them flipped.

As spring unfolded, key negotiators grew closer to a compromise. The tip exemption remained a sticking point. Although some players in $15 for Seattle were open to caving on the issue, the labor negotiators inside the G8 insisted on preventing the exemption. David Rolf of SEIU ultimately came up with the idea to allow a tip exemption and then phase it out (Feit 2014). Two players on the IIAC shared the idea with the group in a document titled "Nick and Eric's Nobody Is Happy Proposal." This seemed to unlock a key sticking point, but the provision ultimately would have an effect beyond Seattle.

On April 22, with the G8—and hence the IIAC—process on the verge of concluding, the pro-$15 players staged a rally, with hundreds surrounding city hall. Although Socialist Alternative had long parted ways with the labor coalition, all the players participated in this public event. They expected an agreement to come out of the IIAC the next day and wanted business players to feel some final pressure, to experience viscerally how popular an exemption-free minimum wage bill was in Seattle.

But on April 23, hours before the mayor's press conference, the inside negotiators hit another snag: the number of employees separating large businesses that had three years to phase in the new minimum wage from small businesses that had seven years. According to David Rolf, we "came into the room and said, 'We think we've got a deal, we have an agreement, we're ready to pop the champagne.' We then went through the exercise of reading aloud what we thought the agreement was, and when I got to 500 employees *nationally* they said, 'No, you said *local*.' Apparently, their notes said [businesses with up to] 500 local employees," would be eligible for the seven-year provision (quoted in Feit 2014). That way, megachains like Walmart might have fewer than 500 employees in Seattle and get the longer phase-in.

Murray had to face journalists empty-handed. Thompson of the *Seattle Times* said, "[W]e all show up and he's like, 'I don't have an agreement.' And it seemed devastating at the time. It seemed like, this is a huge political disaster. He said, 'I'm staking my mayor-ship on this.' . . . [T]he thing's falling apart is what it felt like." The increased responsibility associated with arena creation was on full display. Over the next five days tensions rose in the IIAC, but ultimately the labor-side view prevailed: legislation based on 500 national employees. Mayor Murray announced the final plan on May 1.

The outcome was diverse bundles of gains and losses for the major compound players, as well as for individual players. Socialist Alternative had originally demanded $15 *now*, while "people being born now would have been in college by the time they were making $15/hour if business had had their way," according to one informant. Instead, the three-year phase-in for big business and the seven-year phase-in for small businesses was both a gain and a loss for many players and was interpreted differently by players even on the same "side." Mayor Murray faced a version of the engagement dilemma when he created the IIAC, and all players who entered faced their own engagement dilemmas. May 1 was the culmination of the fraught decision-making in that arena, but it was hardly the end of the strategic interaction.

Murray acutely felt the joined dilemmas of the arena-creation package, as he explicitly created and implicitly owned two new arenas. Of course, he faced the engagement dilemma in choosing to construct and engage the arena at all, but he simultaneously faced the pyramid and powerful allies dilemmas. The pivot from the IIAC to the G8 reflected a new, provisional resolution to the pyramid dilemma—choosing greater control while accepting the risks of excluding some powerful players. In deciding whom to include and exclude, Murray also faced the tradeoffs typical of maintaining—or alienating—powerful allies.

Other participants who shared Murray's ambitions experienced some of the same tradeoffs of arena creation without the responsibility of owning the arenas. Together they were able to manage the strategy's risks by browbeating business players, partly through another engagement dilemma and through radical-flank pressure. Pro-$15 players stuck with the new arenas to get what they wanted. Opponents remained in them to avoid getting a worse outcome.

## It Ain't Over . . . Ever

An outcome in one arena can be a clear end in itself—new legislation—but it is also a capacity that players can carry into other arenas. Although $15 for Seattle and the players that comprised it set the policy agenda in Seattle and won a significant victory, the strategic interactions continued and expanded into new arenas. In the month between when the IIAC presented its final plan publicly and the city council passed it, all involved had agreed not to lobby for changes. Murray's intention was to contain strategic interaction within one arena—the IIAC—over which he held significant influence, but no sooner did it dissolve, then interactions unfolded in other arenas, over which he exercised less control. Throughout May, Sawant denounced the outcome publicly, arguing that the phase-in periods were unnecessary concessions to the mayor's friends in business. At the same time, some (although not all) business players continued to lobby city councilors to weaken the deal. On top of this, SEIU continued its fast-food organizing, staging a strike on May 15. A deal in the IIAC hardly made for peace in Seattle's many other arenas.

On June 2, ultimately with Sawant's vote, the city council unanimously passed the legislation. But even after this seemingly final moment, further rounds of strategic interaction unfolded at the state level. The legislation had included an odd compromise, one that was key to the IIAC's ability to complete its process. During the phase-in period only, businesses would be allowed to earn tip credit—that is, they could count tips toward the minimum wage they were paying their employees. However, in order to elect this option, they had to choose a higher starting minimum wage, making the credit economically meaningless to business owners. Then-State Senator Pramila Jayapal offered a theory:

> I got a lot of flak from some people, because the tip credit piece was seen as being included, even though it started with a much higher wage that negated any credit, and it was phased out over a few years. Economically, it was silly for business to ask for this because they were actually paying a higher wage than without the "credit" but they had a narrative reason to do this. They wanted to say that they had a "tip credit" in there. [T]he people who agree to take the tip credit had to agree to starting and moving at a different schedule than the people who don't take the tip credit. . . . So it was complicated. They would keep saying "we got a tip credit," but I have to explain to my colleagues in the legislature all the time that there is not a tip credit in there, because it doesn't go off a base wage. . . . It's just a way for them to come to the state legislature and say "We got a tip credit." . . . Even within my caucus I had Democrats who were telling me, "Seattle took a tip credit. . . Why don't you take a tip credit here?"

Washington State has the highest minimum wage in the country, with no exemption for tipped employees. A business leader confirmed explicitly that no sooner had the law passed in Seattle, then the business community began pointing to the exemption (of course, not highlighting the fact that it would ultimately be phased out) with state-level legislators in an effort to weaken state law. Gains and losses are often arena-specific. The phased-out tip exemption was a loss for business-side players in the IIAC arena. But that "loss" provided ammunition for battles, and potentially other gains, in other arenas that business players valued highly.

Some business players had still other plans. In addition to being frustrated with the outcome, some were aghast to learn that the Socialist Alternative threat of a charter amendment had not been real, due to a procedural misunderstanding on the organization's part. In Seattle, ballot initiatives can be filed every year, but charter amendments only every other year, meaning that the business community would have had more than a year to prepare to fight the amendment, in the court of public opinion and through various procedural means. Some business players felt they had been duped. A subset of the negotiators broke off to form Forward Seattle. The organization was registered to the address of David Minert, a small business owner who had played a minor part in the IIAC process. Forward Seattle went so far as to file for a ballot initiative to overturn the legislation, although it ultimately backed down.

With the phase-in period now over, every employee in Seattle earns a $15 minimum wage with no exemptions. This is a significant policy gain for labor–community players, a more robust minimum wage than any major US city had yet seen. At the same time, the tip exemption, although to be phased out, enabled the business leaders to pivot quickly to state-level arenas. Moreover, one interviewee suggested that seven years was long enough for them to regroup and attempt to phase out the phase-in, so to speak—that is, to make the tip exemption permanent at the city level. Even the most stable gains (and losses) can potentially be undone.

## Conclusion

In this chapter we have seen multiple cases of the strategy of arena *creation*. No sooner was he in office than Mayor Murray constructed the Income Inequality Advisory Committee. He selected the players; and then he set them loose—too loose—to make a high-stakes decision. When the arena, unwieldy in part because of the sheer number of players and in part because of their antagonism, could not produce the gain Murray desired, he created another arena, smaller, less formal, more temporary, where he could wield his influence with a heavier hand. In the G8, Murray yelled more and got his way.

Any new engagement carries risks, and constructing arenas involves tradeoffs that movement players may experience as dilemmas. In Murray's IIAC, he wielded a great amount of influence over the players in it, including selecting them, a clear gain. But creating the IIAC was not his only option. He could have gone directly to the city council to create the legislation, or indeed to the ballot. Mayor Murray got "buy-in" through the IIAC process from many business leaders who might otherwise have been angry with him for pushing such legislation. But there were risks: he might have alienated the members of city council who were not included, but who would ultimately be presented with the bill that the IIAC created. Or the arena might have collapsed, as it nearly did, damaging his reelection prospects.

The decision to create a new arena, rather than use already-existing arenas, led to a typical package of gains and losses. The expected common gain is increased control—a player who creates an arena largely defines the rules and norms, and may also function as a judge, as Murray did. But there are corresponding losses and risks, especially the alienation of excluded players and increased perception of responsibility.

In this chapter, a powerful player created temporary arenas. In the next chapter, we move to New York, where movement and political players created more permanent arenas as part of an effort to institutionalize participatory budgeting. We identify dilemmas that are common to the process of institutionalization, as movement players ally themselves with elected politicians who ultimately have greater capacity to determine the course of institutionalization. Subsequently, they must decide whether and how to continue to engage in the arenas those politicians have constructed. Nearly all players who seek to institutionalize new systems face these dilemmas, and the paths they choose in their efforts to resolve them create common packages of gains and losses.

# 3

# Institutionalizing Participatory Budgeting in New York City

In 2011, an alliance of New York activists won a cherished reform, empowering city residents to directly allocate $5.6 million in public funds. Four of the city's fifty-one council districts began this experiment in participatory budgeting (PB), an annual process that combines deliberative and direct democracy to reshape public decision-making. The program, Participatory Budgeting in New York City (PBNYC), ambitiously aimed to restore trust in government, improve public spending decisions, and expand civic engagement, especially among marginalized and low-income communities of color. Although applied to a tiny portion of the city's multi-billion-dollar annual budget, PBNYC's creation marked a significant victory for proponents of community control and public participation, whose efforts had been blocked for years by conservative and technocratic mayors.[1]

The experiment grew dramatically in 2014, when twenty-four districts participated. More than 50,000 city residents allocated $31.9 million of public funds in what was the country's largest PB process. This expansion was boosted by an early PB sponsor, Democratic City Council Member Melissa Mark-Viverito, who became council speaker that year. From this powerful position, Mark-Viverito worked with advocates to convert PBNYC from a pilot project coordinated by underresourced civil society groups into a full-fledged, government-led program. Engaging residents in a budgeting process that spanned nearly half the city's districts required significant administrative and outreach capacity. The transfer of these responsibilities

---

[1] This chapter draws on secondary sources, media accounts, original interviews, participant observation, and organizational documents. From 2012 to 2014, Isaac Jabola-Carolus was a staff member of the Participatory Budgeting Project. During the 2015–2016 budget cycle, he observed PBNYC's public forums and steering committee meetings, and conducted fifteen interviews with organizational leaders and officials involved in the participatory budgeting program. Organizational documents were accessed with the permission of the Participatory Budgeting Project and Community Voices Heard. We examine the time dynamics of this case in Jabola-Carolus et al. (2020), upon which we draw here.

*Gains and Losses.* James M. Jasper, Luke Elliott-Negri, Isaac Jabola-Carolus, Marc Kagan, Jessica Mahlbacher, Manès Weisskircher, and Anna Zhelnina, Oxford University Press. © Oxford University Press 2022.
DOI: 10.1093/oso/9780197623251.003.0004

Table 3.1  The Institutionalization Package

| Component Dilemmas | Player Goals | Likely Costs | Risks |
|---|---|---|---|
| Being There | Reduce engagement while bringing stability and resources to a past gain | Less influence over the stakes of an arena | Your priorities are more exposed to resistance |
| Powerful Allies | Leverage the power of players who have resources and standing to advance your priorities | Less control over decisions and resources | Ally pursues own goals, not yours |
| False Arenas | Retain influence, and create or restore real stakes, in an arena | Time and resources | Your time and resources are wasted; you legitimize an arena that has no real stakes |
| Solutions | Install sympathetic players in arena where you reduce engagement. Sustain pressure on powerful allies, or create accountability mechanisms between you and powerful allies. | | |

from civil society groups to central city council offices marked the first major step in PBNYC's institutionalization, its transition from temporary experiment to lasting public institution.

Advocates celebrated the paired expansion and institutionalization as the most significant victory since PBNYC's introduction. Yet within a year, these supporters found themselves confronting unforeseen challenges that threatened the quality of PB implementation and the program's community-led spirit. By examining their experience, this chapter illuminates the tradeoffs that accompany the institutionalization of social movement goals: activists may gain stability and resources for their policy or program, but they cede control to other players and expose their initiative to greater bureaucratic resistance. Table 3.1 summarizes this institutionalization package.

## Creation, 2009–2011

Participatory budgeting emerged as a model for democratic reform in 1989 in Brazil, where the city of Porto Alegre introduced the process as part of a radical agenda pioneered by the local Workers' Party. The innovation represented a historic confluence between social movements proposing new forms of democratic citizenship in the wake of dictatorship and the insurgent Workers' Party seeking to give voice to those movements (Abers 2000; Baiocchi 2005). The model spread throughout Brazil, and soon, across the globe. A flexible tool, it held what some have called "polyvalent appeal"— useful for redistributing funds to poor areas, sparking civic activism, improving public health outcomes, and enhancing government accountability (Ganuza and Baiocchi 2012).

The program appeared in the United States in 2009, arising from a collaboration between Chicago Alderman Joe Moore and a small group of activists and scholars. Moore's district-level program dedicated $1 million of his annual discretionary funds to public decision-making and established the dominant PB model in the United States. In this context, PB enables community control of public budget allocations through an annual, multistage process: community members suggest spending ideas at public assemblies and online, meet over several months to develop feasible proposals, and vote by the thousands for which projects to fund. Unlike their Brazilian forerunners, these PB processes have generally lacked the full backing of political parties or mayoral administrations, confining decision-making to relatively small discretionary budgets.

Looking to both Porto Alegre and Chicago, local groups in New York City began demanding PB in 2009. That year, New York's Right to the City Alliance featured PB in its widely publicized policy platform, which, among other demands, called for part of the public housing authority budget, and all council member discretionary funds, to be allocated through participatory means (Right to the City NYC 2009). Although the alliance dissolved one year later, the effort linked together three players who carried forward these PB goals: Community Voices Heard (CVH), a community-based membership organization of low-income women of color and public housing residents; the Participatory Budgeting Project (PBP), a newly founded organization that assisted the Chicago program and promoted PB nationwide; and the Community Development Project (CDP) at the Urban Justice Center, whose research and policy arm assisted community organizing groups through participatory action research and issue advocacy. These civil society organizations ultimately led the development of PBNYC.

CVH, based in East Harlem, saw PB as a promising tool for empowering public housing residents, a goal that overlapped with PBP's interest in engaging historically marginalized communities. Together, they brought. PB to the attention of local policymakers. Although CVH was inclined to confrontational protest that mobilized members, the two groups decided to begin with what Amenta (2006) calls "minimally assertive" tactics. In September 2010, they organized two public forums about PB, to which they invited all fifty-one members of the city council, as well as officials from the New York City Housing Authority and Office of Management and Budget. Addressing other activists, students, and a handful of officials who attended, speakers from CVH and local civic groups argued that elected officials and typical channels of participation shut out residents from decision-making, to the detriment of community well-being and government legitimacy. In their view, PB could repair the disconnect between officials and citizens; it represented a way to realize commonly held democratic ideals.

The headliner of both events was Chicago Alderman Joe Moore, who shared the impacts of PB on his district, reiterating the benefits of restored trust in government and improved spending decisions. But for the officials in the audience, he added an enticing hook. In a statement that reveals the powerful-allies dilemma inherent to participatory reforms and sheds light on why officials might want to embrace PB, he underscored the basic political rationale:

> You know, politicians by their very nature do not surrender power voluntarily, so I thought I'd try something different. And, you know what, I found that—something that I hope my counterparts here in New York understand—that in many respects, by giving up power, I ended up having more power. Because this is the single most popular thing I have done in my nineteen years as a member of the city council. (Pratt Institute 2010)

This admission from a relatable messenger reached two critical players: City Council Members Brad Lander and Melissa Mark-Viverito (Altschuler 2013). These rising stars, both Democrats, had recently founded a Progressive Caucus "dedicated to creating a more just and equal New York City." Among its nine priorities was "reform to restore confidence and participation in government" (Progressive Caucus 2010). PB offered a promising means to achieve that goal—and to increase their popularity at the same time. In a final piece of strategic event planning, PBP and CVH added further impetus by asking Lander to respond to Moore's presentation. Lander, who had held office for less than a year, later recalled being put on the spot: "I don't know if I fully realized at the time, of course, that I was just being set up to bring participatory budgeting here . . . [It was] very hard to say 'No'" (Pratt Institute 2012).

Within a few months, Lander invited CVH and PBP to discuss plans for the proposed initiative; they had won over their first New York official. Lander then worked within the city council to persuade Mark-Viverito and others to join him, and in 2011, four council members committed to implementing PB, by facilitating public decisions about approximately $1 million in each of their districts. In the months that followed, the officials formed a steering committee with CVH, PBP, CDP, and a host of local organizations to craft the program, which they named PBNYC (Baez and Hernandez 2012).

The biggest winner at this stage was PBP, which, as a newly founded non-profit, was eager to create PB programs and to demonstrate progress to gain funding for more advocacy. The participating council members offered small technical assistance contracts of a few thousand dollars to PBP and CVH, and the two organizations could also now apply for foundation grants to support their work.

For CVH, however, the launch of PBNYC was only a partial victory. Its main target, the city's public housing authority, remained elusive because Mayor Michael Bloomberg had little interest in participatory reforms. The district-based PB model, in which some discretionary funds might be won for public housing improvements, provided a less direct but potentially useful tool for engaging and building power within its main constituency. For similar reasons, CDP, which followed the lead of grassroots groups like CVH, viewed this first iteration of PBNYC as a positive but limited gain.

The council members, for their part, did not yet see gains in public support and were not yet fully convinced of PB's efficacy, but they did begin to garner positive press for sponsoring an innovative program.

Overall, the key players had advanced their stated missions or platforms and had achieved the first step in promoting reforms they deemed valuable, even if the starting point was relatively modest.[2]

---

[2] The initial PB allocations totaled less than 0.01 percent of the city's overall budget (Kasdan and Cattell 2012: 8), an amount far surpassed by PB initiatives in Latin America.

## Implementation, 2011–2013

Policies create new players and arenas (Pierson 1993). Participatory budgeting is no exception; its primary purpose is to create an arena that enables public participation in governmental decision-making. New York's PB program in fact established four arenas which structured implementation in its founding years. Strategic interactions within and across these arenas shaped the program's trajectory.

The first arena was the *street-level* PB process. This was the public site of policy implementation, a "public sphere" situated at the intersection of state and civil society (Baiocchi 2005; Lipsky 1980). Here, individual citizens and diverse civic organizations interacted with each other and with government representatives to discuss, define, and tackle public needs. In October and November 2013, for instance, 223 residents of East Harlem and the South Bronx discussed spending ideas at neighborhood assemblies, a series of open meetings at schools and community centers coordinated by Council Member Mark-Viverito's office. Then, from November to February 2014, fifty of those participants volunteered to gather every two to three weeks to deliberate, meet with experts in city agencies, and determine which projects would appear on the final ballot. Finally, during a week-long voting period in March, a total of 1,715 residents, about 1 percent of the district's population, cast ballots at polling sites in schools, community centers, and on city sidewalks. Equivalent processes unfolded at the same time in the other three districts.

The stakes in this street-level arena were high: how were local needs to be defined, who defined them, and which would ultimately be funded? Was PB going to restore trust in government, promote redistribution, and empower communities most marginalized from the political process? Or, in PB activist parlance, was it going to devolve into business-as-usual, amplifying the voice of more affluent "usual suspects" who already have political power? Mark-Viverito's district, advised by PBP and boosted by CVH's targeted outreach, managed to engage low-income people of color and other traditionally excluded groups. According to PB voter surveys collected by CDP, 46 percent of PB voters had household income less than $15,000, compared to only 9 percent of district voters in the 2013 city council election. Similarly, 24 percent of PB voters could participate in PB but not in regular elections due to citizenship, age, or parolee restrictions. In 2014, this inclusive PB electorate chose to fund projects such as a new air-conditioning system for a

**Figure 3.1** Voters select projects to fund in the 2013–2014 participatory budgeting process in East Harlem. Photo by Isaac Jabola-Carolus.

local school, kitchen upgrades at a senior center, and playground repairs at a public housing complex—needs that had been overlooked in the traditional budgeting process (Kasdan et al. 2014).

The second arena was the centralized PBNYC Steering Committee, a city-wide governance and oversight body for the PB process itself.[3] In designing a PB program specific to New York, CVH and PBP insisted on convening a participatory group of organizations and individuals to decide the rules; this approach, they reasoned, was most consistent with the spirit of the reform.[4] The sponsoring council members consented, with the formal understanding that they were included and with the assumption that they would have veto power. Essentially a "constitutional convention" in miniature, this committee formed both a player that made unified decisions and an arena in which forty-one subplayers interacted strategically to shape PBNYC. Those subplayers included representatives from council members' offices,

---

[3] This arena is common to most PB processes in the United States but less so in other countries.

[4] As PBP leaders have written (Lerner and Secondo 2012: 4–5), the steering committee served to foster local ownership over the process and embodied the conviction that "For PB to more deeply transform government, citizens must have the power to write the rules of the game from the start." As we saw in chapter 2, arena creators mindfully create their rules.

community boards (New York's advisory planning bodies), and leaders from an array of nonprofit advocacy organizations and community-based groups.

The steering committee's authority to establish rules for PBNYC set it apart from traditional advisory bodies. The committee defined the goals of the process, the roles of the players involved, and the parameters of participation. Especially groundbreaking, for instance, were the voter eligibility criteria: undocumented immigrants and all formerly incarcerated individuals were included. As for its own role, the steering committee also decided that it was not just a temporary but a permanent player. Committee members charged themselves with overseeing and supporting implementation and with periodically revisiting the rules.[5] They were led by CVH, PBP, and CDP, which each held terms as steering committee co-chairs between 2011 and 2014.

The third arena was a citywide *coordinating* sphere, an informal arena of recurring meetings that featured behind-the-scenes strategic interactions between CVH, PBP, and CDP, and Council Members Lander and Mark-Viverito and their senior staff members. At stake were the quality of PB implementation and the future direction of the program. In this arena, players decided what issues to bring before the steering committee and how to pressure certain council members to better engage low-income communities.

A fourth, more private arena, *private philanthropy,* proved an important location of interaction beyond the PBNYC sphere. In courting philanthropic foundations, CVH, PBP, and other steering committee members collaborated to secure funding for greater outreach to low-income and otherwise marginalized communities. In contrast to Porto Alegre and other cases of PB in Brazil (Abers 2000), New York did not at first create or restructure municipal offices to manage PB inputs or mobilize participation. Instead, during the first three years, PBNYC's implementation was essentially a government–civil society partnership that leaned on a limited number of decentralized city council staff, private foundation funding, and underresourced nonprofit organizations. Individual council member offices had only small staffs and budgets at the district level (O'Connor 2016), and, for more than two years, the council's central legal office delayed the small technical grants promised to CVH and PBP. In the absence of a centralized, higher-level commitment

---

[5] The steering committee also created "district committees," or decentralized committees in each district tasked with formulating guidelines and aiding implementation. CVH and the council offices recruited members for these local committees, but few became viable players.

to PB, the onus of securing resources to run PB fell heavily on CVH and PBP. To fund their outreach and implementation work, these groups had to raise approximately $150,000 a year for each of the initial PB cycles.

## Expansion, 2011–2013

From PBNYC's inception, several members of the steering committee, including CVH, PBP, and CDP, were eager to see PBNYC expand beyond the initial four districts and the $1 million-per-district model. CVH also held closely to its goal of PB for public housing, and the other groups strongly endorsed that parallel effort. These aims required continued engagement not only in the four main PB arenas but in traditional advocacy arenas.

After securing foundation funding specifically for advocacy, CVH and PBP returned to the *policymaking* arena, extending their use of minimally assertive tactics, persuasive argumentation, and powerful allies as relatable messengers. After PBNYC's first year (2011–2012), which drew six thousand participants across the four districts, CDP's research bolstered the case for PB adoption—its voter survey found that PB engaged a more representative slice of the public than did local elections. Further, by analyzing media coverage of PB, CDP showed that participating council members received an average of 126 percent more press coverage than in previous years, owing largely to PB-related stories (Kasdan and Cattell 2012: 26). Here, advocates took it upon themselves to demonstrate that the promised benefits of PB were materializing.

Paired with the firsthand experiences of the participating council members, these findings renewed the commitment of the initial four to PBNYC. They also helped to attract new sponsors. Prodding from Lander and Mark-Viverito ensured that four more council members signed on for the second year, and one more for the third. The New York City Housing Authority also began to warm to the proposal.

Local elections in 2013 opened the *electoral* arena to PB advocacy and allowed activists to achieve the most dramatic PBNYC expansion yet. Steering committee members developed tactical options, and CVH, through its political advocacy arm, exploited this election-year opening. The group asked all candidates to declare a position on PB, which CVH considered in making endorsements. Ultimately, a total of twenty-one council members who pledged to sponsor PB in 2014 were elected or reelected, up from nine who had participated in 2013 (Participatory Budgeting Project 2013b). The number rose to twenty-four before the next cycle commenced. PBNYC was now by far the largest participatory program in the country.[6]

## Dilemmas Emerge

In 2013, during the months preceding the expansion, Community Voices Heard, the Participatory Budgeting Project, and the Community Development Project reached a choice point. PBNYC's successful expansion led each to decide whether, how, or how fully to remain engaged in the street-level, steering committee, coordination, and philanthropic arenas. These players confronted a being-there dilemma: continued involvement in an expanding program would drain resources, but curtailing activity would diminish their influence. Institutionalization was tempting.

They chose to reduce engagement for many reasons, largely reflecting cultural dispositions and resource constraints that drove a change in goals. At an organizational level, the leaders of CVH, PBP, and CDP increasingly felt as if their intensive, hands-on activities in the street-level, steering committee, and coordinating arenas were diverging from their core identities and missions. Looking back on this juncture, one CVH leader noted that PB created a sense of mission drift: "Our role for a while . . . had [become] more of a 'technical assistant, implementation' role, versus a 'we're organizing to build power' role—which created a complex tension in an organization that's focused on power-building." CDP was similarly dedicated to supporting community-based, power-building groups, but involvement in PBNYC arenas pulled them away from that anchor. PBP also felt distracted, hoping to free up staff for its projects outside New York City.

These players had additional ideological reservations about their continued involvement, seeing long-term engagement in the street-level and coordinating arenas as inconsistent with their political beliefs. The point of PB was to change how government works; as in Latin American cases, PB implementation should primarily be the role of government, not civic organizations.

But the prospect of institutionalization was also a matter of resources. Philanthropic foundation funding was proving inadequate to support

---

[6] A four-district, $4 million initiative in Chicago was the closest rival.

PBNYC's implementation. Players needed a more robust administrative structure to undergird implementation, especially at a scale of twenty-four districts or more. With populations of roughly 160,000 each, the districts now encompassed almost half of New York City's residents. This scale required more resources than three understaffed and underfunded nonprofit organizations could provide. Moreover, if PBNYC were to grow further or to expand into new budgets, centralized capacity within the local government would be critical.

Taken together, these motivations to reduce engagement in New York amounted to a strong case for institutionalizing PB, for creating or adapting an architecture in city government that could sustainably implement PB each year. The organizations had won, and it was now time to step back.

However, by decreasing their involvement—by *not* being there—CVH, PBP, and CDP stood to lose influence over PBNYC's implementation and impacts. A diminished presence in the street-level, steering committee, and coordinating arenas could mean less attention to the composition and quality of participation. Retreating from fundraising could mean fewer resources for targeted outreach and inclusion.

A powerful-allies dilemma complicated these risks. In general, players may leverage alliances with more established, powerful players to achieve common goals, but the overlap in aims is often only partial. At critical moments, powerful allies may subordinate the goals of weaker allies to their own goals. This is a standard, perhaps inevitable, relationship between social movement organizations and state agencies, especially the more successful organizations.

In the case of PB in general, nongovernmental advocates have little choice but to ally with influential elected officials, whose participation is required to sustain the reform. Yet as Chicago Alderman Joe Moore attests in his aforementioned statement about gaining power through PB, officials approach the program with different goals than do nongovernmental activists. Some of these goals overlap, such as restoring trust between citizens and government. But some goals do not; officials have an interest in PB for enhancing their reelection chances, while activists may have a greater interest in PB as a tool for redistribution. In stepping back, PBNYC advocates ceded influence over PB not just to anyone but to powerful elected officials who might be less attentive to redistribution, inclusive deliberation, and other goals of civil society players. Indeed, in 2013, as advocates explored the goal of institutionalization, Mark-Viverito was positioning herself—with Lander's support—to contend for the city council speaker seat, the city's second-most powerful post. The quality of the PB process was not her chief concern.

Yet the advocates' choice over reducing their involvement materialized as an implicit tradeoff, not an explicit dilemma. In interviews, CVH, PBP, and CDP leaders recall no specific moments at which they made a decision. Instead, the arguments for pulling back dominated; it was a nondecision, a "no-brainer." Any risks, leaders recall, were partly masked by their trust in their powerful allies, Lander and Mark-Viverito, who had been PBNYC's foremost governmental proponents. As progressives with demonstrated commitments to PB, these sponsors should be capable shepherds of the program going forward.

The three organizations, however, would not disengage without first ensuring that government players could assume their roles. CVH, PBP, and CDP had been the administrative backbone of PB, and simply dropping out would jeopardize the program.

Consequently, even while the 2013 election season unfolded, CVH, PBP, and CDP had developed a strategy for institutionalization—the transformation of PBNYC from a civil society-driven "pilot" project into a durable, government-led program. With input from the broader steering committee, these three players crafted a memo that called for an enlargement of the budget decided through PB, and for the creation of a new city office and robust staff infrastructure to coordinate PB. After the election, they shared the memo with Democratic Mayor-Elect Bill de Blasio, leading council members, and other influential officials. Meanwhile, Mark-Viverito campaigned for the city council speaker seat, and CVH again used the electoral process to promote their PB goals. In December 2013, CVH cohosted a televised forum on a major local news station and posed a question to speaker candidates about PB. In contrast to her rivals, Mark-Viverito pledged to provide centralized support for PBNYC and to encourage its broader adoption. In January 2014, after weeks of backroom maneuvers steered largely by Lander, the city council elected her speaker (Karni 2013; Taylor 2014).

## Institutionalization, 2014–2015

Speaker Mark-Viverito's PB reforms fell short of the most ambitious targets set out in the advocates' memo, but, combined with the expansion to twenty-four districts, they represented major gains for all key players. Advocates touted the development as the most significant victory to date for PBNYC. In public communications, PBP broadcast the story as one of its biggest wins that year. Like CVH and CDP, the group was able to claim that it had helped "guide the incoming officials on how to turn PBNYC into the largest PB process in the world" (Participatory Budgeting Project 2013a).

Mark-Viverito's office executed four main changes in 2014–2015 that began to institutionalize PBNYC by shifting the locus of coordination and resource provision from civil society to government:

1. In the city council's central offices, the speaker assembled a team of six staff members who assumed much of PBP's and CVH's street-level and coordinating roles.[7] This change also relocated the coordinating arena to the city council offices and enlarged the role of government players, namely, institutional staff, in the process.
2. City funds totaling roughly $20,000 were used to contract PBP to provide training and guidance for the new central staff and district-level staff and participants. This left PBP with a continued but reduced role in the street-level and coordinating arenas.
3. City funds totaling roughly $40,000 were used to contract local organizations (including CVH) across twenty-four districts for targeted outreach to immigrant communities, the formerly incarcerated, and youth. As with PBP, this change left CVH with a continued but reduced role in street-level and coordinating arenas.
4. The steering committee became an official city council body coordinated by city staff. Here, both the location and composition of the governing arena shifted. As with coordination, this arena moved into the city council offices, and city staff assumed a central position. CVH, PBP, and CDP remained players in this arena but stepped out of their leading roles as co-chairs.

Although these measures were limited relative to the original proposals—in particular, a recommended civic engagement office was never created—together they marked a distinct turn toward government-led, centralized coordination of PBNYC.

---

[7] During key moments such as the preparation for the annual PB voting week, council staff in other divisions also assisted.

## Tradeoffs Materialize

In September 2014, as PBNYC entered its fourth annual cycle, public participation in the street-level arena continued much like before but on a wider
scale. Across the twenty-four participating districts, residents came together
in assemblies and online to address problems in their local schools, parks,
housing developments, and other public infrastructure. By April 2015, at the
end of that year's PB process, more than 6,000 New Yorkers had participated
in proposing ideas, 600 refined those ideas into fundable projects, and 51,000
voted for which to fund—more than triple the number of voters in the year
prior. Behind the scenes, however, gains and losses emerged for the leading
organizations and council members, which complicate any simple interpretation of PBNYC's success.

As CVH, PBP, and CDP had hoped, the measures to institutionalize
PBNYC allowed these organizations to decrease their engagement in the
street-level, steering committee, and coordinating arenas. Within each, these
players began to move from the center of action to the sidelines, reducing interaction but not fully abandoning the arena and its stakes.

Lessening their involvement while expanding government's role allowed
these players to realize most of the benefits of not "being there." Freeing up
staff capacity and correcting for organizational mission drift were particularly important. As one CVH leader noted: "We've tried to shift our role, and
I think we've done an effective job this year. [To] leave some of these other
things to central staff . . . [and to say] 'we're focusing on public housing engagement, and that's it,' is a huge thing."

Related gains for the three leading organizations included new governmental funding for implementation, which could prove more sustainable
than foundation grants; basic governmental infrastructure to support implementation across almost half the city and provide for future expansion;
and an ideologically preferable division of labor that shifted implementation responsibility to government. In stepping back and compelling governmental players to be more active, the organizations also achieved one
of their main goals: transforming PBNYC from a pilot program into an
institution.

But the drawbacks of not being there also began to appear. Strategic losses,
both unintended and unforeseen, throw into relief the dilemmas posed by
policy institutionalization. Table 3.2 presents the principal gains and losses
experienced by CVH, PBP, and CDP.

Table 3.2  Gains and Losses for Civil Society Players upon Institutionalization

| Arena | Key Gains | Key Losses |
|---|---|---|
| Street-level and Coordinating | Greater role for government staff, allowing CVH, PBP, and CDP to reduce engagement; increased government funding for program implementation | Lower implementation standards; less monitoring and evaluation; fewer resources per district for targeted outreach |
| Steering Committee | No significant gains | Diminished authority; less influence for civil society players |

Some losses stemmed directly from reduced engagement. In the street-level and citywide coordinating arenas, implementation standards and discourse about PB's goals shifted as city staff, instead of community organizers, led public forums and trained staff and participants. In an interview, one steering committee member lamented that new coordinators tolerated lower participation levels than in the past, inadvertently threatening the inclusiveness of street-level forums:

Staff would say, "Oh, there are 35 people. That was a great turnout for an assembly." Or, "Your district has 100 ideas. Great work. That's all you need." . . . But I think everyone in the past aimed much higher than 35 people in [each] assembly and 100 ideas per district. . . . When the goal is 35 people in [each] assembly and not much outreach is done, you're basically saying, "The goal is to get the usual suspects." That's who comes out.

This problem was extensive in 2014–2015, with the city council's new PB coordinators introducing lowered expectations to the fourteen new districts as the norm. In being less engaged in the PB street-level arena, CVH and PBP gained organizational capacity but lost control over messaging and the setting of standards.

CDP's reduced presence produced a similar tradeoff. As CDP's funding and capacity to evaluate PBNYC decreased, the city council did not provide compensatory means for data collection. Evaluation was thus limited to a slim quantitative assessment of turnout in the public voting—the last and most visible, but least deliberative, stage of the PB process. As a result of this decline in monitoring and evaluation, it became more difficult to assess participation by, and benefits to, marginalized communities.

A third consequential form of reduced engagement was decreased foundation funding to support PBNYC administration. Now that city government was responsible for implementation, foundations were less inclined to contribute. In addition to cutting back CDP's evaluation role, this change hurt other players: (1) steering committee groups that used grants to promote participation through video and multimedia; (2) CVH and local community groups that aided PB outreach, because the council's new targeted outreach budget represented a per-district decrease; and (3) the marginalized communities whose engagement often relied on such targeted outreach.

A more resonant set of losses stemmed from the combination of reduced engagement with arena relocation and bureaucratic resistance: as CVH, PBP, and CDP stepped back, the steering committee became embedded in existing governmental arenas and was exposed to new, less receptive players. The resulting losses presented an unanticipated setback for the three organizations and a new challenge for Speaker Mark-Viverito. These slowly unfolded in the 2014–2015 cycle, and their mitigation became a central focus of the 2015–2016 steering committee.

Almost all PBNYC players, from participants to council members themselves, have struggled with bureaucratic resistance from the program's outset. The main defiance came initially from city agencies, such as the Department of Transportation and the Housing Authority, which are responsible for vetting, approving, designing, installing, and constructing the priority projects that emerge from PB. These players often demonstrated low tolerance for the participatory and innovative spirit of PB (Su 2015, 2018). This is a common challenge in the United States, where PB processes involve large, long-standing, and technocratic bureaucracies. In this case, however, it was not the city agencies but the city council bureaucracy that thwarted the empowering dimensions of PBNYC.

The relocation of the steering committee to "250 Broadway," the city council building in Lower Manhattan, opened the steering committee arena to players who changed its rules and gave rise to a new dilemma. Senior city council bureaucrats, positioned hierarchically between Speaker Mark-Viverito and the newly hired mid-level PB staff, expressed little interest in PB. Some, who were holdovers from the Bloomberg administration and the speakership of Council Member Christine Quinn, a centrist Democratic, saw no place for community participation in budgetary matters.

The mid-level council staff, who served as direct links to the PB players, felt pressure from the senior bureaucrats above them—who had no emotional commitment to the PB process—to limit the role of the steering committee because it challenged their preferred mode of technocratic governance. Recalling a conversation with CVH and PBP about this issue during the transition to council-led coordination, one of these staff members conveyed the difficulties in deciding whether the steering committee should be more or less empowered:

> I just kept saying, "I don't think we have a solution here." You can't do middle-of-the-road. It's either a governance board, which the [city] council is not going to be comfortable with—there wasn't an explicit discussion about that, but I tried to imagine what that would look like, to explain to my higher-ups about what we were doing there, and [they would] say, "Are you crazy?"—[or it's] a place for civil society to plug in to a higher level.

Viewing the options in this way, these staffers proposed to recast the steering committee as a "council-run advisory board [that] acts as a policy-making body and hub for the process" (New York City Council 2014). Ambiguity arose in changing the steering committee's role, as the contradiction between "council-run advisory board" and "policy-making body" suggests. On the one hand, the steering committee was subsumed under the city council: members were vetted and approved by city officials, and their input became merely advisory. On the other hand, it was to remain a "policy-making body," implying real power and authoritative decision-making over matters such as who could participate in the PB process. City staff and civil society leaders recall tacitly accepting this ambiguity as they managed countless other aspects of the administrative transition. CVH, PBP, and CDP, furthermore, were eager to step back from their leading roles in this arena. The players worked out the details as the year progressed.

As PBNYC's Cycle 4 (2014–2015) began, the changing rules of the steering committee arena slowly emerged, and their effect was to undermine its nongovernmental members and constrict the body's authority. Attempting to convene a group of only highly committed members, the staff reduced nongovernmental steering committee membership from forty-four to twenty-two. They also took responsibility for coordinating the body and leading its meetings, a role previously filled by CVH and PBP as formal co-chairs.

Finally, the committee became less productive, as meeting times were halved and multiple working groups were disbanded.

These changes in formal and informal rules led to concrete alterations in the function of the steering committee. First, steering committee documents attest to a shift in concrete *agenda-setting* power. The central staff rarely circulated agendas in advance of meetings or solicited agenda items from committee members. Moreover, staff focused heavily on developing technological tools to aid implementation, even though committee members did not see that as a priority.

Second, the steering committee's *advocacy* function, codified in the PBNYC Rulebook, diminished. For nearly two years, this body ceased to discuss how PB could win new and larger budgets, stalling important goals held by the nongovernmental players (Jabola-Carolus 2017).

Third, the transfer of certain *implementation* responsibilities to government staff lessened the burden on steering committee volunteers but removed core functions of a steering committee whose role was already tenuous, eroding its sense of ownership over the process. Instead of developing new functions for the steering committee, the body's city council leaders had reduced membership and made meetings shorter. Under these conditions, participation became less fulfilling and less engaging for civil society representatives. Their influence, and the stakes of the steering committee arena, had shrunk.

## False Arenas and Powerful Allies

Frustration understandably emerged, as PB advocates realized they were confronted with a false-arena dilemma. Were there still real stakes in the steering committee worth pursuing, or were members just legitimating decisions and actions already taken by other players elsewhere? Members raised this very issue in meetings and interviews. "To my mind there's this question," one member asked: "Is this the council members' process, or is this the people's process?" Another asked, "Are we making decisions, or are we just nodding our heads at the decisions you've made?" False-arena dilemmas often appear in the context of task forces and advisory committees—typically during agenda-setting and content stages of the policy process, but also during policy implementation and institutionalization, as in the present case. With city council bureaucrats intent on limiting the stakes of the steering committee arena, this challenge became acute. And it fueled new emotions—anger, bitterness, disappointment—that shaped subsequent interactions.

Recall that CVH, PBP, and CDP leaders felt comfortable reducing their engagement in 2014 because they believed PBNYC would be in good hands with their allies Lander and Mark-Viverito. What those organizations did not fully foresee was that institutionalization meant embedding PBNYC in new arenas rather than simply handing PBNYC to new players. They mistook arenas for players; these were arenas that might contain new, unsympathetic players. As one advocate reflected, "We probably underestimated . . . how much institutionalizing PB through particular political actors also meant institutionalizing it through institutions that were very distinct from those actors." What mattered more than the general trustworthiness of Mark-Viverito and Lander was that their lack of attention to the strategic conflict between bureaucratic players and steering committee members precluded intervention on the latter's behalf.

In the transition year, 2014–2015, Lander and Mark-Viverito reaped the benefits of PBNYC's expansion but, with little direct involvement in the street-level, coordinating, and steering committee arenas, remained aloof from the rising tensions. For Lander, the primary gain at this moment appeared to be the spread of what he believed to be good policy. Lander did not get the same credit for PBNYC's citywide expansion as Mark-Viverito, but he seemed to genuinely believe in the transformative value of PB, and to take satisfaction in its growth. More than any of his colleagues, he has widely argued for its merits (Lander 2016; Lander and Freedman-Schnapp 2012).[8] During this period, he did not appear to experience any losses around PB, especially as his popular district-level PB process continued much as before.

Speaker Mark-Viverito garnered additional benefits. Beyond promoting good policy, as head of the city council she was now able to take primary credit for the program, with her name prominently attached to PBNYC in all press releases and publicity. PB, in tandem with reforms that gave council members more equitable amounts of discretionary funds, distanced her from the clientelistic image of her predecessor, Christine Quinn, and contributed to her overall image as fair and progressive (Barkan 2014). This branding and

---

[8] Lander's office has also dedicated more staff time to PB than most others. And unlike most council members, including Mark-Viverito, he has often participated in behind-the-scenes PB meetings and deliberations. His ideological motivations are likely coupled with a recognition that PB bolsters his popularity, just as Chicago Alderman Moore had suggested it would.

her growing reputation were valuable, given her ambitions for higher office and nationwide policy influence (Grabar 2015; Ngo 2016).

Interviews suggest that Mark-Viverito was unaware of the mounting frustrations within the steering committee. Although she received regular reports, the layers of hierarchy between her and her PB staff meant that she was not closely apprised of PB developments and did not participate directly in steering committee meetings or coordinating meetings. Lander, too, rarely engaged directly in those arenas, as his primary PB responsibilities lay in his Brooklyn district. To reclaim the steering committee as a meaningful arena, CVH, PBP, CDP, and other steering committee members had to persuade Mark-Viverito and Lander that PBNYC's integrity was imperiled, or that these officials risked their reputations if the problems were not remedied.

## Reform, 2015–2016

When facing a false-arena dilemma, players can either quit the arena or struggle to remake it and revive more meaningful stakes—options analogous to Hirschman's (1970) "exit or voice." This is a form of the being-there dilemma. By withdrawing, players give up their position in the arena and any influence that came with it. By seeking reform, players spend valuable time and resources for uncertain results.

In mid-2015, as Cycle 4 gave way to Cycle 5, frustrations on the steering committee peaked, and its long-time members, many with deep emotional investments in the program, opted to fight for reform. Their concerted response pulled CVH and PBP back into the center of the steering committee arena.

The trouble began with an abrupt personnel change, in which two of the staff members who had managed PB coordination left. In the shuffle, the speaker's office pivoted three other staff positions away from PB, leaving only three part-time positions to assist PB across a new high of twenty-eight districts. This reduction marked another loss, leaving fewer dedicated staff for central coordination than in the civil society-led approach of earlier years. It left the problems of institutionalization intact while trimming the benefits of added capacity.

The remaining staff, overburdened and still without a clear vision for the role of the steering committee, further struggled to moderate bureaucratic pressures on the PB process. Just weeks before the next cycle was to begin, they informed the steering committee and council staff in district offices that, at the urging of a different part of the bureaucracy, the council division that oversaw budget issues, the PB process timeline was going to be compressed to fit the city's main budgeting calendar. This decision openly contradicted past feedback and new protestations from participants, steering committee members, district staff, and several council members, who argued that the existing timeline was already too tight. After heated exchanges and a modest compromise, the timeline was condensed.

In this instance, the diminished authority of the steering committee— brought about by arena relocation—led to a loss for street-level participants, who would have less time to assess community needs and craft budget proposals before the voting stage. By extension, potential beneficiaries of PB funding would also lose insofar as the ballot items would be less carefully developed. Along the way, civil society groups and staff in the district-level council offices would lose, too, forced to conform to a timeline they viewed as objectionable. Mark-Viverito and Lander lost little directly, but advocates endeavored to show them that they, too, stood to lose from such bureaucratic incursions.

In responding to this loss, long-time advocates resolved that the steering committee arena, although increasingly constricted, should be revamped. To revive the arena, they sought to mobilize their powerful allies, whose prior inaction on the steering committee issue had contributed to the present problems. In the fall of 2015, as PBNYC's fifth annual cycle began, steering committee members thus initiated an effort to rewrite the arena's rules and reclaim meaningful influence over the PB process. This effort pulled CVH, PBP, and CDP back into leading positions. CVH (2015) crafted a list of proposed reforms to the steering committee, which included:

1. Rotating meeting locations between the city council building and "more community-friendly spaces";
2. Restoring co-chair positions held by nongovernmental members, to enable greater civil society control of agendas and deliberations;
3. Expanding decision-making power to "major decisions regarding the overall process," including selection of co-chairs and changes to PB voter eligibility, timelines, and other rules;
4. New member recruitment, to involve more nongovernmental groups, district-level participants, and individual council members in governing PBNYC; and

5.  Reestablishing a working group structure that could renew attention to
    issues such as advocacy and expansion.

Together, and advised by the remaining PB council staff, the steering committee reasoned that diplomatic tactics were again an appropriate starting
point. Members collectively sent their proposal to the speaker, who, after
consulting with Lander and her own staff, acted. Overriding the reservations
of her senior aides, the speaker approved the reforms to the steering committee arena and preserved its authority to guide the implementation
of PBNYC.

The speaker's actions on this issue suggest that she came to see a loss or
potential loss in the constricted steering committee and in the grievances of
civil society players. Already steering committee participation had dwindled
as frustration grew, and the top-down timeline decision further offended
the collaborative, democratic spirit that remaining steering committee
members and participating council members valued. The threat of their protest or withdrawal likely gave them a degree of influence that may explain the
speaker's relatively quick concession.

As Rebecca Abers (2000) has observed, in PB processes, civil society
players possess leverage when sponsoring officials desire a public image of
the participatory program as inclusive and empowering. To maintain this
image, and to paint the innovation as a successful policy, sponsors depend
heavily on civil society groups that have a grassroots reach. If such groups
make demands and signal discontent, sponsors often buckle because the
details of the participatory innovation are typically less important to elected
officials than the program's overall image as a successful policy endorsed
by reputable civil society groups. Granting the steering committee greater
power, although it might displease her senior aides, was one such detail. By
conceding to the demand, Mark-Viverito ensured the continuation of gains
at small cost.

The implementation of the steering committee reforms also became an
object of strategic interaction, but by the beginning of Cycle 6 (2016–2017),
the modifications were in place. The steering committee arena was, at least
temporally, salvaged as a meaningful site of contestation. The false-arena dilemma that had emerged during institutionalization receded.

The being-there dilemma, however, had not diminished. CVH, PBP, and
CDP grappled with that dilemma anew, and with greater wariness than before, given the difficulties that resulted from their initial withdrawal. Across

the street-level, coordinating, and steering committee arenas, these players were forced to weigh the tradeoffs of their continued presence.

## Conclusion

The PBNYC story, from 2009 to 2016, shows how a strategy of institutionalization produced a package of gains and losses common among movement-backed public policies or programs (summarized in table 3.1). By integrating newly won initiatives into established governmental arenas, activists gain resources and security for their programs as well as the ability to focus their efforts elsewhere. But they cede control to allies who may not fully share their goals, and decision-making moves into arenas that tend to contain unreceptive players. As a result, the integrity and impacts of their program may suffer. Activist groups that attain policy influence typically face something like this institutionalization package and the strategic dilemmas that structure it.

Institutionalization first poses a version of the being-there dilemma to players temporarily involved in policy implementation, especially in pilot programs driven by civil society organizations. In this dilemma, by reducing its presence in one arena, a player may transfer its work to a more permanent player and, thereby, solidify an existing program while redirecting its resources and attention to other arenas.

The tradeoff in such a withdrawal is that a player loses influence over the stakes of those arenas, namely, the quality of policy implementation and its impacts. Given that institutionalization typically embeds implementation within bureaucracies, a player may therefore leave the fate of a policy or program to players who do not share its goals. Indeed, the being-there dilemma is compounded when institutionalization shifts decision-making into a larger, inhospitable arena. This circumstance can precipitate a false-arena dilemma, whereby one plays in an arena but may no longer have any influence over the stakes, if they still exist at all.

Finally, a powerful-allies dilemma permeates institutionalization, as public officials undergird policy efforts but have goals that rarely overlap completely with those of activists. Powerful allies may aggravate the being-there and false-arenas dilemmas when neglecting a player's particular goals or, conversely, alleviate the dilemmas when coming to the defense of that player's goals.

When bureaucratic intolerance for new programs like PBNYC is a threat to durable policy gains, how might activists respond? PBNYC activists appealed to a powerful ally, but Amenta (2006: 28) offers another approach: "The best case is for movement actors to be installed in a bureaucracy implementing policy chosen by the challenger, affording it great leverage over current and future policy." With insider activists championing the cause, "being there" becomes less pressing for outsider activists. Women's movements demonstrate this strategy's viability; so-called femocrat experiments, in which feminists took bureaucratic posts in key government offices, were critical in advancing movement goals (Banaszak 2010; Eisenstein 1996). Simple players can pursue movement goals outside the movements.

Yet attenuating the being-there and false-arena dilemmas is not enough. Dependence on elected officials, a precondition for any public programs like PB, necessarily poses a powerful-allies dilemma. Not only are those officials subject to pressures that generate goals contrary to those of activists; those officials may also lose office, and support for the program might depart with them. Such was the case in Porto Alegre, Brazil, where the world's most lauded PB program withered after its sponsors lost power (Melgar 2014). One of the chief perils of fighting for progress through government is the dilemma of powerful allies.

In New York, strategic interactions after 2016 yielded mixed outcomes for PB advocates. When term limits forced Melissa Mark-Viverito to leave the city council at the end of 2017, Manhattan Democrat Corey Johnson, a PB supporter, succeeded her as speaker. But in his first year, he proved an unreliable ally: like Mark-Viverito in 2014–2015, he subordinated PB to other political concerns and frustrated civil society groups.

Instead, Mayor Bill de Blasio, sensing an opportunity as he entered his second term, took up the cause of PB advocates. First, he pledged to give public high schools $2,000 each for students to allocate through small-scale PB programs. Then he convened a commission to propose reforms for strengthening civic participation and local democracy. In November 2018, voters approved one of the resulting ballot measures, to create a Civic Engagement Commission tasked with implementing a new citywide PB program spanning all fifty-one districts. PBP, CVH, Council Member Lander, and other supporters hoped that the program would allow PBNYC to transcend the $1 million-per-district model, engaging residents of all districts in much larger funding decisions. However, the expanded program had not yet been launched when the COVID-19 pandemic hit New York in 2020, at which point the mayor suspended the deadline to implement it. No doubt, the dilemmas of being there, false arenas, and powerful allies will accompany future efforts to implement and institutionalize a larger citywide PB program.

With institutionalization, players seek to solidify their gains, to achieve security for the new arenas that result from policy victories or pivotal decisions. Often, however, players aim to win control over long-standing institutions, whether governments or organizations. The following chapter, on a dissident caucus within New York City's Transport Workers Union, explores such a case. By examining how the caucus competed in internal union elections, we track the gains and losses embedded in electoral struggles to obtain institutional power. The case highlights the problems of trying to lead a large compound player, which especially involves the extension dilemma. The caucus grew, but in doing so attracted new players with their own ideas about goals, appropriate arenas, and even how to respond to setbacks. Its electoral victory launched its candidates into new arenas with new resources that eventually brought about the demise of the caucus. A charismatic individual pursued his own goals, increasingly centered on his own power. We will see both the electoral package and the personality package unfold.

# 4

# Dissent in New York's Transport Workers Union

While incremental or gradual gains or losses are common in social movements, here we examine an apparent "touchdown." For a small group of union insurgents to topple entrenched leaders in an election seems like a clear example of success, but this big "outcome" resulted from many gains and losses during more than a decade of struggle. Along the way, players, goals, alliances, and attitudes all changed. The insurgents' electoral victory resolved some long-standing dilemmas about how to build union power but intensified others, affecting the course of subsequent actions. Our microanalysis allows us to see how small gains and losses, strategic tradeoffs, dilemmas, and decisions—often intended to resolve short-term problems—shaped and altered what it meant to win.[1]

More generally, this chapter highlights a string of gains and losses that have to do with winning control of, and then running, a group or organization: what it means to lead. In addition to issues of hierarchy and conflict within any organization, this particular effort came up against the question of whether and how to enter a union electoral arena and what the goal (and therefore the tactics) of the organization should be there. Once that decision was made, means may come to determine ends, as the Sorcerer's Apprentice dilemma reveals. Assembling electoral coalitions, winning an election, and functioning in office after winning are inevitably in tension with each other. Meanwhile, this initially small insurgent group had to deal with a series of extension dilemmas as it gathered adherents and entered larger arenas with more players and subplayers. Table 4.1 summarizes this electoral package. Along the way, the leadership of the organization changed. Although we

---

[1] All internal *Hell on Wheels* and New Directions information, except as noted, are drawn from two sets of interviews with former New Directions members: Goldstein, 2003–2004 and Kagan, 2014–2016. Both are available at Tamiment Labor Library, New York University. Marc Kagan was a transit worker from 1984, a New Directions member from 1995, and on TWU Local 100 staff 2001–2003. In this chapter, we draw on his recollections as an individual player and as an observer.

*Gains and Losses.* James M. Jasper, Luke Elliott-Negri, Isaac Jabola-Carolus, Marc Kagan, Jessica Mahlbacher, and Manès Weisskircher, and Anna Zhelnina, Oxford University Press. © Oxford University Press 2022.
DOI: 10.1093/oso/9780197623251.003.0005

Table 4.1 The Electoral Package

| Dilemmas | Player's Goals | Risks | Likely Costs |
|---|---|---|---|
| Engagement | Access to decision-making or positions of power; Reputation as a serious player; Mobilization of supporters; Media attention | False arena; Playing into the hands of opponents; Reputational damages in case of poor performance | Resource-intensive; Must follow fairly narrow rules of electoral arenas |
| Sorcerer's Apprentice | Win elections as most promising arenas | May prove a poor choice of arenas | Precludes other strategies and arenas |
| Extension | Mobilization of more money, votes, people, networks, know-how | Loss of control over the campaign or loss of previous goals or ideology | Costly internal management Working to other players' advantage |
| Solutions | identity work and education to solidify team; ideological work, such as stoking outrage; demonization of opponents; positive boomerang from other arenas. | | |

will deal most extensively with the "personality package" in chapter 7, we also see it here in the transition to a charismatic and more overtly dominant leader.

Union leaders and the workers, or subsets of workers, they represent often have different interests (Freidman 1982; Hyman 1989). Union insurgency—oppositionists within a union who seek to influence workers or supplant existing leadership—introduces even more complexity. Lacking hierarchical discipline or the ability to offer material incentives, and with frequently changing membership and changing goals, insurgent organizations are a compound player within a compound player. Internally, subplayers vie to make their goals preeminent within the opposition and within the union as a whole.

The *Hell on Wheels* (HoW) newsletter was founded in 1984 by a small coalition of leftist New York City transit workers. Despite various individual goals, their shared intention was to encourage rank-and-file militancy in their workplace, the subway and bus system operated by the New York City Transit Authority (Transit). Sixteen years later, its successor organization, New Directions (ND), won control of the 35,000-member Transport Workers Union (TWU) Local 100, the union for virtually all of Transit's operating personnel, from mechanics to bus drivers to subway car cleaners. During the intervening years, control of the union had come to be seen as a necessary prerequisite for the militant action that its activists espoused.

Making electoral victory their first priority fundamentally changed the character of HoW. On January 1, 2001, the individuals who arrived triumphantly to take their posts at the union hall, and the ideas of union-building they carried with them, differed substantially from those who had begun the journey in 1984. The views and actions of both old-timers and newcomers within the organization had been shaped by perceived gains and losses along the path to success and the microcorrections that resulted. Moreover, in a final push to "win," the group had fractured, resulting in several unintended outcomes after the electoral victory.

We focus on the strategic choices and interactions of HoW/ND activists, Local 100 members, and union officers (and to a lesser extent Transit management) that ultimately led to the electoral victory of New Directions. ND activists chose arenas that they perceived as advantageous sites of struggle, such as electoral campaigns, anticontract agitation, union meetings, and shop-floor disputes—while avoiding arenas they felt would have led to internal division or unacceptable changes in values.[2] When necessary, they played defense in those arenas chosen by their chief antagonists, as when their activists were disciplined or even fired by Transit management, or when incumbent union officers offered small favors or staff positions designed to co-opt dissenters. A third set of arenas were the New Directions meetings themselves, where an increasingly heterogeneous group of individuals formed and reformed alliances and factions to debate and decide on broad strategies and short- and long-term tactics.

All these strategic interactions unfolded in arenas influenced by historical precedent and culture and often created by other powerful players; electoral arenas, for example, are notoriously rule-bound. The leaders of ND tried to understand, respond to, and sometimes change the employer's work organization, the relationships of management to the leaders of Local 100 and its members (or, as management saw it, their workers), the Local's organizational structure and electoral procedures, and the ideas and culture of transit workers. For some context, we briefly examine these arenas.

---

[2] Throughout this chapter, we use "shop" or "shop floor" to designate not only traditional factory-like settings like repair shops but the work conditions of bus and train operators, track and signal mechanics, token booth clerks—what transit workers call "rail and road."

## Buses vs. Subways

In the 1980s and 1990s, New York City Transit ran the city's subway lines and most of its bus lines; Local 100 represented almost all its 34,000 rail and road workers, and 2,000 more working for private bus companies.[3] The president of the Local supervised a treasurer, a recording secretary, and seven vice presidents (VPs), heading four subway and three bus departments. That bureaucratic organization was recent; it was meant to roughly parallel Transit's but had an additional consequence of limiting officer accountability to members. Even though each VP headed a discrete craft or geographic work unit, candidates for these ten offices were elected by the entire membership. As a practical matter, therefore, all the top officers rose or fell as a group, and it was impossible for a single oppositionist, unknown outside their own department, to unseat a VP. Oppositionists often won election to division and section offices (smaller subsections of departments chosen just by the members of those units), only to find their power limited by the VPs and staff appointed by the president.

Within the various departments, work conditions, feelings of oppression, physical work locations that aided or thwarted organization, and the ability to affect service varied by type of work. All these, plus historical experiences sometimes stretching back decades, produced diverse worker responses to management and to the incumbent union leaders. Transit had a history of "autocratic" and militaristic management (Freeman 1989: 14). Since the TWU was first organized in 1934, it had tried to resist with shop-floor work stoppages and slowdowns, sometimes wielding considerable power. One day, every bus might have a mechanical problem that needed to be fixed before it could go in service, or every driver might seem to hit every red light. A stalled train backs up a dozen behind it. Repairs might take far longer than usual. As recently as 1984, workers at a key subway car repair shop plunged the subway system into chaos through a sustained months-long slowdown. All this requires cohesion between leaders and workers: what Margaret Levi et al. (2009) call accountability and responsiveness.

But beginning in the 1970s, union leaders increasingly discouraged the resolution of worksite disputes through job actions, even as Transit was

---

[3] Roughly 1,500 New York City Transit (NYCT) bus drivers and mechanics in Queens and Staten Island belonged to another union. Both management and union structures subsequently underwent expansion and restructuring.

becoming more aggressive, part of a general shift in American workplaces toward more despotic management (Wood 2021). Instead, they urged workers to write grievances that union staff discussed with management, often ineffectively, but always over weeks, months, even years. This was the Transit version of a phenomenon that labor historians have noted: the institutionalization of a "web of rules" that purposefully shifted union power from shopfloor stewards to leaders at the union hall (Dunlop 1958: 27).

This is the kind of organizational bureaucracy that Piven and Cloward feared. Union leaders came to see workplace disputes as potential headaches—potentially punishable contract violations on the union's part—rather than opportunities (Aronowitz 1973; Lichtenstein 2002).[4] Interactions among union leaders and management moved to new arenas such as arbitration hearing rooms and paneled offices with workers increasingly excluded. At that subway repair shop in 1984, union leaders cooperated with Transit to break the slowdown. As a result, some rank-and-file workers (especially frustrated shop-floor activists) were attracted to ND for its "fight back" rhetoric.

Union leaders clearly understood the dilemma that their policy of "comply-and-grieve" posed at election time. Instead of sprinkling some naughty tactics in with the nice, to make greater gains, they focused on winning election by strengthening a culture of loyalty in the bus departments and encouraging apathy in the numerically larger subway departments.

Spanning twenty-four years, four successive presidents of the Local came from the bus departments—three (covering twenty-two of those years) from the same six-thousand-person unit, called OA.[5] They were personally familiar with the lower-level officers and managers there, and intervened to fix problems with which they were conversant.[6] They cut some slack to the "depot chairs," the ranking elected officer in each bus garage. Letting them occasionally exercise some power encouraged managers to cooperate in addressing the everyday needs of the operators and mechanics. A Saturday off, a changed shift, some overtime, and deeming an accident "unavoidable"—little favors hard to procure in subways—were routine in buses. The *quid pro quo* was political loyalty. Their officers warned bus workers that a

[4] In the case of Local 100, this general concern was exacerbated by New York State's Taylor Law, which makes work stoppages subject to a range of legal penalties.

[5] OA was short for MABSTOA, which in turn was an acronym for the Manhattan and Bronx Surface Operating Authority, a sub-unit of the New York City Transit Authority.

[6] In more recent years, the last three presidents have come from the Maintenance of Way department. The result has been a substantial increase in that workforce and a substantial decrease in deaths and injuries there.

victory by the "subway-based" ND would lead to a deterioration in their own working conditions. Gains and losses were overtly spelled out.

In the subway departments, union leaders let organization slide. Some of this was simple unfamiliarity. But they also favored and promoted weak officers who lacked organizational skills. When workers elected militant lower-level officers who might emerge as political opponents, they were largely squirreled away in grievance hearing rooms, out of contact with most members. Although they were constitutionally mandated to "administer the affairs" of their divisions they were excluded from contract negotiations. A vicious cycle ensued. Leadership-appointed staff with no electoral accountability to workers and a mandate to quiet problems, not stir them up, were subway workers' first contacts on shop issues. Contractual pay increases for the membership as a whole were funded with work-rule and wage concessions that victimized discrete sections of subway workers. For the leadership, these were all short-term gains, but it meant that management abuses went unchecked, leaving a vacuum for ND to fill.

Angry subway workers began to vote for ND in the 1990s, voting for ND vice presidential candidates over incumbent VPs in each of the four subway departments. Nonetheless, the incumbents, repudiated by the members they actually represented, and thus with diminished power in disputes at the union hall and with management, were returned to office on the strength of votes from the bus departments. As long as bus workers were relatively content, they overwhelmingly voted to reelect the entire incumbent slate. Subway workers repeatedly felt victimized in contract negotiations and sabotaged in shop-floor struggles, since "their" VPs were not accountable to the members they officially represented. Unwittingly at first, each succeeding election tied the Local's leaders closer to one section of the membership while alienating them from the rest, one of many examples of how gains and losses come tied in complex bundles, in this case a version of the extension dilemma.

Largely excluded from power and responsibility, ND's officers, candidates, and activist-members remained committed outsiders from customary union–management arenas. They had no formal contacts with Transit's top managers. They had few ties or *quid pro quo* working agreements with the leaders of the union; relationships were simply varying degrees of mutual hostility. Just a handful of ND's leaders were ever successfully co-opted, and no important incumbent union leader ever cast their lot with ND, or even offered them a say in important decisions. The contest between ND and the Local's leaders became a death match (Lipset et al. 1956). As we will see, the original ND activists were ambivalent about union electoral politics, but experience, the growth of the organization, and its rank-and-file support drove them toward the electoral arena. Only by winning control of the entire Local did it seem they could secure the interests of members in the ND-leaning divisions and departments. That choice, and the gains and losses that came with an electoral package, utterly transformed the group.

## Founding, 1984–1988

ND's predecessor, the HoW newsletter, was produced by a small coalition of "soft Trotskyites and soft Maoists," who had become transit workers with a general notion of organizing in this strategic section of New York's working class. Almost uniformly, they recall being inspired by Local 100's 1980 transit strike, the result of an earlier wave of dissident organizing. Joining Transit was an unusual version of what union organizers call "salting"—filling a workplace with outsider activists—since these leftists wanted to mobilize already unionized workers to overcome what they saw as the reticence and "class collaborationist" attitude of a passive leadership which had sabotaged the 1980 strike.[7]

The ability of both HoW and the eventual ND caucus to remain largely unified for more than a decade, and for the caucus itself to expand, had much to do with the organizational and intellectual capabilities and the ideology of its founding figure, Steve Downs. Marian Swerdlow, present at the founding, notes in admiration, "he had a coherent theory worked out." Downs was a member of Workers' Power, which in 1986 became the organization Solidarity.[8] "Their project at the time," Swerdlow recounts, "was what they called 'regroupment.' They were going to try to get as much of the fractured left together as possible . . . let's try to get the left to work together on whatever it could." According to Naomi Allen, another early HoW participant, Downs "was the one who decided to make a success of this and was absolutely non-factional."

---

[7] For similar examples of leftists using this outside-inside strategy to reinvigorate unions, see Brenner et al. (2010). For more on 1980, see Kagan (2016).

[8] For Solidarity's current self-definition, see http://www.solidarity-us.org/about. For its current political strategy, see http://www.solidarity-us.org/sot. Solidarity's most long-standing project is the publication *Labor Notes*.

Other members of Workers' Power had participated in the building of the dissident caucus Teamsters for a Democratic Union (TDU), an umbrella organization that welcomed both the left and rank-and-file activists and tolerated different definitions of success within its ranks (La Botz 2010).[9] As often happens, "nonfactionalism" was itself originally a factional theory, adopted for tactical purposes, which gradually outgrew its roots and its initial limited application, and became part of ND's guiding culture. As the organization grew, a nominal annual dues payment entitled any member to full and equal participation at biweekly meetings.

This eagerness to find common ground among individuals and factions on the left became more pronounced as activism declined in the broader culture. With mass movements waning, HoW and later ND became a type of refuge, and also a point of pride, for these leftist transit workers.[10] Participation in ND meant individual activists could continue political work that seemed both effective and potentially radical, when many of their former colleagues had (at best) joined more mainstream or "reformist" social justice organizations. It gave them a place where they might succeed on their own terms and, as a result, encouraged both real sticking power and internal compromise.

It took a long time to organize a workforce as geographically and structurally diffuse as Transit's. With a few exceptions, the early rank-and-file activists of ND came and went, often exhausted by the effort, sometimes put off by its left politics, or, more rarely, won over by Local leadership entreaties.[11] But the leftist core of ND persisted for years, even when gains seemed limited. Their ideology helped them resist the petty bribery which offers dissidents low-level union posts, with the prospect of promotion on good behavior, in return for curbing their criticism of higher officers. This is a form of the engagement dilemma, a choice of arenas; earlier oppositionists had accepted positions, believing they could help their members better from the inside. ND members, observing the limited impact of this practice, rejected it. The

---

[9] TDU ultimately allied itself with, and provided pivotal organizational support for, the indigenous Teamster reformer Ron Carey in his successful campaign for Teamsters president. There, TDU sat in the passenger seat with the map, but Carey drove. Since there was no comparable Carey-like figure in Transit—no powerful Local leader ever threw in, or even flirted, with New Directions—ND never had to decide whether to forego its independent path.

[10] Steve Downs makes the point that "the left as a whole is much weaker". (Goldstein interviews). Both he and Josh Fraidstern note how work within Transit became all-consuming for these activists, to the exclusion of other left activities (Goldstein interviews).

[11] Here, we define "rank-and-file activists" as those who had come to Transit seeking a job, rather than with an explicit political agenda. Some had, or gained, leftist political views, while others did not.

Local's officials were perplexed by their inability to simply wait ND out, to wear it down through exhaustion, or to co-opt key leaders, as they had done with previous dissident efforts.[12]

Yet because HoW was an alliance of different left factions, the purpose of the group, the type of work, and the politics that should be expressed publicly, all had to be negotiated, albeit within a common cultural mindset. Subplayers prioritized different goals and arenas: regroupment, a more general effort to gather together whatever militant rank-and-file forces still existed, worker support for radical politics, reforming the union to pay more heed to members, a workplace fight against management, or simply better contracts. (Downs himself averred in 2016 that regroupment was "a secondary goal for me. The [primary] goal was building the caucus and using the caucus to engage in building the struggle and raising consciousness.")

At first, meetings were by invitation only, and activists from left groups unwilling to act "nonfactionally" were excluded. Individuals—there were no members yet—wrote articles on issues that interested them without any particular organizational guidance or disciplined ideological coherence. Outside of HoW, the founders were all organizing independently in their own workplaces. Some held low-level elected office, some deliberately did not. The newsletter gave each a chance to speak to a wider transit worker audience than any one individual might.[13] HoW was only loosely a compound player, and more properly a media vehicle through which individual activists pursued their own goals.

In his study of the United Farm Workers, Marshall Ganz (2000: 1005) notes that an organization "enhances its intelligence" when "a leadership team includes insiders and outsiders, strong and weak network ties, and access to diverse, yet salient, repertories of collective action, and also if an organization conducts regular, open, authoritative deliberation, draws resources from multiple constituencies, and roots accountability in those constituencies." Leftist transit workers were consummate "inside" outsiders. "The[ir] skills ... the ability to put out a publication, to know how to organize a tough organization, those are gifts," noted Noel Acevedo, one of the first rank-and-file workers to stick with ND for the long term.

---

[12] See Kagan and Acevedo interviews on persistence. Swerdlow (1998) discusses this type of bribery throughout *Underground Woman*. On dissident leader co-optation after the 1980 strike, see Kagan (2016).

[13] In the early years, HoW produced 1,000–2,000 copies of three or four articles, four or six times a year. By the late 1990s, the print run was 15,000 copies of an eight- or twelve-page issue, close to monthly.

In HoW and ND, the left created organizations whose procedures and meetings were distinctly less hierarchical and more free-wheeling than the official union meetings.[14] Eladio Diaz, another early rank-and-file participant, says, "I got to like it because of the democratic decisions, the way . . . issues were discussed and voted on. I'd never seen that before, that atmosphere. And that was the ideal of how I wanted the union to go, that was my idea of what the union should be."

Yet after four years of publication, HoW was, by all accounts, failing to reach its own goals. Polletta (2006) notes that the stories activists tell affect how a movement subsequently unfolds, authorizing some types of strategies and not others. Train operators and conductors in Rapid Transit, HoW's base, read and liked the publication, but it wasn't spurring action or radicalization on or off the job, or fostering a larger and more diverse organization. Actual ties to its supposed constituency were weak. "People were drifting, falling away," says Downs. "We were able to keep putting it out but it wasn't building anything." According to Swerdlow, "What Hell on Wheels did that broke them out of it was that they ran a candidate . . . for President [in 1988], and that broke them out of their stagnation." HoW became New Directions, first provisionally and then permanently.

## Early Gains, Unintended Outcomes, and Growth, 1988–1996

In a long process that began in 1988, three factors pushed ND to make winning control of the union through elections its primary goal. First, frustration grew among the HoW activists about their practical inability to stop contract concessions or to organize resistance in the workplace without controlling the upper echelons of the union. Second, the chances for this type of victory increased. Third, preliminary electoral gains meant that the organization attracted more rank-and-file members. For them, the seizure of union office to better the lives of transit workers on the job seemed commonsense—they were familiar with this idea from previous dissident movements. It was easier for ND to recruit and mobilize on this basis, which was easier to explain and justify in public meetings than any of the other original goals.

[14] Again, the desire among various left trends to cooperate encouraged this culture: an unintended gain.

Strategic players constantly juggle their goals and adapt them to different arenas. In the leftists' recurring dilemma between preserving ideologically correct loneliness and gaining a potentially impure power, the balance swung decisively toward the latter. Jasper (2006: 71) remarks, "Radicals can castigate moderates for watering down their goals in order to make them attainable, that is, adjusting them to available means."

In 1988, none of the original activists anticipated either "impure power" or "victory." Although Naomi Allen recalls coworkers urging her and other critics to run for office, HoW's goal was still primarily educational. Downs later explained his intention. "There's a difference between being electoralist and running for something. I was not opposed to using an election to have a platform, to go out and speak to members, this is what the union could be like." According to Sean Ahern, another early member, "Steve was pretty much more focused on . . . trying to raise class awareness among the workers . . . more than just winning an election. . . . I think he was skeptical about the role of the union . . . do you really want to take this over and be the caretakers of this kind of thing?" Workers are most engaged in union affairs during elections and during contract bargaining and ratifications, and this first campaign extended HoW's advocacy of shop-floor struggle and its critique of the union's leadership to a broader audience. Yet while Swerdlow called it "an opportunity to get your ideas out," she also recalls bitterly opposing the change of tactics, fearful it would lead to Jasper's "watering down."

From both propaganda and electoral perspectives, most HoW activists deemed the 1988 campaign a success. They struck an alliance with a Black-nationalist organization with members scattered throughout the workforce and fielded a partial slate of candidates under the name "New Directions." Running largely as an unknown "other," presidential candidate Tim Schermerhorn won 22 percent of the vote system-wide on a platform criticizing contract concessions and advocating rank-and-file action. In Rapid Transit, ND's base, their vice presidential candidate, Frank Boone, won 58 percent of the votes.

In 1991, the incumbents tried to blunt ND's appeal by running a racially diverse slate with a Latino and an African American woman for Secretary-Treasurer and Recording Secretary, yet Schermerhorn did even better, with 34 percent. New Directions candidates won nine of thirty-six executive board seats, and swept the officer positions in the Rapid Transit division. In 1994, Schermerhorn won 45 percent of the votes including the majority of the vote in all four subway departments; other ND candidates won fifteen executive board seats, and many division and section offices. Workers who voted for New Directions were expressing several sentiments: support for the ND "fight back" platform, rejection of incumbent practices and policies, and the racial politics of voting for a Black presidential candidate, since the union's top leadership was still predominantly white.

The campaigns brought HoW politics to a larger audience, but the exclusive focus on education barely had a shelf life of one election round. For one thing, electoral gains proved tantalizing, encouraging, and frustrating too. In 1991–1992, a delayed contract and proposed work rule changes resulted in unrest and sporadic job actions among members, including system-wide work-to-rule slowdowns in Rapid Transit—an exciting vindication of the shop-floor struggle part of the left agenda. ND's assessment was that, "Even though ND did not initiate the slowdowns, the fact that [ND] officers were in place who would support the action made a clear difference to the people operating the trains" (Downs 2006: 12).

ND leaders believed that potentially activist workers were more likely to organize *themselves* and participate in action if they felt there was some sort of union imprimatur for their efforts. ND electoral visibility and partial success thus drew those activists toward New Directions. By the early 1990s, ND was able to expand its own membership and the HoW distribution network to several other sections of the workforce, gaining credibility and a more holistic understanding of transit workers' grievances. Even among those who saw rank-and-file action—"militancy"—as the main goal, winning positions assumed increasing importance. It turned out that being a "caretaker" had an upside.

But piecemeal electoral victories were also less than the sum of their parts—with some virtually a loss in the short term. "The structure of the union," observed Downs, "the fact that VPs were elected Local-wide, influenced HoW and ND to become a Local-wide opposition rather than an RTO [Rapid Transit] opposition." Boone was a train operator, ran as the VP "for" Rapid Transit workers, and won decisively among those members, but because vice presidents were elected system-wide, the incumbent candidate was returned to office on the strength of votes from other departments. Divisional slates could run and win office on their own, but their ability to fight management and make good on their promises to members was constrained by antagonistic top officers of the Local. "You have to have a local-wide presence," said Sean Ahern. "You can't have a caucus in just one or two divisions."

Initial successes in the electoral arena also affected and channeled subsequent strategic entreaties toward what Jasper calls the "external audiences . . . [of] potential recruits and allies," necessary to expand electoral success (Jasper 2004: 6). This is the extension dilemma. During its first years, HoW had been a coalition of and by the left. Now, as it opened its doors, many electoral allies—people who ran as ND candidates but didn't come to meetings or even become members—were not particularly interested in education or rank-and-file struggle. The lowest common denominator for entry was simply being upset with the incumbent leadership. In the climate that had been created by years of inaction, both activists and workers were out of practice with shop-floor organizing. Action in this arena was risky too; disciplinary punishments in Transit can be severe, and in many cases union leaders were as happy to get rid of a "troublemaker" as management was. Anticontract campaigns were more popular, but generally ineffective. These new recruits to New Directions wanted to win office, whether to get out of a train operator's cab or to provide better representation to workers.

Running full slates of appealing division and section officers, even those whose politics went no further than "throw the bums out!," boosted the prospects of ND's presidential candidate, as well as its ability to circulate election literature and the HoW newsletter. As Schermerhorn became a vehicle for the goals of those lower-level candidates, he was increasingly judged on his vote totals and his coattails. In a few cases, lower-level ND candidates realigned themselves with the incumbent leadership after winning office. Even the militants who won office became more pragmatic: they had to evaluate which fights (with the Local leadership or management) produced gains or might lead to losses. This encouraged a more cautious mindset than did the responsibility-free opposition of the HoW era.

Downs later framed a "tension" within ND between organizing from below and from above: "those who thought that victory in elections would follow from successful organizing around daily issues on the job . . . [and] those who thought no amount of organizing on the job would matter if ND didn't hold the top positions in the union" (Downs 2006: 13–14). Swerdlow observed that, after 1988, ND "attracted a lot of people . . . and not all of those people shared the idea of changing the union—shared the *same* idea of changing the union I should say." Another Solidarity supporter, Josh Fraidstern, noted the drift: "People . . . basically felt that until they actually won the top levels of the union they were not going to make any significant progress. . . . A lot of things became more and more focused over the years about electability and not necessarily militancy and democracy." In this version of the engagement dilemma, seeking gains in one arena inevitably created unanticipated contingencies and impinged on work in others.

It was not just the "rank and file" who prioritized electoral work. Many of the original left core gave lip service to "bottom up" but had actually struggled at it for years, possessing neither the skills nor the enthusiasm for organizing workers in shop-floor militancy.[15] After the 1991–1992 slowdowns, job actions in Rapid Transit dwindled until 1999. Actions elsewhere were sporadic. Electoral success promised an easier path to many goals. Here we see the sorcerer's apprentice dilemma, where means shape how players prioritize ends (Jasper 2006: 97). Before 1988, HoW "means" were newsletter propaganda and organizing shop-floor action. Now, different, electoral, means beckoned, and not only objectives, but the answers to immediate problems, changed in step. Fight management, or fight the union to fight management? In the 1990s, the balance swung toward the latter.

In early 1997, Downs explained his middle-term strategy. After noting the inadequacy of the terms "militants" (supporting "change from below") and "dissidents" (advocating "change from above") to describe two general trends within ND, he argued that both perspectives existed within most ND members.

> Depending on the climate in the union and in the city, depending on the chances for success, depending on the response the "from below" approach has received from among the membership, members of ND have been more or less 'militant,' more or less 'dissident.' . . . I thought that this type of split would be postponed by the prospect of winning . . . and that once we had won, the activity and movement that we generated would swing people back behind a "from below" strategy.[16]

Years later, Swerdlow noted the dilemma that Downs faced. "It seemed that nothing less than winning was going to make any change . . . that reality made it impossible to do anything except run to win. And the logic of running to win is that you start throwing overboard anything that might stand in the way of winning." Then she characterized his strategy in terms similar to Downs's elaboration: "Tim [Schermerhorn] would become president

---

[15] See, e.g., Swerdlow on Downs (2003); Kagan on Allen (2003, 2004); Goodman (2016).
[16] Downs, "Re: Response to—future of ND," email, 1997.

and in close alliance with Steve they would activate the ranks and they would use that position at the top to change the way the members related to the union and get them involved, and, you know, they would somehow create a bottom-up change from the top."

Downs believed he could preserve many of ND's original political goals even while its membership became increasingly electoralist in outlook. That strategy seemed most viable when it looked like ND was building toward ultimate victory, but when ND narrowly failed to win back-to-back elections in 1997–1998, Downs's control over ND ebbed. In the ensuing contest for the heart and mind of the organization, new players emerged, the organization itself became a hotly contested arena, and the tasks facing New Directions— its dilemmas and how to resolve them—were reframed.

## New Blood, New Questions, 1996–1998

Groups without official leaders can be undemocratic in practice (Freeman 1972). After apparently unrestricted discussion, decisions are made behind the scenes, while there are no mechanisms to challenge leaders whose existence is denied. In the mid-1990s, when a scandal gripped the union, the International president met with a small delegation of ND leaders and offered to put the Local into trusteeship, with ND given a prominent role; perhaps even the chance to name the VPs in the subway departments. His stated intent, Downs later reported, was to teach the two factions they could work together. It probably would have worked, Downs opined, except the ND delegation turned him down flat. This critical decision was made without even returning to a general New Directions meeting to report the offer. Within meetings, Downs's traditional practice of circulating drafts of HoW articles for brief discussion at the beginning of ND meetings seemed democratic, since everyone was able to comment and suggest changes. Yet ultimately he retained exclusive editorial control over the content. Similar methods cloaked the invisible hands that shaped New Directions policies until electoral setbacks and an influx of new players suddenly challenged them. In the mid-1990s, three new individuals joined ND, and a fourth long-time member challenged the leaders. With their own personal goals, they gradually changed the nature of the organization, in part by utilizing a heretofore little-used rule of the arena: decision-making by voting.

Roger Toussaint and Marc Kagan were allies, leftists who had remained outside the ND orbit. Toussaint had built a reputation by organizing a group of militant track workers who collectively chose a new work location every six months in order to teach different groups of workers how to fight horrific safety conditions.[17] He was "a rank and file leader from very early on . . . people looked up to him," said Ahern, himself a track worker. The political organization to which they had belonged discouraged running for union office, but when it dissolved in 1994, Toussaint was immediately elected Track Division Chair.

After a showdown with Local leaders, the vice president supervising Track allowed Toussaint and his division officers (rather than appointed staff) to handle member problems. Freed from working on the tracks, Toussaint and his committee were able to cast a wide net. They became experts at stopping work for health or safety reasons, gaining the respect of workers throughout the larger Maintenance of Way Department, and the fierce enmity of management. Even a successful rank-and-file organizer like Toussaint, who had avoided electoral politics for years, now saw the value of union office. Downs and his ND leftists weren't the only ones grappling with the engagement dilemma.

Kagan became a member of New Directions in 1995, and in late 1996 he urged his former party comrade to join him, arguing that Toussaint's Track accomplishments were insecure until friendlier Local-wide leaders were in place. Under normal circumstances, newcomers to an organization need to build credibility before they are heeded, but Toussaint's elected office and reputation as a successful organizer gave him instant standing among ND's two hundred dues-paying members and even among the core of twenty to thirty who regularly attended meetings. Within a year, he was named Recording Secretary on ND's 1997 election slate, although the powerlessness of that post made it just the type of nonfactional coalition-building (without consequence for the direction or goals of the organization) that Downs had arranged in earlier

---

[17] Track workers are the closest thing Transit has to coal miners: considered by management "unskilled" and therefore subject to oppressive discipline, working in small crews in hazardous proximity to moving trains and to the 600-volt "third rail," and breathing the steel dust in the tunnels or risking falls from the elevated structure. Largely without access to union officials when work or safety issues arise, they build strong bonds of solidarity and learn to organize themselves and act independently. Kagan's position in a subway car repair shop of eight hundred workers seemed more electorally "strategic," but these skilled workers tended to look toward the shop's elected union officers to protect them against much more limited abuse; they had largely forgotten how to fight.

campaigns.[18] Together, Toussaint and Kagan formed an influential subplayer within ND, arguing for a reorientation of ND's propaganda work: more emphasis on Transit attacks and worker fights, less on the union's ineptitude and concessions. Toussaint believed this approach would appeal to workers who saw ND as just blusterers.

Another key newcomer, but with quite different politics, was Darlyne Lawson, the Stations Division Chair and a former protégé of an incumbent vice president. She had what the left disdainfully called, "Democratic Party politics." Like many other transit workers, Lawson had a visceral hatred of the Transit Authority. In this sense, there was common ground with New Directions. Yet Lawson and the colleagues she brought with her to ND did not share the left's analysis that gains came from shop-floor organization and militant action. But after Lawson fell out with her VP, Downs advocated asking her and her team of division officers to join ND, with the implicit understanding that this Black woman, a potentially potent vote-getter, would replace white leftist Marty Goodman as ND stations vice presidential candidate. She was a strong voice for pure electoralism.

Respecting his previous work, ND activists deferred to Goodman on the question of whether to make the approach. Eventually, he agreed. "I had a nightmare that if I said no to Darlyne and her people, that we could lose the election." Goodman had been an early critic of the emphasis on electoral work; so his lament that, "I didn't want to be the cause. . . . I could have lost the whole election," if he had blocked Lawson, reflects the pressure that had built within New Directions to win. In the following two elections, Lawson and ND won more than 75 percent of the votes in her department. Lawson and similar candidates were a huge advantage in ND's electoral efforts, but at an unappreciated cost to its previous political perspective.

Different arenas require different qualities and skills. Many of those on the ND slates in 1997 and 2000 were chosen because they were good electoral candidates—with the right job titles, work location, ethnicity, and so on—not because they were good or even committed organizers of rank-and-file engagement. The focus on expansion into new departments and winning elections deemphasized a more sophisticated understanding and consensus about political and organizational goals that went beyond basic slogans. Here was Swerdlow's fear, realized. Downs had thought of elections

---

[18] Toussaint fit several useful electoral criteria for rounding out the top of the slate: his ethnicity (West Indian), a department where ND work had previously been thin, and his reputation and experience as an elected officer.

as "educational," but by the mid-1990s, Goodman observed, "There was no political education [with]in New Directions" for new members. They only knew "all the things that [Local 100 President] Willie [James] was doing wrong ... that doesn't tell you what's right ... doesn't educate you in what you need to do."

Years later, Sean Ahern suggested, "The dilemma you describe as electability versus militancy and democracy ... should be taken as a signal to rise to another level of awareness rather than the signal to line up in factions." But the time constraints of a volunteer organization in which everyone began their day by working eight hours for the Transit Authority, and the multiplicity of seemingly urgent tasks that consumed the biweekly meetings, impeded that type of discussion. At a certain point in the development of the organization, those discussions even became counterproductive, more dangerous to internal cohesion than useful.

ND leaders resolved this dilemma through an intense focus on external goals. Leaders turned a blind eye to political divisions within the compound player. No one was likely to radicalize Darlyne Lawson or make her into a shop-floor activist. Having invited her in and staked their future on this type of alliance, ND leaders had to accommodate her politics.[19] New players precluded, or at least constrained, certain tactics, and opened the door to others.

In the run-up to the 1997 elections, Corine Scott-Mack, a rank-and-filer and a VP candidate three years earlier, challenged Schermerhorn for ND's presidential nomination. Scott-Mack claimed she would be a better candidate, and criticized Schermerhorn as "weak"—an implicit way of saying that he was controlled by his white ally Downs.[20] A united left fended her off, but the episode was revealing. For Scott-Mack, ND was nothing more than an electoral vehicle. She stretched the rules of the ND arena, organizing people to pay the annual dues and join New Directions just so they could vote at the nominating meeting. And although she had no radical or even militant trade union vision, the opposition to her candidacy mostly coalesced around her "disloyalty" to the organization. The previous year, she had accepted a staff job at the union hall despite almost unanimous opposition from ND members who feared this first successful wooing of an important ND leader

---

[19] "So you have this question which is interesting I thought—'is it possible to hold onto original ideals?' I don't think there was *an* ideal—Steve had an ideal, I had an ideal, which was somewhat different but not far off, but Darlyne's ideal is completely different." (Marc Kagan, Goldstein interviews; italics in original, reflecting emphasis in interview).

[20] An even more biting accusation was that Downs and Schermerhorn were "cappuccino socialists," with the dual implication of armchair theoreticians, and white on top, Black below.

would blur the distinction between ND and the incumbents. Scott-Mack proved too aggressive and hasty in pursuing her individual goals, challenging the ND left without first building a solid base among rank-and-file members. In a test vote in early 1997, Scott-Mack and the left both mobilized their forces; Scott-Mack lost, left ND, and subsequently won a VP post on the incumbents' slate.

For the time being, most new activists continued to follow the lead of the original core. Schermerhorn and Naomi Allen filled the first two spots on the 1997 ballot. Victory would bring the left triumvirate of Schermerhorn, Downs, and Allen to Local leadership. With new pockets of influence, most ND members were confident they would seize control of the union. Their opponent, the newly appointed president Willie James, was the Local's first African American president, but otherwise he seemed a weak candidate.[21] Another OA officer, James had never actually held an important union post in his department. A meteoric rise within the union meant he had little experience dealing with Transit. He reopened an existing contract and agreed to a wage freeze and other concessions, pointing to Transit's claims of budget deficits and threats of layoffs. Within months, Transit announced a large budget surplus. Transit had seen its opportunity to outfox an inexperienced leader; apparently, James had been duped.

Despite James's contract millstone and ND's broadened outreach capabilities, ND fell just short in the 1997 election. And when the election was rerun in 1998 due to election irregularities, ND picked up only a few more votes in a brutal, exhausting, and demoralizing second campaign. In part, James's victory was due to his (ultimately unfulfilled) promise that a huge pension improvement was in the bag only if he was reelected, because the state would not make the same deal with the ND radicals. In part, it was due to the incumbents' intense efforts to turn out votes in the bus departments. And James's candidacy negated the never-stated but always implicit idea of "white incumbent, Black insurgent." Scott-Mack's presence on his slate helped too. Cumulatively, this was just enough. Yet in before-the-fact worries and after-the-fact postmortems, ND members laid a large share of the blame on Schermerhorn and, by extension, his ally Downs.

---

[21] The Local's long-time president, Sonny Hall, had recently become head of the International union. His original replacement had a short tenure—"promoted sideways" after failing to reveal the whole terms of an important contract change to the membership. Despite his lack of experience, James was in the right place at the right time to inherit the presidency. Hall later explained that, although he was not enamored of James, it was politically impossible to bypass the Black officer who seemed next in line. The incumbents faced their own dilemmas.

ND activists respected Schermerhorn's work ethic and his years as the public face of the organization. In face-to-face discussions with workers, Schermerhorn was empathetic and won people over, but he was unexciting in front of a crowd. Particularly in the bus departments, where ND had fewer activists advocating for Schermerhorn, he was derided simultaneously as both a lightweight and as a hothead who would lead the union into perilous waters.[22] And in ND meetings, he was mostly quiet. He didn't project leadership and wasn't regarded as a strategic thinker. In Noel Acevedo's harsh assessment, "Tim Schermerhorn was deficient in many ways and he was being artificially sustained by the left." This echoes Scott-Mack's charge of weakness. That a white intellectual seemed to be leading from behind the scenes had rankled some, but with the dual losses in 1997 and 1998, these criticisms gained more currency. ND members valued Downs for his intellectual gifts, but his seemingly dispassionate nature precluded many emotional bonds.

Moreover, the three long years until the next election became increasingly treacherous for New Directions activists. Transit, now fully alert to the prospect of a more militant union, began to pay more attention to influencing internal Local matters. It targeted ND candidates with disciplinary charges, hoping to fire, intimidate, or discredit as many as possible before the next election. Toussaint *was* actually fired on a trumped-up accusation. It took an extraordinary effort by ND members on the Local's executive board to reverse James's preliminary decision to remove him from his union position.[23]

Under these circumstances, the driving question—how to win—became even more urgent. Newer ND supporters saw 1997 and 1998 as a failure, not a near miss. Older activists fretted about how many more years the movement could sustain itself. Collectively, members began to discuss what had

[22] The importance of activists in the work locations was discussed in Kagan, Goldstein interview. "It is my shop after all, my shop. Which, you know, I delivered to New Directions.... It's very personalist actually, you know, you become the leader of a group of people and they trust you. You say—they don't know Roger Toussaint—you say, 'I know this guy, I trust him, you trust me, so vote for him.'"

[23] The best, but partial, account of Toussaint's firing and, generally, the targeting of ND activists is to be found in Kagan, Goldstein interview. The charge—riding in a union vehicle during working hours—and the penalty—dismissal—were on their face absurd, and thus complemented ND's demands for wholesale changes in the disciplinary system—"an end to plantation justice," Toussaint called it. A closely guarded secret that would have raised questions of competency, was that either Toussaint or a member of his committee had failed to appeal the charge in a timely manner, thus "accepting" it—a huge blunder that allowed Transit to avoid the content of the charge in all subsequent disciplinary hearings. A strict reading of the Local's bylaws would have led to Toussaint's removal from union office since he was no longer a transit worker. ND argued that the Local should not allow management to "decide" through its disciplinary procedure who should be representing union members, at least as long as Toussaint's dismissal was being appealed in the courts. Several of James's supporters on the executive board were swayed by this argument.

gone wrong, and how to fix it before the next election cycle. The possibility of a new standard-bearer or a new electoral strategy was increasingly discussed. With electoral success now the organization's overriding goal, the range of choices as to what to do next were limited to those that would lead ND to that promised land. A new arena, an internal struggle for the leadership of New Directions, now opened up.

## Success? 1998–2000

The range of alternatives to Schermerhorn soon narrowed to one. Roger Toussaint fit three key demographic characteristics: male, Black, subways. He was charismatic, spoke with great self-assurance, and seemed to possess a strategic vision for New Directions and the Local, encapsulating the best of both Downs and Schermerhorn. He wasn't weighed down by defeat. That Transit had fired him on a trumped-up charge was not a decisive mark in his favor within ND, but, on balance, members thought that it helped his appeal to transit workers as a whole, playing to their sense of grievance against management. Unlike Schermerhorn, he fit the image of a powerful union leader; no one else would be "run[ning] the union behind the scenes," a charge Lawson later leveled against Downs. To increasing numbers of ND members, Toussaint and Kagan replicated the strengths of Schermerhorn and Downs, but in a more appealing package, with the white expediter clearly subordinate to the Black visionary with an impressive record of action against Transit. By 2000, Toussaint had been a division chair for six years. He produced a document package an inch thick for ND activists demonstrating his record of mobilizing workers and fighting Transit successfully. Leftist supporters of Toussaint believed that he resolved the militancy versus electability dilemma. Rank-and-file ND members believed that Toussaint had a plan and that, in 2000, they would win.

When a player has a charismatic figure like Toussaint available, the personality strategy seems most promising (see Table 7.1). The risks seem worth taking (assuming they are even assessed or considered), especially when the goal is narrowed to something like an electoral victory. So the personality package and the electoral package often go together. The full range of losses and gains comes later.

Like the Scott-Mack-Schermerhorn contest, the underlying strategic and tactical differences between the candidates was not decisive in the choice

Figure 4.1 Photo credit Alan Saly

between Toussaint and Schermerhorn. Partisans of both candidates tried to claim the mantle of militancy while deriding the other as representing a top-down and demobilizing approach, but neither side's arguments resonated with the majority of the activists. Many of the newer rank-and-file members had only a vague idea—and no experience—of how to build shop-floor militancy or gauge which candidate's strategy would be more effective. Even fewer understood the left's subtle disquisitions and distinctive tropes about "top-down *or* bottom-up," "fight management *or* fight the union," and "electoral work *or* class awareness."

That this kind of internal education had never taken place now precluded a real discussion of alternative futures for the activists who chose a path forward for New Directions during the summer of 2000. Downs's accusations, that Toussaint would not respect "union democracy," or would be too authoritarian once in office, were ineffective. Despite its frequent use as a slogan, there was no common understanding within ND of what "union democracy" meant, and therefore how Toussaint endangered it. The second claim also failed to resonate. The earliest members of ND—especially the leftists—were windmill tilters, inclined to "question authority." The newer activists and candidates tended to be more pragmatic, more accepting of hierarchies, and more inured to the ways of a traditional union bureaucracy. ND's seeming lack of structure held no particular charm for them. Charges that Toussaint would wield too much personal authority were reframed by his supporters as the "leadership" that Schermerhorn lacked.

Toussaint's supporters were also unable to explain ideological differences between the two candidates in a clearly comprehensible manner—but they had an alternative. "It was harder for people to grasp the idea that Steve doesn't want to fight or Tim doesn't want to fight, Roger does," Kagan argued later. "What was easier to grasp was that Tim can't win . . . we have to move on, who is there to move on to? That's an easy slogan in a sense for people who don't understand the other piece."[24] What ND members understood, or believed they understood, was that their goal was to win power, that Toussaint could win and then "the union," or transit workers collectively, could fight management. The average ND member did not consider how, exactly, that fight might proceed differently under Toussaint or Schermerhorn.

In the ND nominating meeting before the 2000 election, Toussaint bested Schermerhorn decisively. Opposition was limited mostly to the Schermerhorn-Downs base in Rapid Transit, a handful of Solidarity leftists, and a few individuals whose officeholding ambitions suffered in the new reconfiguration of the top of the slate. In a gesture of healing, Toussaint offered Schermerhorn the Recording Secretary position on the ticket, but he declined and accepted the nomination for Vice President of Rapid Transit instead—a position with more actual power. Acevedo, another Downs partisan, received the Recording Secretary spot. Downs and Allen still carried some heft within New Directions meetings, but wound up far down the ticket, running for offices of little importance. They were the big losers in the reshuffle—"their" organization, which they had built since 1984, was taken from them, on the eve of electoral victory, albeit according to the rules they had established.

The general election was anticlimactic. Toussaint was indeed a far better candidate than Schermerhorn. Although James had negotiated a new contract with impressive wage gains (in return for health benefit concessions which were designed to kick in only after the election), Toussaint won 60 percent of the vote in a three-way race—the incumbents split in a sign

---

[24] Noel Acevedo also confirmed that the choice of Toussaint was based on the belief within "the organization" that he was the best candidate.

of incipient panic and the hope to preserve a few positions. ND candidates secured the vast majority of executive board seats and for the first time even won a majority in one of the bus departments. The new strategy and leader had produced gains beyond most ND activists' wildest dreams. The personality strategy had paid off in electoral victory. The losses bundled with those gains only gradually became apparent.

## 2000–2003: Complex Bundles of Gains and Losses Revealed

Winning an election seems like a relatively objective mark of success. A significant subset of the New Directions movement now had a larger and different arena to work in: as officers of Local 100, they could turn their attention to the struggle against Transit management. Some had hoped for this moment for a dozen years or more. Workers reluctant to fight management unless led by "the union" were now psychologically ripe for mobilization. Financial resources were available to communicate with those members and with the public. The possibility of leveraging action and success in this new arena to blaze a new path for all of New York's labor movement was a tantalizing prospect. Yet even this success had its ambiguities: the choices that subplayers had made to win the election affected the Local going forward, shaping and constraining the decisions that the new officers could and would make.

United for so many years, New Directions began to tear itself apart even before it won, when the transition to new arenas with different rules proved disruptive. The flush of victory only briefly obscured an increasingly bitter dispute between Toussaint and Downs. At the nominating meeting, in what Toussaint and his allies saw as an organized bending of the arena rules, three additional challengers to Toussaint had emerged, all from the Downs-Schermerhorn Rapid Transit base. Each had used his nominating speech to attack Toussaint, forcing Toussaint to defend himself and allowing Schermerhorn to counterpose himself as a peacemaker. More he said/she said incidents—including one in which a Downs ally wrote a letter to a local newspaper accusing Toussaint of constructing a "cult of personality"—led to further bad blood. Having chosen "naughty" over "nice" in a final effort to derail Toussaint, Downs and his ally Allen now suffered the consequences. Neither received a significant staff position and they were soon shoved to the sidelines. Different arenas have different pecking orders. New elected leaders now allocated and legitimized positions and power in "Local 100" based on the union's organizational hierarchy rather than on the quality and quantity of past work, or on ND's historic one person-one vote decision-making. This new arena had its own rules.

Downs and his allies now seemed to become critics of the new administration; these actions unwittingly hastened ND's demise. On the executive board, they sometimes allied themselves with the handful of holdovers from the "old regime." They tried to reappropriate the ND name by issuing leaflets in the name of "New Directions Rank and File." An ND meeting put "the franchise name" in the hands of Toussaint supporters—a gain for that subgroup of players—with the time but not the skills to continue the production of the *Hell on Wheels* newspaper—a loss.[25] When Naomi Allen was purposely bypassed for a delegate spot to the union's International Convention, she assembled her own slate, named it "Hell on Wheels" and publicly attacked her long-time colleagues. (At that convention, held a month after 9/11, Toussaint was condemned from the right, for being a "friend of bin Laden," and from the left for violations of union democracy.) Encouraged by Toussaint, Kagan filed formal charges against Allen, claiming she had fraudulently signed nomination acceptance letters. Toussaint then exercised his unilateral power as president to remove her from staff, returning her to her transit job.[26] She was just the first of many to face this treatment.

The efforts of Downs and his allies proved strategic blunders, allowing Toussaint to characterize them as opposed to the New Directions project. New Directions members—now officers—began to "choose up sides," Kagan noted in 2003. "Roger was very good at . . . moving people to that logical conclusion."[27] "Democratically we decided on something," said Eladio Diaz, an early ND member, expressing the sentiment of the majority of New Directions activists, "and he [Downs] didn't like the way it happened, so he

---

[25] "Roger moved . . . me too, to prevent Steve and Naomi and Noel from taking the franchise but once we had the franchise we couldn't, we just didn't have the time or forces to do anything with it" (Kagan, Goldstein interview). The loss was less apparent at the time, since the new TWU leadership now launched a Local newspaper.

[26] The full sordid history of this attack on Allen can be found in Kagan and Allen, Goldstein interviews. Allen had violated the letter of the law but not its spirit, signing for fellow slate members who had agreed to run. The charges were alternately rejected, upheld, and rejected, depending on the factional interests of the group that dominated each hearing body.

[27] Downs, Acevedo, and Allen later claimed that Toussaint's ability to remove elected officers from staff and return them to their transit jobs was used to coerce support. This was true later, but not in these first few months.

took some people and created their own little group."[28] Again, players did not explore substantial/strategic differences about how to run the union. In the full flush of enthusiasm at their long-sought control of the Local, activists-cum-officers were not inclined to question their seemingly brilliant leader if they were asked—or forced—to choose sides in an internal dispute. New Directions members had consciously chosen a strong personality because he would make a good candidate; few had thought about what type of president he would be.

With its victory, New Directions fractured and dissolved. Toussaint's opponents within ND, unable to reconcile themselves to their loss of influence, goaded Toussaint, inviting him to strike back. They underestimated Toussaint's strategic abilities, now greatly enhanced by the prestige of office and the bureaucratic powers he employed in a muscular and increasingly punitive manner. Since Toussaint wielded power within the Local and also had the support of most ND members, he effectively pulled the plug on New Directions, viewing the continued fight over its soul as a time-wasting distraction. Freed from the moral restraint of ND collectivism, Toussaint and other leaders began to resolve debates within the Local using the hierarchical and institutional power they inherited, rather than through the extended discussion, debate, and voting typical of New Directions. Public disagreement might now lead to effective expulsion from a union position. In this new arena, these players had new powers at their disposal.

When we interviewed him in 2016, labor sociologist Stanley Aronowitz noted that a dissident caucus that maintains its existence *after* an election victory may speak or act in ways politically imprudent or even illegal for the union leaders—giving them another tool to fight management. Potentially, ND could have been a forum for rank-and-file activists to engage with the new leadership, to exert a countervailing pressure against "a more conservative and bureaucratic direction" (Downs 2006: 26). But as internal disputes spilled over into the postelection era, none of its leaders seemed to need New Directions enough to be willing to compromise to save it. If ND was born in a spirit of "nonfactionalism," it ended in partisan warfare. The manner and ramifications of its death affected how the new officers implemented their

---

[28] Oddly, in 2003 interviews, both Downs and Allen seemed oblivious to their own rejection of decisions that were made democratically, albeit against their interests and perspectives, within the organization in 2000–2001. See, for example, Allen talking generically about decision-making: "Everybody has the right to participate in these discussions and decisions but we have no trouble taking a vote . . . and the majority gets to have it their way, the minority gets to fight another day. . . . Next time it comes up for discussion you can re-raise your point (Allen, Goldstein interview).

plans. Within a year, Toussaint began to purge former ND colleagues from the Local 100 staff. In the 2003 elections, Downs and Acevedo, among others, chose to join forces with their long-time political enemies—the remnants of the former leadership—to form a common slate against Toussaint.[29] The rivalries of electoral arenas redirected these factions' goals.

The ferocity of ND's rupture shaped Toussaint's eight years at the helm of Local 100. It turned out that Toussaint's supporters and critics were both partially right. He was a strong leader who wanted to fight management. For several years, the union was far more aggressive than it had been in the past. Management had been right to worry about a ND victory. It organized militant actions and mobilized surprising numbers of workers in large demonstrations. Hundreds of workers volunteered to be trained as shop stewards. It was far more active in building community alliances. It threatened a strike in 2002, and waged a short strike in 2005. Supporters celebrated that strike as a blow against neoliberalism (although critics called it a top-down affair intended to promote Toussaint).[30]

Downs was also right about Toussaint: he did enjoy exercising authority and was increasingly intolerant of dissent, ultimately surrounding himself with yes-men. Many of the new but pragmatic and practical officers were reluctant to take on initiatives that might go wrong and lead to a chewing out by Toussaint. The ambitious shop-steward training program withered when the new stewards were deployed mainly as "gophers" and discouraged from the very kind of shop-floor combativeness that ND had pressed for in the past and for which Toussaint personally had been known. That type of action is potentially empowering but also inherently risky—each one a new arena of multiple players and interests (the engagement dilemma). Mostly lacking an ideological commitment to rank-and-file militancy, the new officeholders saw little reason to encourage shop-floor actions that might go wrong—or to enhance the reputations of stewards who might one day take their place. Lawson, for one, spent the next three years ineffectively arguing with management in meetings instead of organizing her members; she was the rule far more than the exception. There was little "bottom-up change from the top."

---

[29] Schermerhorn and Allen did not join that coalition and left office in 2003 without running for reelection. Even the new opposition ruptured.

[30] The strike has not yet found an authoritative reading. Analyses range from "bold undertaking" to "waged to lose." They agree on one point, however: that transit workers largely perceived the outcome as a defeat.

Within a few years, Local 100's new militancy had atrophied. It was simply a more effective traditional union.

The fight over the soul, the body, and then the carcass of New Directions—the muzzling of certain voices, the loss of potential allies and the search for new friends to replace them—were both cause and effect of Toussaint's increasing paranoia. By 2004, Toussaint was reading the mail of the Local's vice presidents before it was sent or delivered. The organization was no longer "enhanc[ing] its intelligence"; it had placed constraints on itself, it was a diminished vehicle.[31] Eliminating a few opponents may have at first seemed like an easy solution to a classic extension dilemma—a gain of apparent solidarity at the expense of a few people's skills—but the creation of new enemies turned out to have a corrosive effect, the wagons circling ever tighter. By 2008, Toussaint, once a spell-binding, charismatic, and heroic figure, the martyr restored to lead transit workers to the promised land, had worn out his welcome and took a position in the International TWU bureaucracy. Four years later, he was fired for trying to meddle in the affairs of the Local from afar. Today, when ND veterans meet, they shake their heads and talk about the "tragedy" of those years.

## Conclusion

"First, win" might seem a self-evident axiom for social movements, but the electoral package tells us that even apparent gains come freighted with diverse consequences. In 1984, a group of radicals who advocated shop-floor militancy but also had political ambitions to build left movements revitalized a tradition of dissident activity in Local 100. Hopes to win squadrons of workers to radical causes were dashed by national historical trends. The organizing goal thus took precedence, further strengthened because it resonated with rank-and-file anger at management. Hell on Wheels initially wished for an apparent side arena, electoral work, only in order to bolster bottom-up struggles. Yet when workers proved reluctant to fight without the support of "their union," HoW transformed itself into New Directions,

---

[31] "Enhanc[ing] its intelligence is drawn from an observation by Ganz quoted earlier in this chapter. Reading his opponent's mail was reported to Kagan in 2004 by the former editor of the Local's newspaper, and discussed in Kagan, Goldstein interview.

and sought institutionalized power through elections. Other goals soon fell by the wayside.

ND's leaders attempted to attract rank-and-file workers to this project yet feared the costs of an intensive, time-consuming, and potentially risky effort to change their top-down perspective of union organization. Facing a classic extension dilemma, it hoped to postpone the resolution of this dilemma until after it won control of the union. But whether they might have been able, or inclined, to change that culture using the resources of the Local soon became moot. When union elections in 1997 and 1998 brought setbacks rather than expected victories, doubts grew among ND's rank-and-file members about the left's strategies and candidate.

In the following election, relying on Toussaint's personality, ND gained institutional control of the union, but at the cost of its own organizational unity. To consolidate their power in this split, the new leaders turned to the administrative, hierarchical, and bureaucratic methods that both ND members and transit workers were well-trained to accept, while the minority cast itself into the arms of its former opponents, giving up its radicalism also. In the end, neither faction was able to play the role, or uphold the banner, they had both claimed for so long.

In this account, we have focused primarily on the gains and losses embedded in an electoral struggle to gain institutional power, and how the dilemmas activists faced and the choices they made shaped the subsequent outcomes. Virtually all the arenas, and especially the electoral ones, were shaped by long-standing rules, understandings, and processes which tended to regulate players' decisions and responses. Insurgents who had vowed to overturn old rules and culture instead were co-opted by them. Accepting the union's electoral procedures was parallel in many ways to the perils of institutionalization we saw in chapter 3. We might expect to see the same problems in our next chapter, which heads overseas and looks at the Communist Party of Graz, Austria. Instead, it successfully remade itself and changed its long-standing internal culture, producing surprising electoral and policy gains, which then validated further internal changes. And following Amenta's advice to embed itself in the bureaucracy (2006), it seems to have avoided the being-there dilemmas discussed in the previous chapter.

# 5

# Owning an Issue across Arenas

## How the Communists Flourished in Graz

Since the 1990s, Graz, Austria's second-largest city, has witnessed a surprising resurgence of the local branch of the Communist Party of Austria (KPÖ), despite the weakness of radical left players in most of Europe, and especially in Austria. After receiving only 1.8 percent of the vote in 1983, the Communists have since 2012 been the biggest left-wing party in the city council, overshadowing both Social Democrats and Greens—even though the Communists lack political representation in almost all the rest of the country. In the Graz election of September 2021, the party even made international headlines. Attracting 28.8 percent of the vote, the Communists became the most popular party in town, also overtaking the center-right People's Party. In November 2021, a majority of delegates in the city council—Communists, Greens, and Social Democrats—elected KPÖ Graz leader Elke Kahr as new mayor. [1]

Beyond their electoral achievements, the politicians of KPÖ Graz have also been able to make a variety of other gains, mainly on housing issues, which became their main focus. Their gains resulted not only from strategic interaction in the arenas of legislation and government. Some stemmed from engagement outside the arenas that political parties are typically associated with; there, on the fringes of formal arenas, KPÖ Graz looks more like what is typically understood as social movement player.

The Communists achieved gains despite having mostly been outsiders in the political system of Graz. Before entering a coalition with the Greens and the Social Democrats in 2021, the Communists had never formed official coalitions with other parties in the proportionally elected city council. Still, the strength of KPÖ Graz has allowed them to participate in the arena of

---

[1] For this chapter, Manès Weisskircher conducted fifteen interviews with thirteen leading figures and activists of KPÖ Graz in January 2015 (together with Dieter Reinisch) and in January 2016. All quotes from these interviews are translated from German.

*Gains and Losses.* James M. Jasper, Luke Elliott-Negri, Isaac Jabola-Carolus, Marc Kagan, Jessica Mahlbacher, Manès Weisskircher, and Anna Zhelnina, Oxford University Press. © Oxford University Press 2022.
DOI: 10.1093/oso/9780197623251.003.0006

city government since 1998: an Austrian constitutional provision allows all parties above a certain strength in local legislatures to *share* responsibility in local government administration. This system of "proportional government" permitted the Communists to appoint the head of the housing department without joining any governing coalition.[2]

This chapter studies the electoral, administrative, and substantive gains of KPÖ Graz: How has the party been able to make these unlikely gains? And what is the *relationship* between the Communists' gains in different arenas? In answering these questions, we focus on the importance of owning an issue through entering new arenas as well as "boomerang effects" across arenas which increase a player's chances of achieving a variety of gains but also carry risks.

Political parties regularly engage in strategic interaction beyond the formal political system, namely, the arenas of legislature and government. Historically, many labor "mass parties" attempted to care for their members "from the cradle to the grave," reaching out to the spheres of both private and economic life. Recent scholarship has emphasized that contemporary radical left "movement-parties" in Western Europe engage in street politics or have even emerged from them (della Porta et al. 2017). In other words, political parties frequently enter new arenas, such as the protest arena, but also the arenas of direct democracy or courts. Parties are also active in back-stage areas, in places without audiences. There, politicians may be the target of lobbying efforts by other players such as businesses or nongovernmental organizations (NGOs). But politicians may also focus on direct contact with the local population and potential voters.

When players are active in many arenas, their actions in one arena may affect other arenas. Momentum, moods, money, or reputation may move from one arena to another. Gains and losses in one arena may influence the likelihood of gains and losses in another. For instance, political parties with strong ties to "civil society" tend to be more stable in the electoral arena (Martin et al. 2020). To understand such crucial interactions, we adopt a concept from the study of transnational activism, a "boomerang pattern" (Keck and Sikkink 1998), which helps us to understand the relationship between gains

---

[2] The two political arenas that are central to this chapter are the local council (*Gemeinderat*), which is the city legislature of Graz, and the local government (*Stadtrat*), which operates the city govern- ment. Electoral and legislative arenas include not only the city council but the regional legislature (*Landtag*) of Styria, the region of which Graz is the capital, and the national parliament. These three layers point to the federal dimension of the Austrian political system.

and losses in different arenas. Originally, the boomerang pattern referred to activists fostering transnational cooperation in order to put pressure on their own nonresponsive national governments. In our theoretical framework of players and arenas, such a strategy refers to a player entering new arenas partly in the hope of positive "spillover" effects on other arenas where players may struggle to be influential.

The strategy succeeded for the Communists in Graz, despite the risks they ran. We try to discern a boomerang package based on engagement in many arenas in table 5.1. Entries into new arenas can turn out poorly, hurting rather than helping a player: engagement also involves risks. And of course, there is a basket dilemma about spreading time and other resources too thinly, a challenge we analyzed in chapter 3. The new arenas can also become less important than the player had anticipated, turning into false arenas.

KPÖ Graz managed the risks associated with this package well, partly through members' extraordinary contributions of their own time and money. Its key figures developed reputations as reliable politicians on matters of local politics, managing to "own" the issue of housing since the 1990s. This gain became the cornerstone of the party's electoral success. Throughout its

Table 5.1 The Boomerang Package

| Dilemmas | Player's Goals | Likely Costs | Risks |
|---|---|---|---|
| The Engagement Dilemma | Entering an arena to achieve specific gains | Resources and time | Losses instead of gains or maintaining status quo, countermobilization by opponents, disregard of more promising arenas |
| The Basket Dilemma | Spreading across arenas to increase the chances for gains | Resources and time | Lack of focus |
| The Dilemma of False Arenas | Entering an arena to make gains, for example entering a legislature or government to achieve policy change | Time | Legitimation of an arena that does not bring desired gains; limited influence over decisions; loss of reputation |
| Solutions | Find arenas or services where you can build positive reputation that can be exported to other arenas; avoid putting all efforts in arenas where success in unlikely. | | |

rise, the party engaged in different arenas, which were not restricted to the institutions of the political system. Electoral gains provided important resources to the party, but the Communists had to engage in arenas beyond the legislature and government in order to build and keep credibility on housing matters. In many instances, they achieved gains by providing direct help to people in need or after mobilizing broad nonelectoral support. These gains, on housing-related issues and beyond, then reinforced the Communists' strength in the traditional arenas of political parties, the legislature, and administration. To understand this positive feedback loop, we need to examine the work that made effective activism in many arenas possible despite the potential risks involved. At the same time, our analysis of the rise of KPÖ Graz will also shed light on the importance of other dilemmas its subplayers faced over the course of its unexpected rise.

## Shifting Goals when Facing Electoral Crisis

The electoral rise of KPÖ Graz contrasts with the recent experience of most radical left parties in Europe, especially in Austria, where radical left players have been notoriously weak (Weisskircher 2019). KPÖ Graz is a local wing of the Austrian Communist Party, founded in 1918. Since then, the Communists were only represented in national parliament from 1945 to 1959, losing parliamentary representation four years after their former patron and role model, the Soviet Union, withdrew its occupation forces when Austria regained national sovereignty. No other radical left party has ever gained a seat in the national parliament. At the regional level, the situation was similar. After defeats in 1970, the Communists were no longer represented in any of Austria's nine regional legislatures. While some communist parties in Western Europe have had considerable electoral gains, especially in Italy and France, their Austrian counterpart did not.

Similar weakness characterized the Communists in Graz, a city of around 290,000 inhabitants. Since 1945, the city had been governed by mayors from the Social Democrats, the Conservatives, and once even from the radical right Freedom Party. Polling only 2 to 4 percent in the 1960s and 1970s, the Communists managed to continuously maintain one seat on the city council, due to the absence of any threshold requirement. Even after the party's weakest result, in 1983, when it scored only 1.8 percent of the vote, this institutional feature prevented the Communists from disappearing entirely from local politics.

Despite, or perhaps because of, hitting bottom in 1983, the later 1980s were a turning point for KPÖ Graz, which experienced a generational change. Ernest Kaltenegger, then thirty-one years old, became its leader in 1981. In the context of its weak showing and the obvious decay of "really existing socialism" in Russia and Eastern Europe, a situation in which there was little left to lose, the new leaders realized that they needed to shift goals to become politically relevant. Over time, the party turned away from revolutionary rhetoric about unattainable large-scale social change, shifting attention to locally important issues, concrete projects with feasible objectives in the short and middle term. Losses made the player rethink strategic choices. The rise of new individual players within the compound player of the party allowed for innovation.

By the 1990s, the Communists began to focus on housing issues: investment in public housing, a telephone hotline for housing questions, and financial support for tenants in legal disputes with their landlords. Their enduring and consistent commitment to matters of local concern increased the reputation of the Communists in Graz.

Numerous factors shaped the decision to choose this issue, including personal experience and interactions with other players: Kaltenegger himself had changed apartments twelve times by the mid-1980s. In addition, contacts to the local *Mieterschutzverband* (Association for the Protection of Tenants) raised awareness for problems related to housing.[3] The party also benefited from contacts with the Lille branch of the French Communists, who were fighting against evictions. According to Kaltenegger, key party figures wished to engage in problems directly relevant to the electorate instead of calling for large-scale but distant changes:

> Politics mustn't be something happening only inside your head, then you sit down and write something on your computer . . . so that you can think: 'Now I have a great leaflet' . . . [Politics] always needs to happen in connection with the persons concerned; otherwise it won't lead to much.

---

[3] I thank Walter Peissl (Austrian Academy of Sciences) for this piece of information (in an email exchange in September 2021).

This shift exemplifies the importance of biography and taste in political players' choice of strategies (Jasper 1997). The later head of the larger regional party division of Styria, Franz Stephan Parteder, supported the decision, emphasizing that, as a freestanding and distinct problem, housing was a good issue on which to ground the party's political relevance. Improving the housing situation in Graz would allow the KPÖ to underline its "use value as a helpful party for the people," at the same time not requiring a "political-ideological metamorphosis" (Parteder 2013).

Housing policy was also promising because it has a long political tradition in Austria. The construction of affordable housing units for large parts of the population was a key policy of twentieth-century social democracy, especially in the capital, known as "Red Vienna" in the interwar period. Between 1923 and 1934, when the Conservatives completed their coup d'état ending Austria's First Republic, the Social Democratic government of Vienna built more than 60,000 apartments (Seiß 2011: 577).

A glance at other contemporary communist parties in Western Europe reveals that such a shift in goal priorities was not an obvious move; even after the collapse of the Soviet Union, many parties failed to reinvent themselves. Nor did other parts of the KPÖ follow the lead of the Graz branch. The orthodoxy of Austrian Communists—often uncritical toward the Soviet Union (Gärtner 1979)—meant that many of them resisted strategic innovation.

Within KPÖ Graz, only a few individuals initiated the process of reinvention, against the trends elsewhere. Discussions and redefinition of goals always present political players with a whose-goals dilemma (Jasper 2006: 67); no compound player uniformly agrees about how to prioritize its goals. Although the Communists in Graz had not changed their basic political analysis, their attempt to work on a topic of direct local significance implied a different self-conception for party activists. According to Kaltenegger, some of his fellow party members were initially skeptical about the focus on housing issues, underlining the heterogeneity of compound players. Many came around only after the effort proved effective. Current party leader Elke Kahr noted that many younger activists continued to prefer more glamorous political topics:

Only a few had an interest [in housing]. . . . That's also logical, especially when it comes to the young. . . . But that's now changing quicker than in the past: when young people, who regard education and the acquirement of our [Marxist] classics as very important, join [the party], they see that theory is important as backbone, so you do not lose your stance. But they realize much quicker [than in the past] that you can gain access to people only via the medium of local politics. It's not only great theorizing in the pub, also a lot of practical work is necessary—we are really successful in passing this spirit on. [. . .] And of course, with positive results people are easier to convince. And because the elections have also shown, that [our approach] is not wrong and that we have also gained [votes], people understood it. It was not a matter of course; it was a long process.

## Owning the Housing Issue through the Politics of Direct Help

In the 1990s, KPÖ Graz began to slowly but steadily "own" the issue of housing thanks to engagements beyond the legislative arena. In his study of party politics, Petrocik (1996: 826) presents issue ownership as "a reputation for policy and program interests, produced by a history of attention, initiative, and innovation toward these problems, which leads voters to believe that [a specific party] is more sincere and committed to doing something about them." Writing on social problems, Gusfield (1981: 10) understands issue ownership as "[t]he ability to create and influence the public definition of a problem [. . .]. The metaphor of property ownership is chosen to emphasize the attributes of control, exclusiveness, transferability, and potential loss also found in the ownership of property." In chapter 2, for instance, we saw several players jockeying to own the minimum wage issue.

The Communists in Graz began to offer different types of direct support for those with housing problems, moving beyond the formal arenas of the political system. First came the telephone hotline. Then the party offered financial and legal support to tenants in court when landlords threatened eviction. And after they entered government in 1998, they provided financial assistance for people in need, funded out of a portion of their own salaries.

The party introduced the emergency hotline in the mid-1990s well before it entered local government, after meetings with the Lille division of the French Communist Party (PCF), which was active on housing issues and ran a "*telephone d'urgence.*" While KPÖ Graz followed elements of this model, it did not pursue a tactic deemed too radical for the political culture of Austria—the "living walls" that the Lille PCF formed in order to prevent evictions. Initially, the Graz party focused less on evictions, because its members regarded the issue as less salient than other housing problems, such as the bad conditions of many public apartments. As the party advertised the hotline in the local media, word spread, and calls slowly but steadily increased. The party's free advice on a variety of housing issues brought important aid to many individuals.

Initial gains encouraged the party to expand into a related arena, courts. Soon after establishing the emergency hotline, the party started to provide financial assistance for legal representation. Party leaders set up this fund after they realized that many tenants did not challenge their evictions in court, afraid of the financial costs if they lost. Ignoring the law, some landlords tried to evict tenants despite their rental contracts. According to Kaltenegger, "we cooperated with lawyers and said we will cover the financial risk, simply to encourage people to defend themselves. This has worked very well—we hardly ever paid because we almost always won." This form of activism carried the risk of financial costs for the party, but it brought crucial gains to individual tenants.

Beyond these immediate gains, the Communists also attempted to attract media attention to controversial cases in order to raise public awareness of their work. Media attention and acknowledgment are key to owning a public issue; you want journalists to come to you when they need comments on that issue.

KPÖ Graz has also directly supported people with financial problems, using part of the salaries its officeholders receive. Communist members of the government of Graz, and later in other local governments and the regional legislature, decided to cap their personal income at the level of a skilled worker. In doing so, these politicians accepted financial costs, relinquishing key benefits that go along with public office. With the extra money, the party has paid for heating, electricity, rent arrears, the refurbishment of apartments, and even funerals. Every year, the party reports these expenses on an "Open Accounts Day," attracting further media attention. Today, the party annually spends about 100,000 euros for direct housing support, which includes the hotline and the fund for legal challenges. From 1998 to 2020, the party supported 20,039 families or individuals with a total amount of about two and a half million euros (KPÖ Steiermark 2020).

Through these activities, the party built a reputation of being accessible to every inhabitant of Graz. Its deft handling of housing problems encouraged citizens to contact it on other issues too. In 2016 alone, several thousand residents of Graz visited the office of then City Councilor Kahr, reporting their problems and expecting solutions. Its constant availability strongly differentiated the KPÖ from other parties.

Adopting housing issues as a main focus of the party's work required considerable personal efforts by the leading figures within the party. Politicians and their staff had to study legal and administrative details in order to give appropriate advice about provisions in rental agreements, their termination, the payment of utilities, and evictions. In current party leader Kahr's words, "nothing is worse than helpless helpers." The engagements in new arenas related to housing not only required an intellectual effort but also an emotional one. For example, Kaltenegger recounted a late-night call from a person whose eviction was scheduled for the next morning.

The party's politics of direct help shows how political players associated mainly with the legislative and administrative arenas can make gains not only by passing legislation but through more traditional social movement means. Social movement organizations and political parties often provide direct support to beneficiaries and supporters backstage, outside strategic arenas. Also among social movement players using more radical tactics, direct aid is a common practice. Combes (2015: 60) reports that after the repression of the 1968 protests in Mexico, guerrillas "went into hiding [and] worked with disadvantaged populations, offering literacy courses, free medical attention, assistance in land occupation, and help in formulating demands for basic services." Later, the Zapatistas followed similar tactics (Harvey 2001). The relative importance of "nonstate welfare" is particularly high in non-OECD (Organisation for Economic Co-operation and Development) countries, where governments are often not the main providers of welfare services (Cammett and MacLean 2014).

The Communists in Graz adopted tactics similar to these social movements instead of solely or primarily trying to change government policies, as a traditional political party might. They went to work on the less formal fringes of administrative arenas, which led to substantive gains. KPÖ Graz has helped people in need by moving beyond the city council and the city government. In doing so, its politicians came to own the issue of housing in Graz. Yet while engaging in new arenas, the party still leveraged its official positions within the local and regional legislative arenas.

## The Electoral Payoff: Entering Local Government

The decision to focus on housing reversed the declining electoral fortunes of the Communists; its politics of direct help delivered gains in the formal arenas of the political system. In 1993, the first Graz election after the end of the Soviet Union and the broad delegitimization of "real-existing socialism," the party won 4.2 percent; for the first time since the 1950s, the Communists sent a second deputy to the city council. By 1998, the party rose to almost 8 percent of the vote. That year's electoral showing allowed the Communists, by law, to appoint a member of local government even though they were not part of the majority coalition in the city council. The majority parties gave KPÖ control of the housing department, most likely the result of a strategic blunder, with the failed expectation of exposing the radical left as ineffectual and unable to deliver results since it had no control over budget allocations to the department. For KPÖ Graz, the stakes increased: they owned the issue officially as well as unofficially, with more decision-making power but potentially more liability if things went badly.

Party leaders were aware of many of the tradeoffs involved in maneuvering among arenas, facing them squarely as dilemmas. When the party earned the right to appoint a member to the local government, Kaltenegger was skeptical because he understood the Communists as an oppositional force potentially losing their "outside" power by being in the administration. He feared that local government would prove a false arena where the party would have difficulties delivering. But the party managed to use its new formal ownership of housing to reinforce its informal ownership, ultimately reinforcing its electoral success.

The majority soon learned that giving housing to the KPÖ was a strategic mistake. Controlling the department related to "their" issue without being obliged to vote with the majority proved a boon to the Communists. It made the party's activism in the area of housing even more visible. The party has since attracted about 20 percent of the votes three times—in 2003, 2012, and 2017. And in 2021, KPÖ Graz even became the largest party in the city council, with almost 30 percent of the vote.

The electoral gains of KPÖ Graz have also spread to the regional level, allowing the party to enter another parliamentary arena. In 2005, with the popularity of Kaltenegger and the expectation of major vote shifts at the regional level, the party decided to spend scarce resources on the regional election campaign. With Kaltenegger as the leading candidate, KPÖ Styria received the required threshold of votes to enter the state legislature. But as a result, Kaltenegger resigned from his position in the local government in Graz, and his ability to maneuver as the leader of a small oppositional party in the regional legislature was comparatively modest. Kaltenegger's decision to personally focus on regional instead of local politics was also risky because the party could not take for granted that his successor would maintain strength in Graz—a dilemma of engagement. And indeed, in the short run, KPÖ Graz did not do particularly well: in the next local election, the Graz branch dropped from 20.8 (in 2003) to 11.1 percent (in 2008). Engagement in the new arena of regional politics meant losses in city politics. At the time, the result was partly attributed to the less familiar face at the top of the party's list, Elke Kahr. But the setback was short-lived. Already in 2012, KPÖ Graz under Kahr again matched its 2003 results.

Still, throughout history, many left-wing parties and their voters have found that electoral gains do not translate automatically into policies or substantive gains—even when they are in charge of a government department dealing with the issues they own. KPÖ Graz had to search for creative ways to pursue its desired housing goals. To do so, they moved beyond the electoral arena of the city council and city government. Direct aid to citizens in some cases and the mobilization of citizens in others brought substantive gains that boosted KPÖ's electoral success.

## Beyond the Legislative and Government Arenas

Owning the housing issue without controlling the city council required KPÖ to pressure the latter from outside the formal arenas of the political system. The Communists in Graz have been represented in the city council and later even in the government, but until 2021 they were always in a minority position, refusing to join formal coalitions with other parties to be part of an official legislative majority. To promote their proposals from the outside on housing and other issues, the Communists mounted public pressure in three different ways. First, they raised public awareness about their concerns, even in the absence of election campaigns, especially using their own newspaper, thereby entering the media arena. Second, in several instances the party used referenda at the local level, entering the arena of direct democracy. Third, the party entered the protest arena with street demonstrations, especially targeting austerity politics at the regional level. It learned to make gains by leveraging its institutional power and social movement tactics in a virtuous circle. Engagement in arenas beyond the formal political system continued to be a key part of the party's strategy.

The Communists' efforts to raise awareness about local issues stems in part from their dissatisfaction with the mainstream media, but also from the party's long tradition of producing books, newspapers, and leaflets. Kaltenegger maintains, "as a minority in the legislature you are powerless if you do not manage to inform the population about your demands and also about how other parties act." A crucial aspect of the communication strategy has been the publication of the *Stadtblatt* ("City Paper") newspaper, mailed to every household several times a year. Werner Murgg, one of the two current communist deputies in the regional legislature of Styria, believes that the publication of the newspaper is an important element behind the party's electoral success.

Apart from *Stadtblatt*, the party also tried to reach the public in ways more familiar to social movements than political parties, for example, by distributing leaflets after sessions of the local legislature, by hosting cultural events and debates on political matters beyond city politics, and by organizing information stalls and "discussion evenings" in housing complexes or neighborhoods affected by political decisions. The party not only strengthened its ties to its sympathizers, it also signaled to other parties that it is capable of disseminating its demands and criticism to a wide audience. Communications targeting public opinion have been crucial for the party's street mobilization efforts.

Close communication with potential sympathizers has allowed the party to use direct democracy effectively at the local level. In Graz, 10,000 signatures can force the discussion of an issue in the local council or even a nonbinding referendum, the *Volksbefragung*. KPÖ Graz has exploited this legal feature several times. In the mid-1990s, the party collected more than 17,000 signatures in favor of limiting the share of income a tenant must pay for a public apartment. According to Kaltenegger, conversations with people living in financially precarious circumstances raised the party's awareness about this issue. He added that the other parties were surprised that the then-small Communist Party could reach so many people. The party only opted to demand a discussion of the issue in the local council as it was unsure about its chances of winning a referendum, much like the engagement dilemma we saw in Seattle. Still, the public pressure generated through the mobilization led to a 1997 Graz regulation that compensated public housing tenants if their rent was more than a third of their household income.

In the wake of this victory, the Communists increased their vote totals enough to control the housing department, but they continued to face the constraints of being in a minority position in the city council, where budgets are crafted. It was not the Communists but the governing coalition of Social Democrats and Conservatives who controlled the allocation of resources for each department. When the Communists wanted to begin refurbishing public apartments, which in many cases still lacked showers, the department's budget was too small to do so. When Graz was chosen to be the 2003 European Capital of Culture, the Communists saw an opportunity. They advanced the slogan *Auch das ist Kultur. Ein Bad für jede Gemeindewohnung* ("This is culture as well: a bathroom for every public housing apartment"), while privately threatening the governing coalition with a nonbinding referendum on the issue. Ultimately, the Communists received an increased budget to start this work. The Communists' competitors now knew that KPÖ Graz could mobilize enough support to pass the required threshold of signatures to initiate a *Volksbefragung*. As in Seattle, the mere threat of a referendum was sufficient to coerce the majority parties to act. Opening a referendum arena would have posed risks for both sides. The governing coalition decided to concede in the budget-making arena rather than entering a less predictable battle, accepting a small loss instead of risking a larger one in the form of an obvious, public defeat.

In 2004, the Communists used a nonbinding referendum to mobilize against the privatization of public housing. The party won more than 90 percent of the votes—although less than 10 percent of the electorate participated as the other parties recommended that their supporters abstain. These parties faced the being-there dilemma: nonvoting might lead to a landslide for the opposing camp, but they hoped the low turnout would delegitimize the referendum result. In contrast, Communist leaders believed that the referendum, even if nonbinding, would prevent the privatization of public apartments by the governing majority by raising the salience of the issue.

In addition to direct democracy, KPÖ Graz has also organized and participated in street protests. The most prominent was against the austerity policies of the Styrian regional government, led by the Social Democrats and the Conservatives. As part of *Plattform 25*, the Communists protested together with the Greens, trade unions, and many social movement organizations against a proposed 25 percent budget cut. In March and April 2011, more than 10,000 people marched in the streets of Graz, in two of the biggest protest events the region of Styria has recently seen. Ultimately, the Styrian government refrained from some, although not all, of the cuts. In the longer run, the *Plattform 25* mobilization was an important step to ending a controversial law that required close relatives to contribute to the nursing home care of those in financial need. In 2013, the Communists in Styria collected 18,000 signatures against that law, the majority of them in Graz. The law was abolished in 2014. Moreover, party members were also engaged in other street protests, for example, counterprotest against far-right mobilization by the Patriotic Europeans against the Islamization of the Occident (PEGIDA) in the city (Berntzen and Weisskircher 2016), linking again to other civil society groups.

KPÖ Graz moved beyond the arenas of legislature and government with the aim of putting pressure on their elected competitors and effecting political changes. Like direct aid, the tactics of intensive communication work, direct democracy, and protest are often associated with social movements rather than political parties, especially in times of the hegemony of "cartel parties" that do not rely heavily on an organized support base (Katz and Mair 1995). KPÖ Graz has managed to raise awareness for its demands and to mobilize in order to make administrative and legislative gains as well as electoral gains.

## Conclusion

Strategic interaction in many arenas and related "boomerang effects" are crucial to understanding the rise of KPÖ Graz. The gains that the Communists made outside the city council and local government ultimately benefited them in these arenas too, as the party's electoral growth shows. In some instances, the Communists could promote their agenda and convince voters that they were able to deliver results. By owning the housing issue for three decades, the Communists created a reputation of "credibility" and "reliability," which in turn helped them attract voters. Engagement in many arenas helped the party, which was mainly able to avoid the basket dilemma, also due to intensive personal efforts. Due to the party's engagement in new arenas, participation in local government did not turn out a false arena.

Here, the party also benefited from not "being there" in a governing coalition, which allowed it to avoid a series of tough budget and legislative choices upon which many contemporary governing leftist parties have foundered, especially in an era of austerity and widespread anti-immigrant sentiments (Dunphy and Bale 2011). The Communists of Graz did not need to officially moderate their ideology, focusing instead on practical activities surrounding housing.

For some time it seemed that some of its strategic risks eventually caught up with KPÖ Graz. While it again did well in the 2017 election (over 20 percent), the right-wing coalition that came to power removed its control of the city housing department and assigned it two new departments, health and transportation, in which it had little previous expertise. A new member of the governing coalition, the radical right Freedom Party, successfully insisted on controlling the housing department. No doubt the decision was intended to end the positive feedback between arenas that KPÖ Graz had long enjoyed. Given its decision to remain outside the governing coalition—previously a gain—there was little the party could do to prevent this loss, although it has continued its unofficial ownership over housing through its direct-help programs.

Still, the party's reputation and its ongoing activism in different arenas prevented not only electoral losses, but allowed the Communists to become the most popular party in the Graz election of 2021, after a disastrous result for the center-right People's Party. Holding the mayor's office, the Communists will certainly confront new risks, now facing higher expectations and increasing scrutiny by political competitors and the media. Still, their latest electoral peak allowed the party to already make one important gain: The Communists took again control of the housing department.

The story of KPÖ Graz is a story of many unexpected gains that emphasizes the agency of political players. To be sure, however, the gains KPÖ Graz made are small compared to the party's long-term goal of societal transformation. The manifesto of the party's regional organization, KPÖ Styria (KPÖ Steiermark, 2012), remains a far-reaching programmatic statement critical of capitalism. As with the leftist New York City transit workers in chapter 4, the party was not in a position to accomplish radical ideological goals. But in an era when the Left is in broad retreat across Europe, KPÖ Graz stands out for combining, for three decades, electoral success with substantive gains.

All compound players have internal tensions and differences, but gains, as in the case of KPÖ Graz, tend to mitigate them. In our next chapter we turn to a highly divided compound player, Occupy Hong Kong with Love and Peace, more familiar as part of the Umbrella Movement. Unlike New

Directions, though, its internal differences were played out on the most public of stages: in front of, and ultimately engaging, hundreds of thousands of protestors, Hong Kong's political parties, and the local and national state apparatus. The state appears, for the first time in this book, as a true adversary—but containing its own internal divisions. A moderate organization, devoted to due process in civil society, found itself pushed into a strategy of radicalism with a characteristic package of gains and losses.

# 6

# The Radical Package

## The Umbrellas of Hong Kong

When Britain returned Hong Kong to the People's Republic of China in 1997, the so-called Special Administrative Region was promised universal suffrage. Both before and after this transfer, a pan-democratic coalition has fought to turn this promise into reality. In their long effort, they rarely used disruptive tactics; only small, radical factions advocated such methods. But this changed substantially when Occupy Hong Kong with Love and Peace (OHKLP) became one of the first moderate organizations to champion large-scale civil disobedience, culminating in the Umbrella Movement's seventy-nine-day occupation in 2014.[1] Benny Tai Yiu-ting, Dr. Kin-man Chan, and the Reverend Yiu-ming Chu—known as the Occupy Trio—started OHKLP in 2013 to achieve genuine universal suffrage in the electoral reform in-tended to take place before the 2017 election of the territory's leader, the Chief Executive (CE). For over a year, the group tried but failed to reach their goal of 10,000 commitments to conduct a nonviolent occupation of Central, the main commercial district on Hong Kong Island. In the end, the Umbrella Movement that emerged took OHKLP's leaders by surprise.

The Hong Kong Federation of Students (HKFS)—composed of the leaders of the student unions of Hong Kong's eight universities, a secondary school activist group, Scholarism, and members of radical political parties—initi-ated the Umbrella Movement by breaking into Civic Square in Admiralty, part of Hong Kong's central government complex, on September 26, 2014. An estimated one million citizens participated in the movement in some way

[1] For this chapter, Jessica Mahlbacher interviewed forty-two scholars, students, politicians, and activists in the summer of 2016 and the spring and fall of 2018. She also used the archives of the *South China Morning Post* and Radio Television Hong Kong, which have extensive interviews and com-mentary by both pan-democrat and pro-Beijing forces. She consulted government documents avail-able on the Hong Kong government website, as well as the Chinese government website. Mahlbacher also conducted participant observations of pro-democracy rallies and marches in 2016 and 2018, as well as the trial of the "Occupy 9" in November and December 2018.

*Gains and Losses.* James M. Jasper, Luke Elliott-Negri, Isaac Jabola-Carolus, Marc Kagan, Jessica Mahlbacher, Manès Weisskircher, and Anna Zhelnina, Oxford University Press. © Oxford University Press 2022.
DOI: 10.1093/oso/9780197623251.003.0007

over the next three months, nearly one eighth of the city's population. At its height, the movement maintained three large encampments in the city.

Worldwide, encampments caught the world's attention in 2011 with Occupy Wall Street, followed by similar movements in Gezi Park and Tahrir Square. Yet while the seventy-nine-day Umbrella Movement is internationally renowned, it would not have taken place but for strategic interaction both among activists and in their confrontation with Hong Kong and national Chinese authorities in the two-year period prior to the storming of Civic Square. We examine the period leading up to the occupation to explore the strategic package players use when they choose more aggressive tactics. Within this package, stakes are accelerated during strategic interaction, sweeping along more moderate forces, often leading them to get caught up in radical activities. Table 6.1 summarizes the radicalism package.

The focus on the Occupy Trio's efforts also highlights how two key dilemmas discussed in chapter 1, the naughty-or-nice and extension dilemmas, play into the radicalism package. These dilemmas affected the strategies of both activists and government officials, leading them to make choices that bolstered support for radical players within the pan-democratic coalition. The Occupy Trio hoped that more radical tactics would help them

**Table 6.1**  The Radical Package

| Dilemmas | Player's Goals | Likely Costs | Risks |
|---|---|---|---|
| Extension | Create a broad-based coalition to ensure mass involvement in the player's activities | Limited cohesion and lack of efficiency | Spoiler activity or loss of leadership |
| Naughty or nice | Apply public pressure on opposition players | Alienation of potential recruits and repression by government | Reputation is damaged among movement outsiders, lack of resources, and backlash from opponent |
| Janus | Gain control over the campaign and cooperation of movement insiders through radical strategy | Limited recruitment | Player fails to achieve desired movement numbers |
| **Solutions** | present radical tactics as last resort; stoke outrage and develop moral reputation through self-sacrifice; demonize opponents; mediate subplayer conflicts to retain support of moderates. | | |

expand their movement, but this radical approach attracted some kinds of recruits more easily than others. To make the occupation possible, OHKLP players needed a broad coalition, but the coalition's subplayers often had divergent interests and goals that were difficult to reconcile.

The Hong Kong and the central Chinese governments also faced their own naughty-or-nice and extension dilemmas. A similarly large coalition of government actors within both the local and national institutions were tasked with countering OHKLP's activities. Often, however, when one set of government actors chose to act with temperance, the other chose more aggressive reactions to movement activities. Their conflicting strategic choices made it difficult for them to suppress the Occupy movement and often sparked more allegiance to radical activists and their objectives.

## Pro-Democracy Struggle, 1997–2012

The Chinese government refers to its relationship with Hong Kong as "one country, two systems": Hong Kong is part of the country, but it operates with a more pluralistic set of political and economic institutions. This policy was enshrined in the Basic Law, Hong Kong's mini-constitution of 1997. Although the National People's Congress Standing Committee (the NPCSC) in Beijing had the final say in the interpretation of the Basic Law, Hong Kong had considerably more autonomy in managing its own affairs in the 2000s and 2010s. The Basic Law protects freedom of speech and expression, and the rule of law. It also promised that Hong Kong would eventually achieve universal suffrage for the powerful CE and all members of the legislative council (LegCo).[2] But a complicated system containing both geographic and functional bodies excludes the majority from participation; in 2016 only 246,440 people were able to pick the 1,200 members of the election committee for the CE in 2016, out of 3,779,085 eligible voters (Government of Hong Kong Special Administrative Region 2017).

In 2007, the NPCSC created a five-step process to achieve universal suffrage, beginning with the CE submitting a report to the NPCSC

---

[2] Universal suffrage could not be achieved until at least ten years after the handover, but there was no mandatory date for these changes in electoral procedure. The NPCSC made the decision to delay universal suffrage following the Anti-National Security Protests of 2003.

recommending changes in election procedures, based at least in part on public consultation. If the NPCSC agreed to changes and the LegCo passed the legislation by a two-thirds majority, the CE would approve the legislation and send it to the NPCSC for final approval. Members of the pan-democratic coalition were hopeful in late 2012 when the government announced plans to start public consultations. Between their veto powers in LegCo and Beijing's perceived desire to have a popular mandate for the local Hong Kong government, many expected success.

## The Call for Occupation and Coalition-Building (January 2013–Spring 2014)

In January 2013, Benny Tai Yiu-ting, a law professor at Hong Kong University, wrote an article, "The Most Lethal Weapon of Civil Disobedience," in the *Hong Kong Economic Journal*. He advocated nonviolent occupation of the city's financial sector, the Central district of Hong Kong Island, to signal the pan-democratic camp's resolve regarding election reform.

These tactics were aggressive by Hong Kong standards. Historically, most players employed routinized tactics such as marches, vigils, and rallies in the streets, as well as speeches in the legislature. Only a small circle of activists had used more disruptive tactics. Starting in the late 2000s, however, more and more activists concerned with environmental and livelihood issues turned to disruptive tactics. In 2011, there was a small occupation in front of the HSBC Bank headquarters in Central, in solidarity with Occupy Wall Street. In 2012, the secondary school activist group, Scholarism, organized an occupation in Civic Square, in front of the government's headquarters, to stop the implementation of the government's proposed "Moral and National Education" curriculum. More than 100,000 people showed up on the final night of that occupation. As a result, CE CY Leung withdrew the legislation. Despite this rise in disruptive tactics, it was eye-catching for a moderate professional like Benny Tai to advocate breaking the law in the name of further democratization.

Tai himself had little organizing experience and therefore did not want to take a leading position. For most of the 2000s, he described himself as acting as a "lone wolf" in the democracy movement, providing analysis of Hong Kong's situation in his role as a professor. He knew that the leaders of the movement had to hold together a broad coalition of players with a history of mutual mistrust, including political parties, civil society organizations, and student groups engaged in activism.

Pan-democratic parties found it difficult to hold the coalition together because they often competed for the same seats in the legislature. There, they were rarely able to orchestrate policy, leading to disenchantment among civil society groups (Wong 2015).[3] And historically there was little contact between political parties and student organizations like HKFS.

Tai proposed two activists who had relationships with both moderate political parties and civil society organizations to lead an alliance based on his suggested tactics. Reverend Yiu-ming Chu was a veteran of the pro-democracy movement, respected for his work helping Tiananmen demonstrators escape to Hong Kong and enjoying ties to activist networks and religious organizations. Kin-man Chan had worked closely with Reverend Chu and collaborated with civil society groups. As a professor of sociology at the Chinese University of Hong Kong, he had relationships with the student union there and had organized many political activities among academics.[4] Chu and Chan agreed to lead the civil disobedience efforts, as long as civil disobedience was only used as a last resort. They insisted, however, that Tai join them.

In March 2013, Kin-man Chan wrote an article, "May Love and Peace Occupy Central." He emphasized that since civil disobedience pressured the government by arousing public sympathy, disruption must be proportional and activists must remain peaceful and willing to face arrest and imprisonment (Kong Tsung-Gan 2019).

The Occupy Trio hoped to navigate the naughty-or-nice dilemma by escalating beyond past actions but tempering the inherent aggression of an occupation by insisting on peaceful tactics and their willingness to risk incarceration, in other words, by carefully managing public perceptions. They announced the formation of a new organization, OHKLP, meant to be a coalition of pan-democratic organizations, in late March. The emphasis on incarceration suggests that this strategy could work by inspiring a government crackdown, which would in turn arouse further sympathy for the protestors.

With the formation of Occupy Hong Kong, Tai achieved both personal and group gains. He gained widespread media attention. His willingness

---

[3] In interviews, politicians in the pan-democratic camp themselves used the terms "moderate" and "radical" to categorize themselves and other players.

[4] Chan had also cooperated with the Democracy Party in the 2010 secret negotiations with the Beijing government over political reform. Some radical political party members distrusted him because of his involvement in the affair.

**Figure 6.1** The first photo is of the Occupy Trio, Benny Tai Yiu-ting, Kin-man Chan, and Reverend Chu Yiu-ming, during their initial press conference to launch Occupy Hong Kong with Love and Peace in March of 2013. Photo credit Voice of America.

to commit civil disobedience and go to jail to achieve democratic suffrage enhanced his moral standing. The provocative strategy and Chan and Chu's connections persuaded a wide range of democratic players to commit to OHKLP's agenda and coordinate their strategies.

At the same time, Tai's approach had limits: in addition to the naughty-or-nice dilemma, the Occupy Trio also faced a Janus dilemma between appealing to outsiders or to those already in the movement. OHKLP had difficulties recruiting outside existing pan-democratic circles. Few other citizens were willing to risk jail time. Tai's strategy helped OHKLP gain a leadership position inside the movement for political reform but limited its recruitment potential among outsiders fearing government repression.

The Occupy Trio sought to create arenas specific to the public consultation process, including the education and recruitment of the public and negotiation between factions of the pan-democratic camp. Their first step was a series of "Deliberation Days."[5] The first two deliberation sessions explored

[5] Their idea for the arena was based on Bruce Ackerman and James S. Fishkin, *Deliberation Day* (Chan 2015).

democracy, civil disobedience, and possible procedures for nominating the CE. The trio then collected proposals from different civil society groups and invited legal and academic experts to evaluate them. They asked the experts to focus on two criteria in particular: would the nomination process produce a genuine choice between candidates, and would the subsequent election be competitive?

At a third Deliberation Day, participants would discuss and vote on these proposals. The three with the most votes would appear in a citywide referendum, with the winning proposal presented to the Hong Kong government. The trio vowed to launch the Occupy Central campaign only if neither the local government nor the Beijing government offered concessions based on the proposal.

All the more moderate democratic parties and two radical parties took part in OHKLP's Deliberation Days. Prominent nongovernmental organizations (NGOs), religious leaders, think tanks, the social workers' and teachers' unions, and student organizations, particularly HKFS, also participated. Tai persuaded business leaders to participate and to provide financial backing.

The open nature of the arena was important to OHKLP's success in recruiting other movement players. Many chose to participate because the results were not predetermined, allowing them a chance to win. Tai, Chu, and Chan hoped to form a consensus among a wide range of pan-democratic players rather than push their own conceptions of what the reform package should be. They were therefore facilitator-judges in the Deliberation Day arena, as well as strategic players. Tai's "purity," or lack of political affiliation, made him trustworthy as facilitator and judge.

OHKLP attained several objectives through the Deliberation Day arenas. They received the most donations of any group during Hong Kong's annual July 1 pro-democracy march (But and Tsang 2013). The trio also generated hundreds of thousands of dollars through exclusive fundraising dinners where guests met scholars, political figures, and celebrities affiliated with multiple parties. Yet the gains in uniting most of the pan-democratic subplayers in a single arena proved ephemeral and led to corresponding losses based on the extension dilemma in the longer term: so many different groups participated in the arena that it was impossible to reconcile their divergent goals and interests.

## Extension and Janus Dilemmas in Choosing a Reform Proposal (Fall 2013–May 2014)

One of the biggest debates inside the pan-democratic camp was whether to support public nomination of the CE or to focus on improving the representativeness of the nominating committee. According to Article 45 of the Basic Law, a "broadly representative nominating committee" should be the basis for selecting the CE. The wording is general enough that the committee could play a minimum role, vetting candidates nominated by the public, or a decisive role, providing all nominations itself.

While the Occupy Trio sought to preserve the democratic nature of the Deliberation Day arena to entice participation, they also faced another version of the Janus dilemma. They needed to think about how the outcomes of the Deliberation Days affected the legislative and street protests.

Radical parties promoted full public nomination and the elimination of the nominating committee. HKFS and Scholarism, the two student groups, also supported public nomination. Student groups and radical parties were valuable allies because they had more time and ability to participate in street arenas.

Moderate parties rejected public nomination as impossible; the wording of the Basic Law would make it easy for Beijing to dismiss any proposal that did not include a nominating committee (Davis 2016). They preferred to allow parties to nominate potential CE candidates while retaining the existing requirement that a candidate only needed the support of one eighth of the nominating committee to reach the final public ballot. If they could ensure that threshold for candidacy, it would be possible for a pan-democrat to be nominated and win under universal suffrage.

Moreover, moderates were crucial for passing electoral reform through LegCo and thwarting false reforms. The legislative arena was dominated by pro-Beijing forces and therefore would not accept any electoral reform that violated the central government's demands. The two-thirds requirement for passage gave pro-democracy forces the ability to block a bad bill, but only if most moderates cooperated with them.

OHKLP recognzied the naughty-or-nice and extension dilemmas. They worried that if they alienated radicals, these players might launch their own street actions that would thwart OHKLP's strategy of deploying civil disobedience only as a last resort. Yet they realized that more radical measures would alienate the public and depress turnout for Occupy Central.

Despite trying to maintain the open appearance of the Deliberation Day arena, the Occupy Trio elevated moderate players over radical players in their organizational structure. Like Mayor Murray in chapter 2, they created a new arena, a consultative committee, and only invited certain players. The trio sought the input of the consultative committee in tactical matters regarding the Deliberation Days, public promotion of the referendum, and organizing the eventual civil disobedience campaign. Tai, Chan, and Chu dominated this committee, making most of the major decisions rather than merely acting as judges and facilitators.

The trio excluded two of the more radical pan-democratic parties from the consultative committee. While they included members of HKFS, they did not invite Scholarism or its leader Joshua Wong Chi-fung, to participate. While Tai met with Wong at the inception of Occupy and continued to meet with Scholarism frequently throughout the Deliberation Days, the trio argued that since they were too young to vote (under 18), they were too young to participate in civil disobedience.[6] Scholarism was only able to participate in the third Deliberation Day through their collaboration with HKFS on the "Students' Proposal."

While OHKLP had limited student and radical parties' involvement in some arenas, these players scored a major victory on the third Deliberation Day, May 2014. Participants chose three proposals that all included public nomination.

Moderate players who had all submitted proposals publicly denounced the outcome as undemocratic. A representative of the moderate think tank Hong Kong 2020 lashed out against the trio: "A relatively small and unrepresentative group have effectively disenfranchised a large section of the community who do not want to be led down a path towards direct confrontation with the central government" (Cheung and Chong 2014). They noted that fewer people had voted for the winning proposals than for CE CY Leung in 2012.

The trio once again faced Janus and extension dilemmas regarding the need to appeal to a broader public and manage the divergent interests of their subplayers. If OHKLP did not honor the radicals' Deliberation Days victory, they might be accused of having set up a false arena, and the referendum in June would be weakened. At the same time, they were anxious

---

[6] Joshua Wong recalled in an interview that Benny Tai had taken him to lunch early on and tried to convince him not to pursue public nomination. Tai told him that he was "too idealistic—there was no sense in demanding public nomination of the Chief Executive, the people of Hong Kong wouldn't accept it" (J. Wong 2015: 47).

to appease moderates, considering their importance to the legislative arena, and wanted to ensure that the Occupy Central campaign did not appear too extreme to the Hong Kong public. There was no easy solution, no way to balance outcomes in different arenas.

In the end, OHKLP decided that individuals would pick among the three public nomination options but also answer a second question: Should the LegCo vote down the government's proposal if it did not meet international standards for choice and competition? The implication was that pan-democratic legislators could vote for the government's proposal even if it did not contain public nomination, as long as it met international standards. Even though the three options with public nomination were still on the ballot, radical players were incensed that OHKLP had changed the rules with this extra question.

In a coordinating committee meeting, Kin-man Chan tried to mend the schism, warning that if the moderates remained hostile, the turnout for the referendum would be low. The Hong Kong government would view the public as ambivalent, and they would not be in a strong position to deal with Beijing. When he further threatened that the Occupy Trio might withdraw from leading the movement, many of the key stakeholders abstained from admonishing the leaders. But radical players, particularly students, began to lose faith in the trio and became more willing to commit civil disobedience without the sanction of OHKLP.

## The Government's Naughty-or-Nice Dilemma (Summer 2014)

While the pan-democratic camp debated within their own arenas, compound government players had their own differences and dilemmas. The central government apparatus and its affiliates, the Hong Kong Macau Affairs Office of the State Council and the Liaison Office of the Central People's Government in Hong Kong, all had a clear interest in ensuring China's sovereignty and control over Hong Kong. CY Leung was only in his first term as CE and planned on running for a second. Chief Secretary for Administration Carrie Lam Cheng Yuet-ngor was the principal official in the Hong Kong government under CY Leung, and a member of its executive council. She headed the political reform task force that ran the public consultations in 2013 and 2014. Pro-Beijing political parties, the Federation of Trade Unions, and functional constituency representatives benefited from their dominance over the election committee. Finally, several pro-Beijing grassroots organizations emerged in late 2013, hoping to outperform OHKLP and the pan-democratic movement in street arenas.

Government players face many of the same strategic dilemmas that their social movement counterparts confront in interacting with allies and opponents. Just as Occupy faced a naughty-or-nice dilemma in maintaining internal cohesion and rallying public support, so did the government: if it cracked down on peaceful protesters, it risked public outcry and international condemnation, but if it negotiated with protesters to prevent street action, it might encourage future disruptions.

State players often have different, even conflicting, cognitive frames and strategies (Duyvendak and Jasper 2015; Roxborough 2015). Like social movement players, government players can experience extension dilemmas about which state organizations and societal allies to enlist in fighting off challenges. Engaging more state (and nonstate) players as allies may create "efficiencies of scale" but result in a loss of control and coordination, since state agencies—like social movement players—have different tastes in tactics for dealing with the opposition. The local and the central government each sought to respond to OHKLP, but they differed over the naughty-or-nice dilemma, one often using milder tactics where the other preferred more aggressive strategies.

Beijing responded with aggressive tactics. First, they asserted the central government's sovereignty over the region in government statements. On June 10, less than two weeks before Occupy's referendum, the Information Office of the State Council of the People's Republic of China issued its first white paper since the 1997 handover. The paper claimed that Hong Kong autonomy depended on the will of the Chinese government, since "[t]he Constitution of the PRC and the Basic Law together constitute the constitutional basis of the HKSAR" (The State Council, People's Republic of China 2014).

Beijing's aggressive statements interfered with the local government's strategy of coopting moderate pan-democratic forces and delegitimizing OHKLP's referendum. In LegCo, the local government needed to woo a small number of moderate and independent legislators to pass its electoral reform proposal. Lam publicly admitted that it had become harder for the Hong Kong government to convince moderate pan-democratic legislators to sign onto proposals approved by Beijing (Lam 2014). Moderate political parties began to promote the referendum in media outlets. Some moderate politicians, who had originally denounced the results of Deliberation Day, now advocated that people should vote to show that they valued Hong Kong's autonomy.

Hacking was Beijing's second aggressive strategy. Three days after the white paper appeared, murky players within the mainland government attacked the preregistration website that the Public Opinion Programme, University of Hong Kong (HKPOP) had set up for the referendum, launching over ten billion distributed-denial-of-service (DDOS) attacks. The Internet Society of Hong Kong traced at least 40 percent of the strikes to IP (internet protocol) addresses of Mainland firms (Lam and Zhai 2014).

The assault on the referendum once again interfered with strategies of other pro-Beijing Hong Kong government players, further eroding public trust. The dismissal of the referendum by pro-Beijing parties as a glorified public opinion poll with no legitimate legal standing rang hollow, since Beijing had dedicated so many resources to thwarting it. Even for citizens aligned with the pro-Beijing parties, the cyberattacks appeared intrusive and heavy-handed. The Hong Kong and Macau Affairs Office had argued that participating in the referendum was akin to conspiring to commit a crime, in this case, civil disobedience. Yet the lack of a serious investigation into the hacking made this accusation seem hypocritical and arbitrary.

Government aggression can produce feelings of outrage and shock in public audiences, helping movement players in their recruitment. The cyberattack immediately helped OHKLP, which received more international attention and resources. The large international companies Cloudfare and Google helped HKPOP to overcome the DDOS attacks. The Occupy Trio argued that voting in the referendum was not necessarily a commitment to participate in civil disobedience, but it sent Beijing a message in support of Hong Kong autonomy.

In the end, nearly one third of the voting population participated in the referendum, a triumph for the pan-democratic movement and OHKLP. An overwhelming 87.8 percent of participants voted that the LegCo should veto any proposal that did not meet international standards (Public Opinion Programme, University of Hong Kong 2014).

The most moderate of the proposals—which allowed candidates for the CE to be elected through three mechanisms—nomination by the public, by political parties, and through the nominating committee—scored a narrow victory. The trio prepared to present this proposal to the government.

Figure 6.2 The second photo is of volunteers conducting the referendum in June of 2014. Photo credit Edward Chin (used with his permission).

## The Civil Disobedience Campaign Faces the Janus Dilemma (July–September 2014)

After the referendum, the pan-democratic coalition faced internal disputes about how to build momentum from their recent victory. Student groups, radical parties, and some NGO players wanted to capitalize on the success of the referendum with civil disobedience. OHKLP had decided from the beginning to call for an occupation only if the government failed to provide a plan that met international standards for democracy. They would have to wait, possibly a long time, until Beijing came up with their final proposal for how the CE would be nominated.

From the start, the government and its allies had tried to frame OHKLP as dangerous. Only a month after Tai's article came out, a pro-Beijing member of LegCo suggested that people could die as a result of civil disobedience. "There are many unintended consequences, and even in a well-planned activity involving 10,000 or 30,000, people may not necessarily come under control" (Leung 2013). Shortly before the referendum, Silent Majority for Hong Kong released a video called "They can kill our city!" They claimed that within one hour of the occupation, 1.3 million people would be trapped on Hong Kong Island, violence would erupt, and emergency medical care and police would be totally unavailable (Silent Majority for Hong Kong 2014). The trio worried that occupying before they had exhausted their options in the government's reform process would reinforce these narratives with the public, aware that more members of the public accept radical tactics if they see them as a last resort.

The public consultation process proved slower than expected. Although it had announced its plans at the end of 2012, the Hong Kong government did not initiate the process until December 2013, a full nine months after the trio had publicly announced Occupy Central and founded OHKLP. The consultations did not finish until the end of July 2014. The central government's statement about what form of election was permissible was not unveiled until the end of August 2014—more than nineteenth months after the initial calls for Occupy Central.

HKFS and representatives of civil society organizations grew frustrated with the pace of the buildup to the occupation. These players reduced their coordination and communication with OHKLP in the spring of 2014, coming to reject the consultative committee as a false arena. One student leader remarked, "what Benny and the other two project publicly is totally different from what is discussed in the meetings. . . . When they say something different than what has been discussed in the committee, then it becomes, 'Well, what am I for?'" Student groups also complained that the trio was more responsive to political parties' interests than to theirs.

By July, only 3,000 people had signed an oath pledging to take part in the sit-in and to be arrested, far short of the original goal of 10,000. Yet, there was little effort to promote the pledge after the June referendum. One frustrated volunteer could not find a form despite working with OHKLP for two months.

Several student groups, such as Scholarism and HKFS, and civil society organizations such as the Civil Human Rights Front (CHRF), decided to hold a practice occupation in Central immediately following the July 1 march.[7] They planned to stay until morning and to turn themselves over to the police peacefully at 8:00 A.M. In an interview, members of HFKS and CHRF reasoned that if they demonstrated how civil disobedience worked and the impact it could have, people would want to join. Scholarism was also eager to initiate civil disobedience, since it believed the calls for action had dragged on too long, dampening support for the occupation.

The Occupy Trio objected to the practice sit-in. They thought it was not the right time, as the government had not yet responded to their proposal. But they did nothing to stop their supporters from joining the planned action.

Five hundred people participated. Since the majority of Scholarism students were in secondary school, many did not want to get arrested and destroy their chances of getting into a good university program. So most of the participants were from HKFS, along with members from NGOs and radical parties. A few moderate politicians participated; many more party members watched the sit-in to ensure student safety and arrange legal services if needed. Leaders considered it a tremendous success because it was peaceful and lasted all night.

Although the July 1 occupation was a big victory for HKFS, it produced more diverse gains and losses for OHKLP and the larger pan-democratic movement. The action garnered media attention, demonstrated that civil disobedience could be peaceful, and conveyed that mass action was feasible. At the same time, it indicated to both the public and the government that OHKLP was not in control of the pan-democratic movement's radical faction. OHKLP had reiterated that civil disobedience would only take place as a last resort, yet the sit-in happened before the government's reform package was unveiled. This might have led to radical-flank gains, where government players are more inclined to bargain or produce a more favorable plan for fear of more aggressive action (Haines 1984). In this case, however, radical-flank losses were more apparent. Pro-Beijing politicians and organizations argued that this action proved that OHKLP was contributing to radicalization and tension in society. Radical flanks pose the naughty-or-nice dilemma

---

[7] The convener of the CHRF was a former leader of HKFS.

for their movements; the usual risk—fulfilled here—is that the reputation of the entire player is damaged.

After the referendum, weeks went by with no word from the Hong Kong government. Earlier in 2013, the Hong Kong Executive Council had expressed an interest in meeting with OHKLP, but the trio declined. Kin-man Chan stated that they did not want to come to the bargaining table without a popular mandate (Chan later regretted this decision). Chief Secretary Carrie Lam met with all the other groups that had submitted proposals before finally making an appointment to meet with Tai, Chan, and Chu at the end of July 2014.

The meeting between the local government officials and the trio was strained. Lam asked the three to desist in their actions and not conduct a civil disobedience campaign. She left the proposal that Benny Tai handed her untouched following the meeting, which both Tai and Chan interpreted as her unequivocal rejection of their ideas. She refused the trio's request that she make a counteroffer that they could discuss with their constituencies.

Even after this encounter, the trio did not initiate civil disobedience. Tai still thought there was a chance Beijing would offer a reform package with some room for negotiation. OHKLP had even budgeted money raised from the July 1 march for a second referendum.

On August 31, the Deputy Secretary-General of the NPCSC, Li Fei, came to Hong Kong to announce Beijing's plan for universal suffrage in Hong Kong. The nominating committee was to be based on the current election committee. Only two or three candidates would be chosen if they received the consent of 50 percent of the nominating committee. All candidates must "love Hong Kong and love China." Essentially, the proposal meant there would be no chance of a pan-democratic candidate winning office.

Beijing's announcement caused many players to reevaluate the NPCSC's five-step process. It now appeared that the earlier public consultation had been a false arena, since most of the proposals and suggestions from the consultations did not even make it into the report. Beijing did not intend to negotiate, despite the pan-democratic forces' ability to filibuster in LegCo. One member of a think tank who had engaged in the public consultation said, "If this is what they always intended, why bother? The whole thing was a farce ... it is insulting to the Hong Kong people."

While false arenas can sometimes still build public awareness, in this case OHKLP's participation seemed to have backfired because the process had lasted so long. Moreover, OHKLP's initial reaction to Li's announcement caused confusion and may have imperiled recruitment for the occupation. Benny Tai told several news outlets that Occupy had "failed," only later clarifying that he meant it had failed to sway Beijing.

OHKLP and the pan-democratic coalition took several actions to build upon outrage over Beijing's decision. The pan-democratic coalition held a vigil on the night Li Fei announced the political reform package. The next evening, Scholarism protested in front of Li's hotel. Pan-democratic legislators protested Li's September 2 speech on political reform in LegCo wearing black with yellow ribbons; police ultimately escorted them out of the building. Two weeks after the August 31 decision, OHKLP held a silent march. Demonstrators all wore black and held signs charging that Beijing had broken its promise and warning that civil disobedience would soon begin.

There were violent encounters between pro-democracy protesters, demonstrators who supported Beijing, and the police. The police used pepper spray on members of Civic Passion, a radical political party, when they tried to force their way into a hall where Li Fei was speaking. A week later, when the Occupy Trio and forty-three other activists shaved their heads to protest the political reform package, pro-Beijing activists who interrupted the event injured an OHKLP supporter.

Tai still tried to ensure that the occupation would appear restrained and self-sacrificing to the public by minimizing its disruptive nature. Many veteran activists, such as Reverend Chu, were fearful of another Tiananmen Square and wanted to do everything possible to avoid violence. Moreover, increased physical conflict fed into the narrative that government players had repeated since the beginning of the movement: the occupation would cause chaos, rather than fight injustice.

The Occupy Trio therefore guaranteed that the eventual "banquet" (the code name for the occupation) would in no way affect Hong Kong's thriving financial sector. Tai announced that the Central occupation would begin on the Chinese holiday of National Day, October 1. Since the trio anticipated the action taking only a few days at most (however long it took for the police to carry away all the protesters), the streets would be cleared by the end of the holiday weekend.

Once again, the trio's Janus dilemma led to losses in their control of the pan-democratic movement. Some veteran activists were disappointed with this tepid version of Occupy Central. They wanted to force the government to use more aggressive tactics that would alienate the public. "I want to go to jail," one activist declared, asserting that Tai's plan would not force the government into the overreaction necessary to swell the movement. Their actions would probably result in no more than a suspended sentence.[8] Public sympathy and indignation required more suffering. These activists still supported the Occupy Trio, however, and followed their lead through September.

Members of student groups were more annoyed with OHKLP leaders. They felt the trio had telegraphed every action that would be taken during the Occupy Central campaign, allowing Beijing to anticipate and undermine their actions. One prominent student leader implied that the Occupy Trio was confusing the goal, democracy, with the tactic, nonviolent civil disobedience. OHKLP faced an articulation dilemma related to the naughty-or-nice dilemma: The more clearly they stated their goals and actions, the easier it was to communicate and negotiate, but the more constrained they were in switching objectives and tactics if problems arose (Jasper 2006: 78).

Members of radical political parties also considered OHKLP's tactics self-defeating. One radical leader explained, "We believe that for any political movement . . . it is not like a concert, where ten thousand people 'attend.' . . . You have to create conflict and confrontation and then people will respond." While some members of these radical parties were willing to take independent action that would steer the movement in a more confrontational direction, the parties were internally divided about doing so. One leader said "The Trio are like the 'Three Wiseman;' it wouldn't work without them." Yet, after leading the pan-democratic movement for nineteen months, the trio lost control to its more radical elements.

## Students Initiate the Occupation (September 22–28, 2014)

Despite widespread public outrage, it was still not clear whether OHKLP would find 10,000 recruits for its occupation. By their own count, actions from August 31 to Septembers 14 drew between one thousand and five thousand participants. HKFS and Scholarism organized student strikes, running from Monday September 22, through Friday, September 26, that were supposed to build momentum for the occupation on October 1. After protesting at their home campuses on Monday, demonstrators spent Tuesday through

---

[8] While participants in the July 1, 2014 occupation had been arrested and detained, none were formally charged, adding to the sense that a similar occupation would not result in significant legal consequences for activists.

Friday in Admiralty, next to the central government complex and Civic Square, just over a kilometer away from Central. Admiralty had been the site of the successful Anti-Patriotic Education Movement in 2012, in response to which the Hong Kong government had placed fences around the square and restricted hours of access.

The first day of the strike satisfied organizers' expectations, with four thousand to six thousand participants. By midweek, HKFS and Scholarism found their numbers dwindling. They began to worry that even if the numbers increased on Thursday and Friday, the occupation was still five days away. Participants might not come back once they left.

Leaders did not have a plan for the last night, Friday, September 26. HKFS and Scholarism leaders made a last-minute decision that night to "take back" Civic Square. Radical party members facilitated this action, hoping that the takeover would force OHKLP into a more disruptive occupation. The government was not expecting them to launch the occupation early, and therefore would be caught off guard. They felt that if the students took action, OHKLP would have to support them. The radical flank could bring the larger player along with it down the disruptive path.

While many protesters were immediately arrested, others were able to open the gates, get to the center of the square, and link arms. Most protesters demonstrated outside the Civic Square fence, blocking the roads around LegCo. Successfully taking Civic Square not only encouraged student activists to stay and participate in ongoing demonstrations but also drew new recruits.

This time it was the local government's heavy-handed tactics, rather than the central government's, that increased sympathy for HKFS and Scholarism. Riot police showed up to clear out protesters the following morning and, without warning, used pepper spray on students who tried to block access to the demonstrators in Civic Square. Pictures of students with bruises and swollen ankles flooded social media on Saturday, September 27. The image of police violently attacking young people encouraged more citizens to come out and defend the students.

Tai equivocated. At first, he told reporters that he would not start Occupy Central early. The Occupy Trio went to Admiralty that morning, however, wanting to support and protect the students. Activists there implored them to start the occupation immediately, while there was momentum and people were already holding the space around the government buildings. Tai agreed. He worried that OHKLP would be blamed for not acting when these students

**Figure 6.3** The third photo is of protesters at the initiation of the occupation, after the students had been arrested for breaking into Civic Square. Photo credit Suzanne Sataline. (Used with her permission.)

were suffering for the Occupy principles. The trio announced the beginning of Occupy Central in the early hours of September 28, following the second night of the occupation.

Events had already slipped beyond the trio's control. On the one hand, the leaders of HKFS and Scholarism resisted leaving the Admiralty area and relocating to Central until their comrades had been released from police custody. HKFS welcomed the support of the Occupy Trio but tried to warn them not to announce the initiation of Occupy. They wanted to leverage OHKLP resources to help them with their current occupation. On the other hand, Tai's announcement caused the crowd surrounding Civic Square to begin to disperse; Occupy Central meant agreeing to be arrested, which many were unwilling to do.

To be effective in their protests, the trio needed to keep the crowd intact, which meant relinquishing leadership to Scholarism and HKFS. The students' prior entry in the arena allowed them to prevail. The trio agreed to support rather than lead the movement, ending their tenure as the perceived leaders of the civil disobedience campaign.

This proved an unexpected gain for the pro-democracy movement. While the tension around leadership did produce some infighting within the larger pan-democratic compound player, the Hong Kong government once again used repressive tactics in an attempt to clear the streets on the afternoon of September 28. Students, OHKLP, and other members of the pan-democratic camp continued the occupation while awaiting the release of student activists, who had been held for more than thirty hours. Police closed a nearby park, forcing protesters to gather around the government buildings and to occupy more and more of the road. In response to the swelling crowds blocking traffic, the police used tear gas on the peaceful occupation. CY Leung apparently thought about pursuing further measures to disperse the crowd, but this time Beijing stepped in and ordered the local government not to use force. But even the tactics they did use on demonstrators caused widespread public outcry; that night, hundreds of thousands of citizens came to Admiralty, initiating the Umbrella Movement. Having failed to gain commitments for 10,000 arrests, the movement grew far beyond that over the next two months.

## The Radical Package

Occupations are aggressive tactics, a radical choice to play more naughty than nice. One benefit is media attention, which can bring influence, resources, and new recruits. The attention Benny Tai and the Occupy Trio received for pledging to commit civil disobedience helped them shape the trajectory of the pan-democratic camp's approach to electoral reform. And it kept the fractious pro-democracy circles largely united for nineteen months.

But aggressive actions such as occupations run afoul of the Janus dilemma: they appeal to committed insiders more than to most outsiders. The radical package becomes embroiled in the extension dilemma: you only need a small, committed group to occupy a space or conduct some other aggressive tactic, but you need a larger coalition to take advantage of many other arenas, especially electoral arenas. Because their strategy involved direct confrontation with the government and a commitment to incur legal penalties, the trio faced limits on recruiting new participants and maintaining the adherence of the more moderate forces within the coalition. They hoped to resolve this issue by starting with a string of "nicer" actions, by generating sympathy through their willingness to sacrifice themselves, and by framing the occupation as a last resort.

That kind of sympathy is precarious; the success of aggressive strategies depends on how other players respond to them. By publicizing their plan to occupy, OHKLP forced the state into its own naughty-or-nice dilemma: whether to make concessions or clamp down on the protest. The public's perception of aggressive tactics depends on the counterresponse. The more aggressive the government responses were, rejecting even the "nice" overtures, the more people participated in OHKLP and other pan-democratic initiatives. Correspondingly, when the government chose milder tactics, the trio felt they had to limit their own disruptive actions. But many radical members of the coalition found this deescalation distasteful. They sought to increase pressure by taking independent action.

That is, OHKLP had its own Janus problem. As we saw in Seattle, a common tactic for moderates is to distance themselves from the radical wing but use the latter to threaten opponents. In contrast, OHKLP tried hard to hold the pan-democracy movement together. OHKLP was initially able to foster consensus through creating a moderate arena, the Deliberation Days. For a while, it incorporated the radicals, until the regime's sharp rebuff.

The perils of the extension, Janus, and naughty-or-nice dilemmas did not disappear during the occupation but became issues of retaining participants. People could literally vote with their feet. Maintaining leadership structures internal to movement organizations remained difficult.

## Conclusion

While Benny Tai and OHKLP ultimately lost control of the occupation, their efforts led to the largest civil disobedience campaign in Hong Kong's history. In the end, the occupation did not change the government's reform package, but the coalition succeeded in blocking the government's proposal in LegCo following The Umbrella Movement. Pro-Beijing forces failed to win over any of the moderates as they had originally hoped.

OHKLP's gains and losses were a product not only of internal movement dynamics but of interactions with government players. The local government and central government made different decisions in response to the naughty-or-nice dilemmas they faced. Their divergent strategies made cooptation of moderate players impossible, and at times facilitated recruitment to protest. Moderates' outrage over the white paper and the DDOS attack increased their support for the referendum even though they had felt betrayed by the outcome of Deliberation Day. The local government's use of naughty tactics against student protesters also drove Benny Tai and moderate political parties to Admiralty to protect them. Further use of tear gas sparked the Umbrella Movement.

The extension dilemma continued during the Umbrella Movement. New protesters became organized to defend the three encampments. HKFS could not get them to leave on command, limiting its ability to negotiate with the police. Just as student groups felt empowered when they broke into Civic Square, a new wave of "Localist" protesters felt empowered by the continued fight in the street.

Following the Umbrella Movement, more than two hundred protestors were prosecuted on various charges. The Occupy Trio and six others, known as the "Umbrella 9," endured a two-year trial and were finally convicted of public nuisance in April 2019. The trio each received sixteen months of jail time, although the sentence was suspended for the older Yiu-ming Chiu. As the Occupy Trio predicted, outrage over their sentencing sparked mass mobilization in the early stages of the Anti-Extradition Protest of 2019. These protests sought to stop legislation that would allow extradition for criminal offenses into Mainland China.

As with the Umbrella Movement, the police's initially violent crackdown on protesters led to widespread protests and support for the Localist players that arose out of the 2014 encampment. Police used unprecedented levels of tear gas and enlisted local gangs to suppress protest, leading to several activists' injuries. The perception of police actions' as unwarrantedly aggressive helped the pan-democratic coalition weather disagreements over whether to use radical tactics during the summer of 2019. They maintained high levels of mobilization through December of that year, prior to shutdowns on public activity due to COVID-19.

In contrast to the Umbrella Movement, however, both the central government in Beijing and the local Hong Kong government agreed on using more aggressive tactics against protesters. The laws of Hong Kong were changed with the National Security Law, which made it easier for the central authorities to impose long sentences on pro-democracy protesters and prevent activists' activities. Ultimately, government actors in authoritarian arenas have greater ability to withstand the long-term consequences of reputational damage to reap the rewards of aggressive action.

While this chapter investigated the internal dynamics and gains and losses within compound players, especially the dilemmas of the radical package, the next chapter primarily examines the package that results when a movement relies heavily on the charismatic personality of its leader. The Russian government has become increasingly authoritarian following the "Winter Revolution" of 2011–2012. While coalition building proved hard in the face of increased oppression, some pro-democracy players, notably Alexei Navalny, made gains by contesting elections after 2012.

# 7

# The Personality Package

## Opposing Putin in Moscow

To participate in elections, political players need personalities: individuals who can run and win positions at stake in electoral arenas. Personalities can become central to collective efforts beyond elections as well, as the symbols and examples of movement and proposals. Martin Luther King Jr., for instance, embodied the moral aspirations of one segment of the civil rights movement. As "public characters," personalities matter in all sorts of ways (Jasper, Young, and Zuern 2018, 2020). Compound players struggle over how dominant and influential a personality should and will be. The hopes, risks, and outcomes that accompany decisions to rely on charismatic individuals represent a "personality package."[1]

We look at the case of Alexei Navalny, critic and challenger of Vladimir Putin's regime. Navalny was propelled to fame by anticorruption investigations and street politics during the Winter Revolution of 2011–2012 and has remained the "celebrity oppositionist" ever since: his personality and what he stands for attract more supporters than abstract political ideas do, and his efforts have energized oppositional politics. He managed to attract new people into politics, most importantly as volunteers and activists working for his electoral campaigns, investigations, and street actions.

The personality package is a special case of outcomes related to the pyramid dilemma, over how much hierarchy should exist in an organization.

---

[1] The chapter is based on eight interviews that Anna Zhelnina conducted in 2016 with coworkers of the Anti-Corruption Foundation and activists involved with the foundation during their campaigns, along with media and social media research, video recordings and transcripts of meetings, and observation of public events. Under authoritarian regimes, it is difficult to piece together an interactive picture with all players' points of view, since the actions and motivations of the ruling political forces are concealed, at least partially, from the public, including the researcher. Much information about their internal dynamics and reasons can only be reconstructed based on rumors or on the interpretations of other players. The latter are especially important, as in their strategic interactions, the players make their decisions on such (partial and sometimes biased) interpretations of the powerful actors. As a result, this chapter focuses on the interpretations of the events by the interviewees from Team Navalny and their close allies. Quotes are from interviews with Team Navalny members, whom we do not identify in any other way to protect their anonymity.

*Gains and Losses*. James M. Jasper, Luke Elliott-Negri, Isaac Jabola-Carolus, Marc Kagan, Jessica Mahlbacher, Manès Weisskircher, and Anna Zhelnina, Oxford University Press. © Oxford University Press 2022. DOI: 10.1093/oso/9780197623251.003.0008

Navalny is the head of the "Anti-Corruption Foundation," a nonprofit that is unimaginable without him, and the basis for "Team Navalny," a network responsible for mobilizing support for his electoral efforts. This network is built around Navalny's reputation, which is both its strength and a weakness. Putting all or most power in the hands of one person is the most centralized organizational strategy. The charismatic leader helps maintain the emotional commitment of supporters, attracts attention, and can act as a role model. This centralized strategy may also lead to certain efficiencies.

But there are costs and risks. Central players can't run for "small" positions, like parliament: they can only be seen as leaders such as mayor or president.

Other team members have less room for their own development and initiative.

The team comes to be seen as subordinate and working for the individual rather than as a political force on its own.

Relying heavily on a single leader is like putting all one's strategic eggs in a single basket. If a leader dies, defects, or is otherwise unavailable, it is hard to replace her. In addition, strong leaders often substitute their own goals for the group's goals (a version of the powerful-allies dilemma). We saw this at the end of chapter 4, as a strong new leader reshaped the culture of New Directions with little notice or debate.

The "personality package" is a way to talk about leadership and charisma that allows us to consider not only the internal dynamics within the movement related to the leader but also the interactions of the movement with other players. Weber's notion of charisma is one of the oldest ways to analyze leadership, although, as Morris and Staggenborg (2004) observe, scholars sometimes forget that charisma is interactional, and not simply a personality type: followers of a leader actively participate in building and maintaining her charisma. Moreover, a preference for a particular type of leadership is deeply connected with the type of movement organization (e.g., hierarchical or horizontal) and its environment.

Movement leadership is a matter of strategic choices and decisions, embedded in the social and political contexts in which it emerges. In this chapter, we take these observations about movement leadership and organization further by employing the strategic interaction perspective and demonstrating that by choosing a certain type of leadership and its public presentation, a movement faces a specific package of gains and losses. It affects the tactics available to the movement, their possibilities for building alliances, and the resilience of the organization. Charisma is a solution to several strategic dilemmas.

We explore Navalny's development as a political player and identify the specific gains and losses he made in electoral arenas, first of all, in the 2013 Moscow mayoral campaign, where Team Navalny exploited most advantages of the personality package (see table 7.1). During this campaign, the electoral

Table 7.1  The Personality Package

| Component Dilemmas | Player Goals | Likely Costs | Risks |
|---|---|---|---|
| Engagement | The usual opportunities available in existing or new arenas | Reactions from other players who now feel threatened | Charismatic figure risks blame for things that go wrong |
| Powerful Allies | Find individual with name recognition, resources, and persuasive powers | Concede control and media attention to that person | The strong player takes over and pursues own goals, not the team's |
| Pyramid | Organizational efficiency and control; benefits from reputation and resources of leader | Subordinate team members may feel undervalued, ignored, or powerless | Appearing undemocratic to both internal and external audiences; if the "hero" is knocked out (jailed, killed, discredited), the player collapses |
| Basket | Win by identifying crucial arena | Fewer opportunities to advance in other arenas | Death, defection, or discrediting of the charismatic leader |
| Extension | Avoid risks associated with potential allies: reputational costs (only responsible for own reputation), transaction costs, etc. Only focusing on own goals: "whose goals" dilemma solved | Being blamed for noncooperation, losing supporters who look for a more consolidated effort | The personality may become part of "powerful allies" dilemma for potential allies: attracts too much negative attention, potential allies will be less eager to cooperate |
| Solutions | Reassure insiders and outsiders that the charismatic figure is sincere and strong (a hero): concerned with others, not selfish; willing to co-operate; having special insights not available through more dispersed channels; strong enough to protect followers; and a perfect representation of the group. | | |

package (see chapter 4) also appeared through a combination of engagement and extension dilemmas that the opposition had to solve. The aftermath of this iconic campaign exposed additional costs and risks of the personality package: a court sentence against Navalny blocked him from entering electoral arenas, and the team and collective effort behind him could no longer benefit from his popularity where it seemed most natural: in elections.

## The Winter Revolution and the Origins of "Navalny"

Vladimir Putin was president of Russia for the two terms permitted by law from 2000 to 2008; his close ally Dmitry Medvedev then replaced him, although informally Putin remained in charge of Russian politics. When, in September 2011, Putin announced he was going to run for president again the following year, many citizens' hopes for liberalization of the regime were dashed. In their view, this was shameless manipulation of the law, and they focused their indignation on the upcoming parliamentary elections in December 2011. Opposition activists and parties called for Russian citizens to show up at the election polls, increase the turnout, and vote for any party other than Putin's United Russia. Many people signed up to observe the elections, reducing the civil inattention that had dominated elections in previous years.

Activists exposed the electoral fraud that had prevailed in Russian elections for many years. In 2011, many more people paid attention as citizens publicized the scale of fraud on social media, such as YouTube videos of electoral committees stuffing ballot boxes for United Russia. Others reported election committee members' harassing observers, violating the counting procedures, and rewriting the result sheets in favor of United Russia. This evidence of electoral deception produced indignant protests in many Russian cities, which continued through spring 2012, accompanied the presidential elections in March 2012, and then declined under severe repression in May.

The protests of 2011–2012—known as the "Movement for Fair Elections," the "Snow Revolution," or the "Winter Revolution"—did not result in a revolution at all: Putin's regime did not fall, and did not even allow review of the parliamentary election results, the protestors' main demand. Instead, the political system became more authoritarian. Worried by the protests, the regime imprisoned rally participants, passed legislation to make antiregime events costlier and scarier, and forced nongovernmental organizations

(NGOs) receiving foreign funds to register as "foreign agents" subject to frequent investigations.

At the same time, Medvedev's government implemented several positive reforms: it simplified the rules of political party registration and reintroduced direct elections for mayors and governors, who since 2004 had been appointed by the president. Officials denied that the reforms were related to the protests, and political scientists have noted that they were in preparation before the demonstrations began (Golosov 2012).

These decisions created new electoral arenas of mayoral and gubernatorial elections where opposition forces could benefit from the increased indignation and politicization. Opposition candidates entered these arenas, and several won. The protests also brought previously apolitical people into politics (Magun and Yerpylyova 2014; Volkov 2012) and became an arena for new political leaders and groups to emerge.

This opposition persisted after the most active phase of the street protests in 2012. The "Russian opposition" is itself a large compound player with many internal contradictions and opposing subplayers, what Mische (2015: 55) calls an "internally fractious movement arena," similar in many ways to Hong Kong's diverse opposition. Even though many spectators and new participants in the protests in 2011–2012 wanted the opposition to act as a unified player, multiple attempts to "act as one" against the authoritarian regime failed, leading to more frustration and disappointment among those involved.

Subplayers in the opposition ranged ideologically from nationalist groups to liberal democrats to left-wing activists and anarchists; these players had conflicting preferences about goals, leadership, tactics, and the level of assertiveness necessary to win. These subplayers included the representatives of the "traditional opposition"—the "Parnas" (Party of Popular Freedom) and "Yabloko" parties whose leaders had long experience in professional politics; many had been elected to the Parliament before or had occupied government positions at some point in their careers. The left end of the spectrum included one leader of the street protests with a long history of antigovernment activism, Sergey Udaltsov, along with the group "Avant-garde of the Red Youth." The unofficial party "The Other Russia," a successor to the banned "Nationalist Bolsheviks," was also active in the street protests, calling for more assertive acts of disobedience than the moderate wing of the opposition, which sought approval from the government for rallies.

Alexei Navalny and his Anti-Corruption Foundation, also referred to as Team Navalny, made more gains than any of the others.[2] Navalny emerged as a fresh face of opposition during the protests, managed to establish and develop an organization, and maintained some of the enthusiasm of his supporters several years after the demobilization of the Winter Revolution. Unlike most others, Navalny did not return to oblivion but remains active and visible in political arenas, which makes his case an interesting example of a player managing to make gains despite unfavorable outcomes in the broader movement. At least some of his gains should be attributed to his personal charisma and the public personality he created during the Winter Revolution.

## Alexei Navalny

Navalny, trained as a lawyer, was no novice to politics in 2011: he had started his political career when he joined Yabloko in 2000, the year Putin was first elected president. He worked in the party apparatus of Yabloko's Moscow regional branch and got to know young politicians in other opposition parties and movements. Navalny was expelled from Yabloko in 2007 for allegedly damaging the party's reputation because of his nationalist activities. He had participated in the Russian Marches—rallies of right-wing forces with a broadly xenophobic agenda, including organizations with radical and even extremist views; one of them, the Movement Against Illegal Immigration (DPNI), was later officially banned. Association with DPNI became a cloud over Navalny's reputation in the eyes of liberal oppositionists. In 2007, Navalny had even co-founded a nationalist movement, "The People" (*Narod*), which framed its ideology as the "new political nationalism," and was part of the "Russian National Movement" along with the DPNI. Navalny never officially abandoned or disavowed this ideology, although he was more discreet about it later, when he emerged as the leader of the opposition to Putin's illiberal government.

---

[2] Navalny was the undisputed leader of the foundation, and most of the political efforts discussed in this chapter revolved around him. Some members of the team were also notable political personalities in their own right. However, even when they disagreed, they still acted in accordance with the general line and strategy of the organization.

**Figure 7.1** Alexei Navalny at one of the Protest Rallies in Moscow in 2012.
Photo Credit: Mitya Aleshkovsky. https://commons.wikimedia.org/wiki/
File:Alexey_Navalny.jpg

By 2011, Navalny had developed a reputation as a blogger who exposed corruption in large, state-owned companies. He and his supporters were often mocked as internet "hamsters" (internet slang for someone who is very active on the internet, follows the crowd in protesting and criticizing, and is subject to manipulation); Navalny's opponents insinuated that being a blogger was not a serious occupation. But Navalny transformed himself from a blogger into a popular politician, in the process building a stable political organization, a loyal cadre of supporters and activists (the Anti-Corruption Foundation), and recognition from other opposition players.

The mixed elements of Navalny's public character are not unusual for a charismatic leader. Even the nationalism, while a taint in the eyes of liberal allies, bolstered his image of strength in the view of some voters, as did his willingness to stand up to the regime. He had the makings of a hero: strength and—by battling corruption—morality (Jasper, Young, and Zuern 2020). His allies tolerated his populism because it promised to work well in electoral arenas.

## Investigations and Street Politics: Gaining Political Capital (2010–2012)

Navalny started his anticorruption investigations as a private initiative with the help of only a few coworkers, and in 2011 he registered the "Anti-Corruption Foundation" as an NGO and hired additional staff through crowdfunding. Their investigations first targeted state-owned companies and later high-ranking officials involved in shady financial practices. Navalny drew on an ideology that attributes Russia's political and economic troubles to a corruption that permeates all levels of government and public service. Exposing high-level corruption has the potential to undermine the legitimacy of the political regime itself, and the foundation's mission is to keep the public alert to the topic of corruption at all times.

Navalny's decision to crowdfund his efforts rather than apply for grants was a smart strategic move that helped him avoid allegations of being a "foreign agent." Navalny's social media activities gained him name recognition and the trust of some opinion leaders. Several important public figures expressed their support with financial contributions to the foundation.

In August 2011, several months before the parliamentary elections, Navalny started a campaign on social media, asking people to vote for "Any Other Party but the Party of Crooks and Thieves"—a nickname for Putin's United Russia. The campaign caused a stir, and many voters followed his advice; the "Party of Crooks and Thieves" became a popular nickname. With this and similar rhetorical devices, Navalny stoked a feeling of betrayal that led many to vote for different parties rather than boycotting or destroying their ballots. New participants entered the electoral arena and confronted its corrupt rules of the game. Russian elections were not false, but certainly underused, arenas before the movement of 2011–2012 encouraged opposition candidates and voters to engage in them more intensively—and to utilize them for other purposes than winning.

The events of 2011–2012 transformed Navalny from an anticorruption blogger into a politician and visible opposition leader. His blog became a platform to call for action, announce rallies, and suggest strategies for the opposition. He also built political and social capital in street politics arenas. A handsome and charismatic fresh face, he gained the support of young urban protesters, many of whom became enthusiastic and hopeful about politics for the first time in their lives. Navalny spoke at rallies, was always present at street events, and, like hundreds of ordinary Muscovites, was arrested for participating in illegal rallies, which helped people relate to him. He talked in informal language (calling the authorities "scumbags") and was a compelling speaker, connecting with the crowd and speaking in slogans and short phrases. He yelled his signature "yes or no?" at the crowd after each statement, provoking an emotional response: "They said we were going to shout a bit and then we'll just walk away. But we shout and don't go away. Yes or no? Yes or no?" Navalny created the image of a brave, sincere, and energetic leader.

The risks of the personality package appeared almost immediately. Some people in the pro-democratic camp expressed concern that Navalny put too much emphasis on himself, hijacked the oppositional agenda to promote himself, and wouldn't allow for competition. They represented him as an authoritarian leader not so different from his rival, Vladimir Putin. The fear of a personality cult and rejection of the single-leader party resonated with the Russian liberal intelligentsia, evoking memories of the Soviet past and comparisons with Putin's authoritarian rule.

The regime exploited another weakness of the personality package: indispensability. As Navalny became a significant player in political arenas, the Prosecutor General's Office started several criminal investigations into his business practices. It was not only a scare tactic: as a potentially powerful player, Navalny might be excluded from elections. Citizens convicted of crimes are not allowed to run for office once their sentences begin.

Most notorious and consequential was the so-called Kirovles case: an investigation of Navalny's involvement in a suspicious sale of timber by the state-owned forestry enterprise Kirovles to a private company in 2009, when he had been a pro bono adviser to the governor of the Kirov Region. In 2012, the local court in Kirov found a director of Kirovles guilty of embezzlement. Navalny's actions were investigated too—allegedly, he gave incorrect advice to the director in favor of the private company—but the charges were dropped. Several months later, the Investigative Committee, a federal authority responsible for investigations of corruption in governmental bodies, including police and local authorities, brought the charges anew. Navalny's team and supporters interpreted this as revenge by those whom he implicated or attacked and a move to stop him from running for official positions.

Navalny thus had to operate in at least two arenas simultaneously, the mayoral campaign and the courts, which exhausted the personal and financial resources of Navalny, his team, and his family. This benefited his opponents but also included a tradeoff: the court hearings sparked public outrage and kept attention on Navalny, producing some gains. His personal fame was helping to protect him. From the government's perspective, its prosecution of Navalny backfired.

In July 2013, Navalny officially registered as a mayoral candidate in Moscow, and soon after, the judge in the Kirovles case announced a sentence of five years' imprisonment. The same day, crowds (estimates vary from 2,500 to 20,000) gathered in the center of Moscow to protest this sentence as unreasonable and repressive. Smaller protests emerged in several other Russian cities, too. The next day, the judge suspended the sentence until October, effectively allowing Navalny to participate in the mayoral elections scheduled for September. This revision was based, surprisingly, on a request by the prosecution. It is still not clear what the motivation was—perhaps fear of public displays of discontent.

Different players on the government side were not coordinating their actions very well: the prosecution and the court system seem to have come up with a punishment that did not correspond with the anti-Navalny strategy of the president's administration and the mayor's office. We saw a similar lack of coordination between the branches of government in the previous chapter on Hong Kong. Both cases involved the naughty-or-nice dilemma, forcing the government to decide how democratic (and legitimate) or how repressive (and menacing) it would like to appear. In Moscow, the "democratic" choice momentarily prevailed, to Navalny's advantage.

Overall, Navalny had become an influential opposition player. In joining street protests and fighting the investigations against him, he earned public support, which gave him some protection against the regime's repression. He built a new compound player—the Anti-Corruption Foundation—and developed a capable team of staff and allies to help him with investigations and electoral efforts. He gained recognition from other members of the opposition political elite who accepted him as a player with legitimate claims for leadership. The arena where he hoped to formally achieve such leadership was the Coordinating Board of the Russian Opposition, an attempt by opposition groups to build a unified movement after the street protests ended in June 2012.

## Coordinating Board and Electoral Strategies (2012–2013)

The coordinating board was intended to be a unified player that could also serve as an arena for collective decision-making and strategizing. It was meant to coordinate the actions of different subplayers within the opposition and to help them plan protest actions together and make joint statements. It was also supposed to be a platform for negotiations with the authorities. Navalny played a central role in the board's creation. He faced the extension dilemma that always accompanies the creation of larger coalitions, but he was ready to accept the coordination and communication costs in the hopes of increasing his own legitimacy and prestige in the opposition.

After a long discussion about how to choose the board's members to ensure diverse opinions, the Organizing Committee of Protest Actions (the informal group that coordinated the opposition's activities during the White Revolution) decided to hold internet-based elections with supplementary offline polling stations. The organizing committee suggested that citizens select representatives from four lists: thirty from a "general" list and five each from three "ideological" wings, namely, left, liberal, and nationalist—a procedure to ensure that every ideological branch of the opposition received some seats. The decision ran afoul of the extension dilemma, as the board could never develop the collective identity necessary to maintain itself and minimize its coordination costs.

The coordinating board election was basically a "mock" parliamentary election: the idea was to build a Parliament-like structure parallel to the existing State Duma, which was closed to the opposition. In this "training" arena, members planned to perform the same tasks that they would in a real parliament—discussing pressing issues, working with ideological opponents, and making collective decisions.

Ultimately, 81,801 voted in October 2012 to elect forty-five board members, representing all parts of the political spectrum within the opposition, including the left and nationalist poles. The majority of the elected were the "faces" of the Winter Revolution: opinion leaders and celebrities without explicit political career ambitions, long-time political activists, and party leaders. Navalny got more votes than any other candidate: more than half the voters chose him. Two other members of his team were also elected. These elections gave antiregime protesters enthusiasm and a sense of purpose; for that reason they later exacerbated the general disappointment in the antiregime protests.

The new board met once a month throughout the 2012–2013 season. It shared no clear agenda, and the first meetings revealed that those elected had no common understanding of their responsibilities or potential powers. The board tried to outline the strategy for the opposition, made statements about political prisoners, planned actions to support their families, called for international support, and spent most of its time trying to formulate a common political position. Due to ideological and personal differences, it was difficult for members to make any decisions. Transcripts of the assemblies show that cooperation among the different subplayers was fragile, and almost every issue produced more contestation and polarization than consensus. Procedural questions and infighting consumed more time than planning or strategizing. Gradually members began to drop out, either officially leaving the board or just not showing up to meetings.

One of the last issues the board addressed before it collapsed was choosing a single opposition candidate for the Moscow mayoral elections. In June 2013, Moscow's mayor, Sergey Sobyanin, unexpectedly resigned and then announced he would participate in the special election in early September, even though the regular election was due soon after. As we have said, the reasons for government actions are often opaque. Oppositionists believed the decision to speed elections was meant to limit the opposition's organizing and preparation and to suppress voter turnout. As one informant from Team Navalny recalled, there was also a rumor that the authorities had decided to "measure the temperature," to test support for the opposition. Sobyanin even ran as an independent candidate, despite being a member of United Russia.

Navalny's team embarked on what we described in chapter 4 as an electoral strategy: a player broadens its appeal to win votes, in the process potentially watering down its ideology and alienating long-standing core members of the team (see table 4.1). It concentrates on electoral arenas to the exclusion of other arenas, and it usually must suppress radical flanks. In this case, the personality package was a variation on the electoral package that solved some of the radical-flank problems. Navalny's nationalist past probably helped with voters. But it created another problem: liberal allies needed to be reassured.

As part of the electoral strategy, Navalny faced an engagement dilemma: was this election an opportunity or a trap? The election looked suspicious, and it had the signs of a false arena: with little time to prepare and facing the current mayor's capacity to manipulate the campaign and the voting, doing badly was a substantial risk which would allow Navalny's opponents to claim that he didn't have much popular support. But refusing to participate in the "real" action of elections would disappoint Navalny's supporters, who wanted the opposition candidates to keep doing something, demonstrating that they were serious about their political ambitions. Not "being there" would look like admitting his powerlessness.

The coordinating board faced the same engagement (and being-there) dilemma: should they support entry to an electoral arena that they thought was false? Board members used the nicknames "special operations" and "so-called elections" to emphasize the fake nature of elections in Russia, and some called for a boycott of the elections, so as not to legitimize the inevitable victory of the regime. This discussion echoed the same dilemma in the parliamentary elections of 2011 when opinions had split between boycotting and voting for "any other party." Some board members realized that an election, even in an illiberal political system, is a mobilization opportunity:

> Some people think we should boycott the elections. But I would like to re-mind you, that if not for the "special operation" in December 2011, staged by Putin and Churov, we would not have the protest actions, we would not have this Coordinating Board. We must understand very clearly, that this special operation mobilizes our supporters; and if we don't work on the mobilization of our supporters, we are no one: an interest club with various political views. We must participate in it, for mobilization's sake. (Boris Nemtsov, speaking at the 9th meeting of the Coordinating Board, June 15, 2013)

Another consideration made the elections more attractive: Team Navalny intended to use them not only for their normal purpose of electing a candidate but also as a platform for agitation and information. Navalny suggested using the formally hopeless electoral arena to inform citizens about the opposition, spoil the easy victory for the government and pro-Kremlin players, and maintain the enthusiasm of the opposition's supporters by giving them hope and some real action. Furthermore, as one of the board members said, many ordinary Muscovites had already signed up to be election observers, and not having a candidate from the opposition would betray them. This shows that almost no arena is ever entirely false.

Navalny seems to be the only person who gained something tangible from the board's existence. In the board elections, he got more votes than any other candidate, bolstering his legitimacy and political capacity. The board supported his candidacy in the mayoral election as the lone oppositional candidate. In supporting Navalny, the board provided a candidate and a plan of action for their constituency—the gain was the continuing mobilization of supporters.

But the coordinating board never really solved the extension dilemma: the opposition tried to maximize its resources and impact by coming together, but it suffered from constant disagreements over the means and ends of collective action. It did not facilitate a division of labor between different subplayers in different arenas, producing more disagreement than coordination. The board lost many individual players who did not want to participate in permanent squabbles without tangible outcomes, and the new arena became meaningless.

## The Mayoral Campaign 2013

No one, including Team Navalny, expected Navalny to win office: their goal was political capital and recognition. The decision carried risks—running and failing could harm Navalny's image as an up-and-coming politician, since this would be the first real-life test of his political ability. For such a big task, the campaign initially had few resources.

Team Navalny also faced the false-arena dilemma, potentially legitimizing the illiberal government that controlled the electoral arena. Informal encouragement from the mayor's office partly confirmed that the government wanted Nalvany to run. According to some respondents, Navalny received a phone call in June 2013 from a fellow opposition activist, who informed him that the mayor's office anticipated that Navalny might be interested in running and that they would not try to prevent him from registering as a candidate. "Nobody said that openly, that Navalny can try and register, but they talk about it there (. . .) Well, at least, they gave him a go-ahead, that if he wants it, he can register."

Navalny was one of six candidates, along with incumbent Sergey Sobyanin, three representatives of the parliamentary opposition (from the Communist Party, the Liberal Democratic Party, and "A Just Russia Party"), and the leader of the traditional opposition Yabloko party, Sergey Mitrokhin. Navalny was the only opposition candidate who campaigned seriously, which won him a significant share of popular support—even though he failed to get advertising time on the main TV or radio stations. Outdoor advertising companies also refused to accept Navalny's banners.

With Navalny in the race for mayor, the regime faced a naughty-or-nice dilemma typical of electoral authoritarianism (Smyth and Soboleva 2016). Too much repression can cost the regime legitimacy, but allowing opposition players too much freedom of maneuver risks instability and loss of control. Allowing Navalny to run for mayor almost turned into a strategic mistake by the regime: it expected him to win the typical 3 to 5 percent of the traditional opposition candidate. When he received 27 percent, Sobyanin barely managed the 50 percent necessary to avoid a second-round run-off. Sobyanin gained the legitimacy of a real election, but Navalny garnered enormous attention.

## Alliances

Before Navalny could submit his mayoral application, he had to build alliances and secure support from other opposition players. To avoid having to collect signatures to qualify for the ballot, Navalny sought the official nomination of a registered party, Parnas, whose leader was one of the members of the coordinating board. The party's board disagreed over his candidacy, with some resisting due to Navalny's nationalism.

Whatever the motivations of the Parnas leaders, the conflict demonstrates the difficulties that opposition leaders had in accepting and supporting other players, especially an emerging personality who could overshadow them and claim the gains as his own. The more experienced representatives of the traditional opposition were cautious about letting a charismatic newcomer become a strong player in opposition politics. Ultimately, the party's board voted in favor of Navalny's candidacy six to three, although the exact conditions of their agreement remain unclear (there has been a rumor about informal agreements between Navalny and some of the Parnas leaders, but no evidence of it exists). Navalny's tangential connection with his "official" party reemphasizes how much this campaign was about personality.

The interaction of Navalny and his team with other players in the opposition reveals some important features of the personality package. The personalized nature of Navalny's movement made it impossible for other individuals in the opposition to detach Navalny from the potentially uniting values and goals he claimed to pursue. Furthermore, this personalization, to some players in the opposition, seemed incompatible with their own electoral ambitions and chances, increasing the sense of individual competition.

A second barrier was the municipal filter—a new requirement, introduced in 2012, for candidates for governors and mayors to collect the signatures of (in the case of Moscow) 6 percent of the municipal deputies in their region. While 110 signatures were needed to register, only thirty-five deputies were independent in 2013. This required extensive negotiation and coordination with representatives of United Russia. Fortunately, the regime was seeking election legitimacy and so acted "nice." Sergey Sobyanin, the incumbent mayor, quickly collected 160 signatures and then called for deputies to support the opposition candidates, signaling that there would be no punishment if they did, and that he was interested in winning a truly representative election.

Despite this "permission," collecting the deputies' signatures was a tedious and time-consuming task, which had to be completed parallel to the ongoing Kirovles court hearing. Navalny talked to all the potential signers on the phone and arranged meetings for signing the papers. As this was the peak of the summer season, some of the deputies were traveling. The team looked for volunteers in the regions where the sympathetic deputies were on vacation and had the papers signed. Getting the necessary signatures required not only secret negotiations with other professional politicians, as in the case of Parnas, but also the enthusiasm and commitment of volunteers.

## The Janus Dilemma and Emotional Resources

Team Navalny's personality strategy relied heavily on the support of volunteers, mobilizing young activists who had participated in the protests of 2011–2012. Two headquarters were formed, based on the tasks and proximity to the decision-making core. The first worked directly with Navalny on collecting the signatures of the municipal deputies, on developing campaign strategies, designing campaign materials, preparing leaflets and newspapers, and so on. This first headquarters was based in the office of the Anti-Corruption Foundation, and its core staff were foundation employees.

The second headquarters was located in another neighborhood, drew relative newcomers, and organized street agitation. The foundation later reproduced this dual system ("core" and volunteers) in other electoral campaigns. But Navalny spent considerable time in both offices. For the volunteers, contact with Navalny and the opportunity to snap a selfie with him were important rewards. As one interviewee recalled, Navalny patiently stood for endless photos with volunteers.

Energizing supporters was a crucial part of Navalny's campaign: after the deputies' signatures were collected, Navalny used the bureaucratic procedure of officially registering with the election committee as an opportunity to organize an emotionally charged public event for his supporters. His team arranged a march, beginning with several streams of people at different locations but eventually merging near the election committee. They filmed the march, and posted a rousing video on YouTube of Navalny talking with a crowd of supporters before submitting his application (Yakovlev 2013).

The core tactic of Navalny's campaign was an intensive program of meetings with voters across Moscow: three meetings a day in different neighborhoods for the entire campaign. This might not seem impressive in countries with developed democratic electoral systems, but in Russia, it is unusual for candidates to meet voters in person.

Volunteers worked "on the cubes," Team Navalny's innovation: "Navalny Cubes" were mobile constructions of four banners and a frame, used for street propaganda. The cubes could be moved freely around the city, establishing a convenient and visible area where activists would stand and reach out to pedestrians. The cubes were a creative way to avoid the limitations imposed on political activity in public spaces. They did not require complicated approval procedures from the police as they were not seen as fixed constructions. Volunteers also campaigned in the private spaces of their own buildings, turning familiar spaces into political arenas.

Volunteer enthusiasm was essential, and Navalny's charisma and reputation acquired during the street protests engaged people in the campaign. The established opposition did not generate such enthusiasm, and Navalny was one of the few who managed to draw on the emotional political mobilization of the 2011–2012 antigovernment protests.

Because movements relying on volunteers can offer their supporters few material benefits, they "must devote a tremendous amount of time and effort to soliciting and maintaining the commitment of its members" (Mansbridge 1986: 120). This includes formulating a strong, "black and white" ideological message that activists will identify with, and rewarding volunteers with community, solidarity, and identity. In the Janus dilemma, organizations that turn inward to satisfy volunteer activists may lose broader support. Some critics, and even core insiders, saw this risk in Team Navalny and their second headquarters: Navalny's mayoral campaign inherited the emotional

**Figure 7.2**   Alexei Navalny meeting with voters in one of the Moscow's neighborhoods, August 2013, with a "Navalny cube" in the background. Photo Credit: Ilya Isaev. https://commons.wikimedia.org/wiki/File:%D0%9D%D0%B 0%D0%B2%D0%B0%D0%BB%D1%8C%D0%BD%D1%8B%D0%B9_9.jpg

power of the Winter Revolution, and the black-and-white vision of the antiregime protests: everything associated with United Russia and Kremlin was seen as evil. The campaign became an opportunity for young protesters to identify with their comrades; the "volunteer headquarters" became a place to hang out, meet interesting people, and discuss politics—for many young volunteers, a new and beguiling experience. At the same time, the volunteer headquarters still had to accomplish the ongoing tasks of the campaign: selecting the locations of the Navalny cubes; managing the storage, delivery, and installation of the cubes; and tending to other routine needs of the street campaigning process.

Maxim Katz, an activist and politician who joined Team Navalny in July 2013, organized the volunteer headquarters. Katz later posted a detailed description of his efforts and the dilemmas he had faced. He believed that the volunteers' emotional enthusiasms were secondary and even detrimental to the routine tasks of the campaign:

The headquarters' coordinators thought that it was necessary to create a nice atmosphere for the people who come there, to make it good for them. Then they will help us and do the campaign. I was certain that the headquarters is not a place for activists pondering over strategy, not a place for a hangout ("*tusovochka*"). Nobody should drink tea in the kitchen and dispute about the Motherland's faith, there must be no lectures about the political configuration of the Russian Federation— it must be something like McDonald's: young people, who know their functions well, must bake absolutely standard hamburgers and give them to the arriving supporters, who take them and get out of there and come to our help. (M. Katz 2013)

Katz worried about what Mansbidge calls the "iron law of involution": in the long term, movements relying on the solidarity and commitment of volunteers, looking inward, can turn into sects. According to Katz, the "nice atmosphere" threatened the efficiency of the campaign. Although the campaign required a well-organized effort, volunteers often resisted hierarchy and centralization and were not as focused as the paid staff.

Katz later claimed that his unwillingness to defer to the feelings of volunteers helped build an efficient campaigning machine. The cubes were installed; the meetings took place; the volunteers did their work. His team built "an ideally working system" thanks to their ability to "ignore the emotions," but this also led to conflicts, resentments, and ultimately Katz's expulsion from Team Navalny "the next moment after the last truck with the cubes had left" (M. Katz 2014). Katz's strict, efficiency-based methods alienated many, including some close to Navalny; enthusiasm, emotions, and belonging—the advantages of Team Navalny—were threatened by a dry, businesslike approach.

Team Navalny's final report about the technologies used in the mayoral campaign rejected Katz's argument; it concluded that volunteers did better work than paid distributors of leaflets: the paid promoters who were hired to distribute the materials to car drivers in traffic jams were often rude and sometimes threw away the leaflets instead of distributing them. When volunteers began supervising the groups of hired promoters, the situation improved (Report 2013: 25). Volunteers' enthusiasm and loyalty to the cause were the campaign's main assets. As the volunteers worked the streets ("on the cubes," distributing leaflets at traffic jams and in the subway, delivering leaflets and newspapers to mailboxes), the team carefully monitored and analyzed the effectiveness of each action. In addition to its detailed report (Report 2013), it created a series of educational videos (Volkov n.d.) explaining the techniques, information they hoped would start a cascade of opposition campaigns outside Moscow.

Team Navalny grappled explicitly with the Janus dilemma, whether to concentrate on its members' interest and enthusiasm or to turn outward to expand, recruit new supporters, and persuade the undecided. Allowing the volunteers to "hang out," the campaign risked some short-term inefficiencies, but if stripped of solidarity and fun, the campaign would risk losing the long-term commitment of the members. As one of the activists in the mayoral campaign stated in an interview, working with the volunteers and keeping their enthusiasm going was an important task, which kept the machinery going; without this crucial emotional resource, the best strategizing would not work. Without at least some inherent pleasures, the volunteers would not return.

The decision to participate in the elections helped Team Navalny to recruit and expand, because elections require reaching out to wide audiences, not just cultivating an inward identity and fun atmosphere for the sake of those already active. But the movement also depended on the reputation of one central personality, Navalny.

The conflict with an ally, Maxim Katz, shows another effect of the personality package: centering on Navalny put some techniques off limits. It was not possible to work for Navalny's campaign without acknowledging its personalized nature and the dynamics within the movement that it produced. It also shows that other ambitious individuals were limited in their own personal advancement. On the other hand, some players in the opposition learned from Navalny's innovations in the electoral domain, and later tried similar techniques in municipal and parliamentary elections—independently of Team Navalny's support.

The emotional and personal dynamic between the charismatic personality and his team is also part of the personality package: one cannot remove the personal relationships and emotions from a campaign built on such a foundation. The increased commitment to the cause comes with the personal fascination with the central character; refusing volunteers the opportunity to feel part of it restricts the potential gains. The right charismatic leader can solve the Janus dilemma at least temporarily by appealing to insiders and outsiders alike, although sometimes in different ways.

## Learning the Tactics

The Navalny campaign's main activity was outreach to the undecided Muscovites and promoting Navalny in the world beyond social media. Since the team did not expect victory, the main goal in the elections was to build Navalny's political base. With this in mind, the campaign built an operation that spread the word and eventually earned a good share of votes.

The scale of Team Navalny's activities made his state opponents wary, and they used their administrative resources to reduce the impact of the agitation techniques. For instance, janitors, who are in most cases employees of the local administration, removed Navalny's newspapers from mailboxes and newsstands. Despite these countermeasures, Team Navalny estimated that at least half of Muscovites received at least one Navalny newspaper (Report 2013). The Levada Center found a steady growth of pro-Navalny voters in Moscow as a result of his campaign: in July, only 8 percent of respondents said they were going to vote for Navalny; by September, 18 percent did (Levada Center 2013).

In the official results, Sobyanin received 51.37 percent of the votes, thus avoiding a run-off, with Navalny second at 27.24 percent and the other candidates splitting the remainder. Because Team Navalny's own polling service showed that Sobyanin had not legitimately received 50 percent of the vote, Navalny had to decide whether to claim electoral fraud and to call on his supporters to protest. His team prepared for a challenge, although some were secretly hoping he would let the results stand after such an exhausting campaign. Supporters' opinions were split on the issue.

An important feature of the personality package is the tendency of the key individual to make decisions and resolve dilemmas on their own; the loyal team and committed supporters would accept it. Until the last moment, apparently nobody knew what Navalny would announce at the big rally that gathered on Bolotnaya Square, the spot of the mass protests of 2011–2012. He decided against open protest at the results. As one team member recalled, "And then he says: 'when the time comes to turn the cars over—I will tell you.' We all exhaled. Not everybody, some wanted it. People brought tents; they were very determined."

It is difficult to say why Navalny made this decision. Personal exhaustion after a long campaign was one reason (he called the rally on the Bolotnaya square "a rally of the tired people"). Another was the wish to leave the arena with some sort of victory; persisting meant risking a greater loss. He could reframe 27 percent as a win for an opposition candidate campaigning in the face of a state-media blackout. Framing the result as partial victory allowed him to maintain some enthusiasm in his supporters and point toward future electoral victories. The result proved that the electoral arena was not absolutely hopeless.

Navalny instead filed a complaint of fraud with the electoral committee, asking for the results to be canceled. Unsurprisingly, the committee refused. Compared to the Duma elections of 2011, which sparked the street protests that boosted Navalny's rise, the electoral fraud during the mayoral elections was more limited: "Golos," the main independent organization tracking violations and fraud in Russian elections, issued a statement about the surprisingly low level of recorded fraud at the election, concluding that the incumbent candidate used his administrative resources while campaigning, but less than is usually done in similar situations (Golos 2013). According to Team Navalny members, it was still enough to guarantee Sobyanin a first-round victory. However, the closeness of the race and Navalny's strong result showed the government that allowing the opposition into electoral arenas is a risky move, which they learned to prevent in future elections.

## Disappointing Elections after 2013

Despite the loss, the process of organizing and campaigning benefited Navalny and his team as players, with political recognition, organizational development, and recruitment. Navalny and his supporters became serious politicians and politically engaged citizens, instead of remaining "bloggers" and "internet hamsters." The foundation attracted more supporters and donations which helped it to grow, hire new staff (from ten in 2013 to thirty in 2016), and fund anticorruption investigations. Team Navalny expected to ride their momentum into election arenas beyond Moscow.

But without Navalny in the race, the personality approach reached its limits. Opposition candidates increased their vote totals in regional elections but only won two mayoral races. Even those wins proved temporary. One new mayor was impeached by the local legislature, the other was found guilty of taking a bribe. Even elections are not always final outcomes (Moses 2015; Semenov 2017).

Navalny was the charismatic dissenter in the most "charismatic" media market, Moscow. Because of its symbolic importance as the capital, and the biased perception of national journalists who are mostly located there, events there draw more attention than those in smaller cities.

Nor was Navalny always so charismatic in other regions. He built a reputation as a "radical critic" of the existing political system, unwilling to compromise with the establishment; he has always rejected the strategy of "changing the system from the inside" through administrative appointments. Such black-and-white politics earned him the respect and admiration of his followers but scared off more moderate activists and politicians and made Navalny-related activities a "red flag" for most local electoral committees. His choice of the naughty option in Moscow, driven by the Janus tradeoff (his refusal to compromise or enter any deals with the government pleased the existing supporters, but limited the opportunities to recruit more followers from the moderate pool of liberals), cost him elsewhere.

His supporters' excitement over Navalny made the results in other regions more disappointing. They felt their excitement turn to frustration. They had invested energy and hope in the campaign, which they described as the "first real electoral campaign in Russia." "In some sense we became hostages of this miracle—we are responsible for what we have tamed, and the supporters, with their mouth open with amazement, demanded repetition of this," said a team member who was actively involved in the post-2013 elections. Charismatic candidates often help allies in minor races, but mostly when they are running themselves.

The weak regional results contributed to apathy and disappointment, and eventually depoliticized many of his supporters. Feeling "trapped," Team Navalny blamed the "structural factors" that were out of their control; they attributed their troubles to the government's administrative machinations, not to their own decisions around the personality package.

There were plenty of government tricks for them to blame. Electoral boards can reject the registration of an opposition candidate or party list. Their supporting signatures can be excluded as fake. They can find it difficult even to rent an office for their headquarters. If they manage to register as candidates, they are denied the same media time as the candidates backed by the ruling party. In many cases, voting results are simply falsified.

In the face of defeats in 2015 and 2016, Team Navalny rethought the extension and Janus dilemmas, turning against their former allies. Fellow opposition forces had nothing to offer them: "[they are] all bullshit, all these coalitions—it was a mistake. We gave and invested in it so much, but never got anything; we did not get more opportunities for our agenda." Having acquired recognition and political capital, Team Navalny decided to abandon other opposition subplayers. They now felt they had more potential on their own and did not want to accept the costs of coalition-building.

While Russian elections can induce apathy, Team Navalny understands one of its key tasks as sustaining emotions, including outrage, in the political sphere. Investigations disclosing corruption and the level of luxury consumption among state employees and individuals close to Putin seem to do this effectively. One respondent summarized the goal of this tactic as "causing the maximal political damage" to the authorities, exposing their financial and consumer practices. The well-made, entertaining videos posted on Navalny's YouTube channel help to maintain people's interest and outrage and, unlike elections, don't require difficult negotiations or alliances with other opposition forces. The personality strategy can be detached from the electoral strategy, transforming the political leader into an influential celebrity.

## Conclusion

In this chapter, we have explored how two interrelated packages of gains and losses—the personality package and the electoral package—worked well in some ways for Alexei Navalny and his team during and after the mayoral elections in Moscow in 2013 but failed in subsequent elections.

The decision to participate in elections brings along the goals, risks, and costs of the electoral package. It involves several dilemmas: the engagement dilemma (whether to participate in the arena), the extension dilemma (building new connections and attracting new publics), the Janus dilemma, and prioritizing some goals over the others in the "whose goals" choice. Whether to engage with governmental institutions or become part of the government is a common dilemma for several of the players we have seen in this book: for PBNYC, the Communists in Graz, and $15 in Seattle, becoming part of the government had its advantages, helping to promote their causes or to secure future electoral gains. But the electoral path usually excludes other, more aggressive strategies; winning elections becomes the overriding objective.

The focus on Navalny's personality during the Winter Revolution and the creation of a team loyal to him bore fruit in 2013. The personality strategy, a collective effort centering on Navalny, had advantages: a single person can make decisions faster, and his authority makes supporters accept his decisions. The team could stick to their own agenda instead of engaging in difficult alliances and negotiations; they did not have to take responsibility by association for actions of other opposition players. It is easier for one person to be impeccable than to control how everyone in the collective behaves. Personal fame also brought some protection to Navalny. Charisma can alleviate the Janus and extension dilemmas, among others.

The personality package also includes risks and costs. First, anyone can make mistakes. Diverse perspectives and sources of information are usually thought to generate better decisions than powerful individuals do (Ganz 2000). Second, to rely heavily on a single figure is to put all your eggs in one basket. When a criminal investigation against Navalny effectively removed him from the electoral arenas, there was no one available to replace him. In regional parliamentary elections in 2016, the Navalny-centered organizing did not produce enough support for liberal candidates who were not Navalny, even if they were associated with him. Losing the player (due to death, incarceration, defection, or exclusion from an arena) means that the collective effort behind this personality could collapse. With the Communists in Graz, we saw a similar, although temporary, loss in the party's electoral results after a well-known leader moved from the local up to the regional level.

A final risk of the personality package is the reluctance of potential allies to associate with someone who is too strong: a powerful-allies dilemma for them. Realizing that Navalny's personal reputation would overshadow everyone around him, some political players, including Parnas party leaders, were loath to associate with him. Even the active participants of the Winter Revolution, who were "on the same side" as Navalny, hesitated: they feared he would become "like Putin," authoritarian and mistrustful of competition. Compared with New Directions in chapter 4, we have less information about the level of internal debate and democratic decision-making within Team Navalny, but whatever its extent, from the outside, they always looked like a team consolidated behind their leader, arousing suspicions of authoritarianism. Such players are often dismissed as "cults."

Risks, gains, and losses are never distributed equally across the subplayers that make up a movement or government. With a personality strategy, Navalny himself took greater risks. He might be assassinated, like so many of Putin's critics, or jailed for a long term. In 2020, Navalny was poisoned and fell into coma, barely surviving. Team Navalny investigated the assassination attempt and made several highly popular videos based on this investigation. They also published a video directly targeting Putin for the first time, exposing the sophisticated corruption schemes used to build a secret palace for the president on the shores of the Black Sea. Shortly after, Navalny was imprisoned and sent to a remote prison for three years: the regime decided to fully embrace the "naughty" option, unwilling to bear the costs of having Navalny active anymore.

Team Navalny can continue working without their charismatic person available, but it remains to be seen how this will play out.

# Conclusion

## Following the Interactions

We have seen a variety of strategic players pursuing their goals across a number of arenas. Three attained most of what they wanted: $15 an hour in Seattle, participatory budgeting (PB) in New York, and electoral success in Graz. Even in these three cases there were losses sprinkled among the gains. The fight over Seattle's minimum wage—and Washington State's—continues at the state level. Pro-PB organizations gave up control in exchange for institutionalization, in a tension that continues to unfold. The Communists in Graz still own housing informally as an issue, but their decision to remain outside the governing coalition cost them power over funding and their official position as head of the department of housing.

The other cases had more complex outcomes, mostly losses. New Directions (ND), in addition to traditional economic goals, had hoped for cultural–political transformations inside and outside the union. An electoral strategy seemed the best way for them to accomplish this. It was not. It led to a package of outcomes they had not fully anticipated. That choice, and the subsequent compromises they made to win union elections, changed the nature of the organization and allowed a strong personality to control the union. Winning elections cost ND most of their original substantive goals.

Occupy Hong Kong with Love and Peace (OHKLP) experienced a radical package that we often see among protest movements: they were able to mobilize crowds in a memorable pageant but had little impact on the election rules they sought to change. Occupations are a dramatic example of radical protest strategies, which sometimes succeed but more often do not. They often energize a core of activists at the expense of broader public sympathy. Sometimes, if government players respond with aggressive tactics themselves, public sympathy remains favorable to radical protestors, a dynamic that reemerged dramatically in 2019. The public supported the occupation of the legislative council (LegCo) chambers after the police used tear gas, rubber bullets, and

*Gains and Losses.* James M. Jasper, Luke Elliott-Negri, Isaac Jabola-Carolus, Marc Kagan, Jessica Mahlbacher, Manès Weisskircher, and Anna Zhelnina, Oxford University Press. © Oxford University Press 2022. DOI: 10.1093/oso/9780197623251.003.0009

beanbag guns on young protesters and journalists. But there is no certainty of this. We have emphasized throughout the book that each loss or gain, whether small or large, sets conditions for future rounds of interaction. In the long run, partly under cover of the pandemic, the Xi government further tightened its grip on Hong Kong.

Alexei Navalny sustained the mobilizing potential of the Winter Revolution through the construction of his heroic public character. But by pursuing a personality strategy, he and his team had a hard time helping other candidates, especially after Navalny was neutralized. Members of Team Navalny were more able to help themselves, through fundraising and the strengthening of his foundation. Careers are a far cry from structural reform, but they were still a gain for those individuals, including for a while Navalny. Like OHKLP, Team Navalny created media credibility, networks of donors and followers, and other infrastructure for future fights. And Navalny has survived despite challenging Putin. But only barely. As we finish this book, he has endured another poisoning and is now in prison. In June 2021, the Moscow City Court disbanded his Anti-Corruption Foundation. Future reformers may be able to use some of the pieces Navalny built, but they are mere pieces.

We have tried to make sense of these six engagements by linking the dilemmas that central players faced in each, observing how decisions cluster and lead to packages of outcomes. The ability to create new arenas, in Mayor Murray's case, gave him ownership over the minimum wage issue, which heightened the stakes for him. For this reason, when the first arena failed to deliver, he persisted by creating a new, smaller, and tighter, arena. Creating new arenas is a strategy open to mayors and other top officials more often than to protestors. Arena-creation sets in motion a familiar package of risks, gains, and losses, and even when they cannot create new arenas, all players face similar choices about entering arenas. If they work hard they may come to own an arena, reshaping it without having to create it from scratch.

We have seen other familiar strategic packages, each based on a cluster of underlying dilemmas. Go down an electoral path, and you need to reach out to new audiences, perhaps alienating either your core supporters or a radical wing of your team. More attention to winning elections means less attention to occupations or other insurgent tactics. Because packages of outcomes are linked to strategic choices, they help us see the agency and decision-making underlying the correlations between strategies and outcomes identified by scholars like Gamson and Piven and Cloward.

In all cases, selecting strategies is also about choosing allies and teammates: the identity of a player depends on what leaders and subplayers want them to do. Some will be drawn to a strong personality, others repelled. Electoral and institutionalization packages also incorporate some individuals and exclude others. Individuals are emotionally and morally attached to certain tactics, or they may have special expertise in using them. Who you are and what you do always unfold together.

Just as strategic dilemmas are typically entwined, so packages may be linked to one another. You can pursue an electoral strategy with a strong personality or with a less personalistic approach. You can pursue a radical strategy, too, with or without a strong personality. And yet electoral and personality strategies *tend* to be found together, no doubt because elections feature individuals in a way that strategies such as occupations do not.

Packages like these begin as strategic intentions and decisions on the part of players, who see risks, hopes, and potential gains from their portfolio of activities. As they evolve, sometimes in predictable ways and other times in surprising ways, the packages encompass a distribution of gains and losses across the players that make up a movement or a coalition. The personality package highlights a leader, allowing her to gain publicity and attention, frequently at the expense of her followers and allies. The package suggests one extreme of the powerful-allies dilemma, in which the leader (the powerful ally) can go her own way if she wishes. The radical occupation package puts leaders in a more precarious situation, positioning radical subplayers to have more control over coalition strategy. The electoral package gives more power to large numbers of voters; the institutionalization package grants more to government bureaucrats charged with operating the programs. By defining players more carefully, we avoid the obfuscations of talking about "a movement" as winning this or losing that. The subplayers are the ones who gain and lose.

Strategic decisions do not automatically generate fixed packages of gains and losses. Players on all sides try to maneuver in response to other players. Protestors try to resolve their dilemmas, such as by finding a charismatic leader to appeal to multiple audiences. Their opponents try to invent new ways to block them or even destroy them as coherent players. But packages like these may represent common tendencies in strategic engagements.

We have labeled these six packages, loosely and tentatively, not because we expect other researchers to recognize identical packages in their own cases but because we expect them to find different variations of packages (as well as some idiosyncratic bundles of outcomes). It is those differences that will help scholars to sort out the winding pathways of strategic interaction. The packages are meant to suggest connections between dilemmas, or between tradeoffs. At the level of details, there is an infinite number of paths; at a broader level, we expect some familiar patterns, with family resemblances.

, If nothing else, we can distinguish packages that are primarily about the control of arenas—who creates or owns them, who staffs them or writes the rules—and packages mostly about the definition and reputation of players—how radical are they, how centered around one person, and are they machines for winning elections or something else? The language of players and arenas remains useful for understanding these different packages. We can also distinguish between owning an arena (like Mayor Murray did) and owning an issue that spills over various arenas (as the Graz Communists did). The concept of an "issue" reminds us of cultural processes and reputations that flow across arenas, even while they are attached to players.

If there is an overarching theme to our cases, it may be the tension between following the rules, accepting the system, and cozying up to power on the one hand and challenging, breaking, and pressuring powerful players from the outside on the other. In other words, naughty or nice. But even this contrast oversimplifies the many ways that each can be done, especially in and across diverse arenas. The simple question that began the long tradition of research on protest's impacts in the 1970s—does disruption work?—cannot really be answered in such a simple form.

———◇———

Although a players-and-arenas framework is meant to incorporate both structure and agency, we have leaned slightly toward the latter, toward a theory of action more than a theory of structure. We have highlighted the points of view of players, their feeling-thinking processes, and the ways that they anticipate barriers and try to deal with them. It is not that we do not believe in structures, but we feel they have been overemphasized in recent theories. We hope the concept of arenas captures what we know about structures but also makes them present in interactions.

The risk of interactionism is that it does not go beyond the "here and now," falling into "hodiecentrism," as Duyvendak and Fillieule (2015: 308) call it (literally, todayism). They also point to the solution: the dispositions that players carry with them, forged in previous efforts to test the limits and permeability of arenas and other structures. A player's past interactions, outcomes, and interpretations all shape their future actions, via skills, tastes in tactics, and other dispositions. Widely shared dispositions, or conventions, they say, "are both a restrictive framework for action and a strategic issue in the struggle for actors" (Duyvendak and Fillieule (2015: 312). Structures are not immutable, just damned hard to change. Nor are they hidden and mysterious; strategic players are typically well aware of the constraints they face.

Any fine-grained attention to players and arenas requires that we include players outside the movement coalition, whether these are elected officials, bureaucrats, funders, targets, or opponents. Mayor Murray was the key player in the battle over $15 in Seattle; city councilors were salient in Graz, New York, and Seattle. By focusing on arenas, we must pay attention to all the relevant players operating in them. Most of the time, protestors play smaller roles than elected officials, bureaucrats, corporations, and political parties.

This kind of microanalysis does not preclude explanations of "big" outcomes. One pattern of gains and losses will be widely recognized (and even more often, claimed) as a success for a player or a movement; another will be viewed as a failure. A series of arena changes may add up to a revolution, or it may fall short. Redefinitions of players and of arenas over time may entail the kind of incorporation of new groups into the polity that once interested political-opportunity researchers. Big outcomes like these are comprised of many smaller changes in players and arenas. Gains and losses can add up and fit together in big ways.

Because our building blocks are smaller things, they should apply to various kinds of regimes, as we have seen by including more authoritarian governments among our cases. Players in all sorts of strategic settings face similar dilemmas, such as which arena to prioritize or how many allies to recruit. Their resulting strategies and packages of outcomes will interact with the arenas they face. For instance, many of our cases featured electoral strategies with common challenges. Both KPÖ Graz in democratic Austria and Navalny's allies in authoritarian Russia faced electoral declines following the loss of a celebrated leader. In Graz's case, they were able to win back some of those seats in the long term, but in Navalny's, the government restricted opposition access to electoral arenas in subsequent years. The Russian government had considerable power to change electoral rules. In Hong Kong, the fierce competition over the limited geographically elected seats made it easier for a political outsider like Benny Tai to lead the efforts toward universal suffrage than for anyone associated with a political party.

Those arenas, electoral and others, differed significantly for the different cases. Regime types can be understood, perhaps even defined, through the language of players and arenas. First, they entail different rules within arenas, of how players can maneuver in pursuit of their goals. Second, they entail different relations between arenas, ranging from a balance of powers at one end to domination by a single arena at the other. Finally, regimes differ in the relationship between players and arenas. Arenas can be designed so that a single person can have—at least on paper—enormous influence over all arenas, including the power to create or eliminate arenas. A single player, a dictator, may also have informal influence that does not appear in the official rules, for instance, by paying or coercing other players to act as directed in the arenas. The rules of political arenas are often framed as the rule of law, but there are many ways they can be twisted, broken, and applied selectively.

Microdynamics transcend regime types. At some level, political action looks the same in royal courts, universal elections, and one-party regimes; in nations, cities, and unions. There are payments, persuasion, and coercion, as well as players jockeying for position; tradeoffs over alliances, tactics, and speed; emotions of pride, hate, and outrage; and the construction of heroes, villains, and victims. This is the stuff of any approach that is cultural, strategic, and interactive.

Even so, arenas differ. Most of the arenas we have examined are city-level. Smaller in scope and in numbers of players than national arenas, they typically provide access to more grassroots players. For that reason, we need to be cautious about generalizing from our results, as our portrait of strategic interaction may grant more influence to protest groups than they have in bigger arenas. But this is simply a variable to be included, not necessarily a scope condition. Similar dilemmas, strategies, and choices may face players in national arenas, but the packages may look different because the arenas may be larger, may be more rigid, or may harbor more powerful players. The gains and losses may add up differently in larger or smaller arenas, but the logic of following the interactions is the same. We may simply end up at different kinds of places, with different kind of packages.

When writing about politics, it is always tempting to derive practical lessons as well as explanatory ones. Do the lessons of Graz offer suggestions for other left-wing parties in Europe? Does Seattle provide a blueprint for other American movements in favor of a higher minimum wage or greater economic equality? Perhaps we can point out some tradeoffs to expect, some packages to try to manage. Identifying dilemmas may make them easier to manage, all the more so if players can learn about how others have grappled with the same issues. Strategic advice from scholars to players is usually fairly lame. But armed with lists of tradeoffs, dilemmas, and packages, we can offer checklists of hazards to look out for, mistakes to avoid, and risks to plan for. Half the game is avoiding your own blunders; the other half is recognizing and taking advantage of your opponents' blunders.

Our central lesson is sobering, hardly the stuff of hortatory rhetoric: yes, players—and movements—make gains, but no gains are pure: they are usually accompanied by some losses. We selected these cases because they had some prominent gains, more than the average protest movement. But all six cases reveal *combinations* of wins and losses. Even revolutions, which promise to change all players and arenas at once, entail complicated packages of gains and losses. When the dust settles, players of all sorts remain—strategizing, hoping, stumbling, and struggling.

# References

Abbott, Andrew. 2005. "The Idea of Outcome." In *The Politics of Method in the Human Sciences*. Edited by George Steinmetz. Durham, NC: Duke University Press.

Abbott, Andrew. 2007. "'Mechanisms and Relations': A Response to the Comments." *Sociologica, Italian Journal of Sociology Online*, no. 2 (Sept.–Oct.). https://doi.org/10.2383/24750.

Abers, Rebecca Neaera. 2000. *Inventing Local Democracy: Grassroots Politics in Brazil*. Boulder, CO: Lynne Rienner.

Accornero, Guya. 2021. "Contentious Buildings: The Struggle against Eviction in NYC's Lower East Side." *Current Sociology*. Online. https://doi.org/10.1177/0011392121 1012738.

Ahlquist, John S., and Margaret Levi. 2013. *In the Interest of Others*. Princeton, NJ: Princeton University Press.

Alexander, Jeffrey. 2006. *The Civil Sphere*. New York: Oxford University Press.

Alford, C. Fred. 2001. *Whistleblowers: Broken Lives and Organizational Power*. Ithaca: Cornell University Press.

Alford, Robert. 1998. *The Craft of Inquiry*. New York: Oxford University Press.

Altschuler, Daniel. 2013. "Participatory Budgeting in the United States: What Is Its Role?" *Nonprofit Quarterly* (April 18). https://nonprofitquarterly.org/2013/04/18/participat ory-budgeting-in-the-united-states-what-is-its-role/.

Alvarez, Sonia, and Arturo Escobar, eds. 1992. *The Making of Social Movements in Latin America*. Boulder, CO: Westview.

Amenta, Edwin. 2006. *When Social Movements Matter: The Townsend Plan and the Rise of Social Security*. Princeton, NJ: Princeton University Press.

Amenta, Edwin. 2014. "How to Analyze the Influence of Movements." *Contemporary Sociology* 43: 16–29.

Amenta, Edwin, Neal Caren, Elizabeth Chiarello, and Yang Su. 2010. "The Political Consequences of Social Movements." *Annual Review of Sociology* 36: 287–307.

Amenta, Edwin, and Nicole Shortt. 2020. "How Targets Influence the Influence of Movements." In *Protestors and Their Targets*. Edited by James M. Jasper and Brayden King. Philadelphia: Temple University Press.

Amenta, Edwin, and Michael P. Young. 1999. "Democratic States and Social Movements: Theoretical Arguments and Hypotheses." *Social Problems* 46: 153–168.

Andrews, Kenneth T. 2001. "Social Movements and Policy Implementation: The Mississippi Civil Rights Movement and the War on Poverty, 1965 to 1971." *American Sociological Review* 66: 71–95.

Andrews, Kenneth T. 2002. "Movement-Countermovement Dynamics and the Emergence of New Institutions: The Case of 'White Flight' Schools in Mississippi." *Social Forces* 80: 911–936.

Andrews, Kenneth T. 2004. *Freedom Is a Constant Struggle: The Mississippi Civil Rights Movement and Its Legacy*. Chicago: University of Chicago Press.

Andrews, Kenneth, and Sarah Gaby. 2020. "Protest Episodes: Shifting Actors and Targets in Local Movements." In *Protestors and Their Targets*. Edited by James M. Jasper and Brayden King. Philadelphia: Temple University Press.

Aronowitz, Stanley. 1973. *False Promises: The Shaping of American Working Class Consciousness*. New York: McGraw-Hill.

Baez, Nancy, and Andreas Hernandez. 2012. "Participatory Budgeting in the City: Challenging NYC's Development Paradigm from the Grassroots." *Interface* 4: 316–326.

Baillot, Hélène. 2017. *"Nous ne devons rien, nous ne paierons rien."* Jubilee 2000 et la redéfinition du mode de problématisation de la dette des pays pauvres (1996–2000). PhD diss., Université Paris 1 Panthéon-Sorbonne.

Baiocchi, Gianpaolo. 2005. *Militants and Citizens: The Politics of Participatory Democracy in Porto Alegre*. Stanford, CA: Stanford University Press.

Banaszak, Lee Ann. 1996. *Why Movements Succeed or Fail*. Princeton, NJ: Princeton University Press.

Banaszak, Lee Ann. 2010. *The Women's Movement: Inside and Outside the State*. New York: Cambridge University Press.

Banaszak, Lee Ann, and Heather L. Onderlin. 2016. "Public Opinion as a Movement Outcome." *Mobilization* 21: 361–378.

Barkan, Ross. 2014. "City Council Rejects Quinn Era with Rules Reform." *Observer*. Accessed September 15, 2016, http://observer.com/2014/04/city-council-rejects-quinn-era-with-rules-reform/.

Beach, Derek, and Rasmus Brun Pedersen. 2013. *Process-Tracing Methods*. Ann Arbor: University of Michigan Press.

Beckwith, Dave. n.d. "Community Organizing: People Power from the Grassroots." https://comm-org.wisc.edu/papers97/beckwith.htm.

Beckwith, Karen. 2016. "All Is Not lost: The 1984–85 British Miners' Strike and Mobilization after Defeat." In *The Consequences of Social Movements*. Edited by Lorenzo Bosi, Marco Giugni, and Katrin Uba. Cambridge: Cambridge University Press.

Bernstein, Mary C. 1997. "Celebration and Suppression: The Strategic Uses of Identity by the Lesbian and Gay Movement." *American Journal of Sociology* 103: 531–565.

Bernstein, Mary C. 2003. "Nothing Ventured, Nothing Gained? Conceptualizing Social Movement 'Success' in the Lesbian and Gay Movement." *Sociological Perspectives* 46: 353–379.

Berntzen, Lars Erik, and Manès Weisskircher. 2016. "Anti-Islamic PEGIDA beyond Germany: Explaining Differences in Mobilisation." *Journal of Intercultural Studies* 37: 556–573.

Biggs, Michael, and Kenneth Andrews. 2015. "Protest Campaigns and Movement Success." *American Sociological Review* 80: 1–28.

Bloom, Joshua. 2015. "The Dynamics of Opportunity and Insurgent Practice: How Black Anti-Colonialists Compelled Truman to Advocate Civil Rights." *American Sociological Review* 80: 391–415.

Bob, Clifford. 2012. *The Global Right Wing and the Clash of World Politics*. New York: Cambridge University Press.

Bosi, Lorenzo. 2016. "Social Movements and Interrelated Effects." *Revista Internacional de Sociologia* 74: e-047. http://dx.doi.org/10.3989/ris.2016.74.4.047.

Bosi, Lorenzo, Marco Giugni, and Katrin Uba, eds. 2016. *The Consequences of Social Movements*. Cambridge: Cambridge University Press.

Brenner, Aaron, Robert Brenner, and Calvin Winslow. 2010. *Rebel Rank and File: Labor Militancy and Revolt from below in the Long 1970s*. London: Verso.

Brockett, Charles D. 2005. *Political Movements and Violence in Central America*. Cambridge: Cambridge University Press.

Burstein, Paul. 1998. "Interest Organizations, Political Parties, and the Study of Democratic Politics." In *Social Movements and American Political Institutions*. Edited by Anne N. Costain and Andrew S. McFarland. Lanham, MD: Rowman and Littlefield.

Burstein, Paul. 1999. "Social Movements and Public Policy." In *How Social Movements Matter*. Edited by Mario Giugni, Doug McAdam, and Charles Tilly. Minneapolis: University of Minnesota Press.

Burstein, Paul. 2014. *American Public Opinion, Advocacy, and Policy in Congress*. New York: Cambridge University Press.

Burstein, Paul. 2020. "The Influence of Public Opinion and Advocacy on Public Policy." In Thomas Janoski, Cedric de Leon, Joya Misra, and Isaac William Martin, eds., *The New Handbook of Political Sociology*. Cambridge: Cambridge University Press.

Burstein, Paul, Rachel L. Einwohner, and Jocelyn A. Hollander. 1995. "The Success of Political Movements: A Bargaining Perspective." In *The Politics of Social Protest*. Edited by J. Craig Jenkins and Bert Klandermans. Minneapolis: University of Minnesota Press.

But, Joshua, and Emily Tsang. 2013. "Occupy Central Poised to Top July 1st Donation Chart." *South China Morning Post*, July 3. http://www.scmp.com/news/hong-kong/arti cle/1274135/occupy-central-poised-top-july-1-donation-chart.

Cammett, Melani, and Lauren MacLean. 2014. "Introduction." In *The Politics of Non-state Social Welfare*. Edited by Melani Cammett and Lauren MacLean. Ithaca, NY: Cornell University Press.

Case, Benjamin S. 2021. "Molotov Cocktails to Mass Marches: Strategic Nonviolence, Symbolic Violence, and the Mobilizing Effect of Riots." *Theory in Action* 14: 18–38.

Chan, Kinman. 2015. "Occupying Hong Kong: How Deliberation, Referendum and Civil Disobedience Played out in the Umbrella Movement." *International Journal of Human Rights* 12: 1–7.

Chenoweth, Erica, and Kurt Schock. 2015. "Do Contemporaneous Armed Challenges Affect the Outcomes of Mass Nonviolent Campaigns?" *Mobilization* 2: 427–451.

Chenoweth, Erica, and Maria J. Stephan. 2011. *Why Civil Resistance Works*. New York: Columbia University Press.

Cheung, Tony, and Tanna Chong. 2014. "Occupy Central Accused of Disenfranchising Moderates in Vote." *South China Morning Post*, May 7. http://www.scmp.com/news/hong-kong/article/1506490/occupy-central-founder-denies-deliberation-day-vote-was-hijacked.

China, State Council of the People's Republic of. 2014. "The Practice of the 'One Country, Two Systems' Policy in the Hong Kong Special Administrative Region." *Chinese Government Website*. http://english.gov.cn/archive/white_paper/2014/08/23/content_281474982986578.htm.

Combes, Hélène. 2015. "Political Parties and Legislators: A Latin American Perspective." In *Breaking Down the State*. Edited by Jan Willem Duyvendak and James M. Jasper. Amsterdam: Amsterdam University Press.

Combes, Hélène, and Olivier Fillieule. 2011. "De la répression considérée dans ses rapports à l'activité protestataire." *Revue française de science politique* 61: 1047–1072.

Community Voices Heard. 2015. "Draft Revision Proposal—Cycle V: Participatory Budgeting NYC Steering Committee." Unpublished memo.

Creasap, Kimberly A. 2022. *Making a Scene: Urban Landscapes, Gentrification, and Social Movements in Sweden*. Philadelphia: Temple University Press.

Davis, Michael. 2016. "Promises to Keep: The Basic Law, the 'Umbrella Movement' and Democratic Reform in Hong Kong." In *Information Politics, Protests, and Human Rights in the Digital Age*. Edited by Mahmood Monshipouri. Cambridge: Cambridge University Press.

della Porta, Donatella, and Daniela Chironi. 2015. "Movements in Parties: OccupyPD." *Partecipazione e Conflitto* 8: 59–96.

della Porta, Donatella, Joseba Fernández, Hara Kouki, and Lorenzo Mosca. 2017. *Movement Parties against Austerity*. Malden: Polity.

Dobry, Michel. 1986. *Sociologie des Crises Politiques*. Paris: Sciences Po.

Downs, Steve. 1998. "New York Transit between Old and New Directions." *Solidarity Newsletter*. https://solidarity-us.org/node/860.

Downs, Steve. 2006. *Hell on Wheels*. Detroit, MI: Solidarity.

Drury, John, Christopher Cocking, Joseph Beale, Charlotte Hanson, and Faye Rapley. 2005. "The Phenomenology of Empowerment in Collective Action." *British Journal of Social Psychology* 44: 309–328.

Drury, John, and Steve Reicher. 2005. "Explaining Enduring Empowerment." *European Journal of Social Psychology* 35: 35–58.

Dunlop, John T. 1958. *Industrial Relations Systems*. New York: Holt.

Dunphy, Richard, and Tim Bale. 2011. "The Radical Left in Coalition Government: Towards a Comparative Measurement of Success and Failure." *Party Politics* 17: 488–504.

Duverger, Maurice. 1954. *Political Parties. Their Organization and Activity in the Modern State*. New York: Wiley.

Duyvendak, Jan Willem, and Olivier Fillieule. 2015. "Patterned Fluidity: An Interactionist Perspective as a Tool for Exploring Contentious Politics." In *Players and Arenas*. Edited by James M. Jasper and Jan Willem Duyvendak. Amsterdam: Amsterdam University Press.

Duyvendak, Jan Willem, and James M. Jasper, eds. 2015. *Breaking Down the State*. Amsterdam: Amsterdam University Press.

Eisenstein, Hester. 1996. *Inside Agitators: Australian Femocrats and the State*. Philadelphia: Temple University Press.

Ellefsen, Rune. 2021. "The Unintended Consequences of Escalated Repression." *Mobilization* 26: 87–108.

Elster, Jon. 1989. *Nuts and Bolts for the Social Sciences*. Cambridge: Cambridge University Press.

Elster, Jon. 1998. "A Plea for Mechanisms." In *Social Mechanisms: An Introductory Essay*. Edited by Peter Hedström and Richard Swedberg. Cambridge: Cambridge University Press.

English, Richard. 2016. *Does Terrorism Work?* Oxford: Oxford University Press.

Evans, Erin. 2015. "Stumbling Blocks or Stepping Stones? The Problems and Promises of Policy Reform Goals for the Animal Advocacy Movement." *Sociological Perspectives* 59: 835–854.

Faludi, Susan. 1991. *Backlash*. New York: Crown.

Fantasia, Rick. 1988. *Cultures of Solidarity*. Berkeley: University of California Press.

Fantasia, Rick, and Judith Stepan-Norris. 2004. "The Labor Movement in Motion." In *The Blackwell Companion to Social Movements*. Edited by David A. Snow, Sarah A. Soule, and Hanspeter Kriesi. Malden, MA: Blackwell.

Feit, Josh. 2014. "What Do We Want? $15! When Do We Want It? In a Little While!" *Seattle Met* (July 30). http://www.seattlemet.com/articles/2014/7/30/history-of-seattles-minimum-wage-law-august-2014.

Fetner, Tina. 2008. *How the Religious Right Shaped Lesbian and Gay Activism.* Minneapolis: University of Minnesota Press.

Fillieule, Olivier. 2010. "Some Elements of an Interactionist Approach to Political Disengagement." *Social Movement Studies* 9: 1–15.

Fillieule, Olivier, Sophie Béroud, Camille Masclet, and Isabelle Sommier, eds. 2018. *Changer le Monde, Changer sa Vie.* Paris: Actes Sud.

Flesher Fominaya, Cristina. 2010. "Creating Cohesion from Diversity: The Challenge of Collective Identity Formation in the Global Justice Movement." *Sociological Inquiry* 80: 377–404.

Fligstein, Neil J., and Doug McAdam. 2012. *A Theory of Fields.* New York: Oxford University Press.

Freeman, Jo. 1972. "The Tyranny of Structurelessness." *Berkeley Journal of Sociology* 17: 151–164.

Freeman, Joshua. 1989. *In Transit: The Transport Workers Union in New York City, 1933–66.* Philadelphia: Temple University Press.

Gamson, William A. 1975. *The Strategy of Social Protest.* Homewood, IL: Dorsey.

Ganuza, Ernesto, and Gianpaolo Baiocchi, 2012. "The Power of Ambiguity: How Participatory Budgeting Travels the Globe." *Journal of Public Deliberation* 8: art. 8.

Ganz, Marshall. 2000. "Resources and Resourcefulness: Strategic Capacity in the Unionization of California Agriculture, 1959–1966." *American Journal of Sociology* 105: 1003–1062.

Gärtner, Heinz. 1979. *Zwischen Moskau und Österreich. Analyse einer sowjetabhängigen KP.* Vienna: Braumüller.

Gitlin, Todd. 1980. *The Whole World Is Watching.* Berkeley: University of California Press.

Giugni, Marco. 1999. "Introduction." In *How Social Movements Matter.* Edited by Marco Giguni, Doug McAdam, and Charles Tilly. Minneapolis: University of Minnesota Press.

Giugni, Marco. 2007. "Useless Protest?" *Mobilization* 12: 53–77.

Goldfarb, Jeffrey. 2006. *The Politics of Small Things.* Chicago: University of Chicago Press.

Goldstein, Sarah. Interviews. 2003–2004. Transport Workers Union Local 100: Noel Acevedo, Naomi Allen, Eladio Diaz, Steve Downs, Josh Fraidstern, Darlyne Lawson, Clarence Little, Roger Toussaint, Marian Swerdlow. New York: Tamiment Labor Library, New York University.

Goldstone, Jack. 1980. "The Weakness of Organization." *American Journal of Sociology* 85: 1017–1042.

Golos. 2013. Predvaritelnoye zayavlenye po itogam nablydeniya za vyborami mera Moskvy 8 sentyabya 2013 (A preliminary statement on the observation results at the Moscow Mayor election on September 8, 2013). https://www.golosinfo.org/ru/articles/204.

Golosov, Grigory. 2012. "The 2012 Political Reform in Russia: The Interplay of Liberalizing Concessions and Authoritarian Corrections." *Problems of Post-Communism* 59: 3–14.

Grabar, Henry. 2015. "New York City's Second-Most Powerful Politician Isn't Waiting in the Wings." *Next City*, September 7. https://nextcity.org/features/view/new-york-city-powerful-council-melissa-mark-viverito.

Gupta, Devashree. 2009. "The Power of Incremental Outcomes." *Mobilization* 14: 417–432.

Gusfield, Joseph. 1981. *The Culture of Public Problems. Drinking-Driving and the Symbolic Order*. Chicago: University of Chicago Press.

Hagen, Ryan, Kinga Makovi, and Peter Bearman. 2013. "The Influence of Political Dynamics on Southern Lynch Mob Formation and Dynamics." *Social Forces* 92: 757–787.

Haines, Herbert H. 1984. "Black Radicalization and the Funding of Civil Rights: 1957–1970." *Social Problems* 32: 31–43.

Halfmann, Drew. 2010. *The Rules of War*. Chicago: University of Chicago Press.

Han, Hahrie, and Dara Strolovich. 2015. "What the Tea Party and Occupy Wall Street Illuminate about Bystander Publics as Proto-Players." In *Players and Arenas*. Edited by James M. Jasper and Jan Willem Duyvendak. Amsterdam: Amsterdam University Press.

Harvey, Neil. 2001. *The Chiapas Rebellion: The Struggle for Land and Democracy*. Durham, NC: Duke University.

Helander, Sofia. 2016. "Movement and Empowerment: Explaining the Political Consequences of Activism." *Revista Internacional de Sociologia* 74: e-049. https//:doi. dx.10.3989/ris.2016.74.4.049.

Hirschman, Albert. 1970. *Exit, Voice, and Loyalty: Responses to Decline in Firms, Organizations, and States*. Cambridge, MA: Harvard University Press.

Holden, Dominic. 2014. "Leaked E-Mail Shows Big Business Trying to Use Small Businesses to Weaken $15 Minimum Wage." *The Stranger*, April 8. http://www.thestran ger.com/slog/archives/2014/04/08/leaked-e-mail-shows-big-business-trying-to-use-small-businesses-and-workers-to-weaken-15-minimum-wage.

Hong Kong Special Administrative Region, Government of. 2017. "Voter Registration Statistics: Geographic Constituency 2007–2016." Government of Hong Kong Special Administrative Region Website, https://www.voterregistration.gov.hk/eng/statistic2 016.html.

Hyman, Richard. 1989. "The Politics of Workplace Trade Unionism: Recent Tendencies and Some Problems for Theory." In *The Political Economy of Industrial Relations*. Edited by Richard Hyman. London: Palgrave Macmillan.

Jabola-Carolus, Isaac. 2017. "Growing Grassroots Democracy: Dynamics Outcomes in Building New York City's Participatory Budgeting Program." *New Political Science* 39: 109–125.

Jabola-Carolus, Isaac, Luke Elliott-Negri, James M. Jasper, Jessica Mahlbacher, Manès Weisskircher, and Anna Zhelnina. 2020. "Strategic Interaction Sequences: The Institutionalization of Participatory Budgeting in New York City." *Social Movement Studies* 19: 640–656.

Jasper, James M. 1990. *Nuclear Politics*. Princeton: Princeton University Press.

Jasper, James M. 1997. *The Art of Moral Protest*. Chicago: University of Chicago Press.

Jasper, James M. 2004. "A Strategic Approach to Collective Action: Looking for Agency in Social Movement Choices." *Mobilization* 9: 1–16.

Jasper, James M. 2006. *Getting Your Way: Strategic Dilemmas in the Real World*. Chicago: University of Chicago Press.

Jasper, James M. 2010. "Social Movement Theory Today: Toward a Theory of Action?" *Sociology Compass* 10: 965–976.

Jasper, James M. 2012a. "¿De la Estructura a la Acción? La Teoría de los Movimientos Sociales después de los Grandes Paradigmas." *Sociológica* 27: 7–48.

Jasper, James M. 2012b. "Introduction: From Political Opportunity Structures to Strategic Interaction." In *Contention in Context*. Edited by Jeff Goodwin and James M. Jasper. Stanford, CA: Stanford University Press.

Jasper, James M. 2015. "Introduction: Playing the Game." In *Players and Arenas*. Edited by James M. Jasper and Jan Willem Duyvendak. Amsterdam: Amsterdam University Press.

Jasper, James M. 2018a. "Afterword: Comparative versus Historical Research." *Social Movement Studies* 18: 130–136.

Jasper, James M. 2018b. *The Emotions of Protest*. Chicago: University of Chicago Press.

Jasper, James M. 2021. "Linking Arenas: Structuring Concepts in the Study of Politics and Protest." *Social Movement Studies* 20: 243–257.

Jasper, James M., and Jan Willem Duyvendak, eds. 2015. *Players and Arenas*. Amsterdam: Amsterdam University Press.

Jasper, James M., and Brayden G. King, eds. 2020. *Protestors and their Targets*. Philadelphia: Temple University Press.

Jasper, James M., and Aidan McGarry. 2015. "Introduction: The Identity Dilemma, Social Movements, and Contested Identity." In *The Identity Dilemma: Social Movements and Collective Identity*. Edited by Aidan McGarry and James M. Jasper. Philadelphia: Temple University Press.

Jasper, James M., and Jane Poulsen. 1993. "Fighting Back: Vulnerabilities, Blunders, and Countermobilization by the Targets in Three Animal Rights Campaigns." *Sociological Forum* 8: 639–657.

Jasper, James M., Michael P. Young, and Elke Zuern. 2018. "Character Work in Social Movements." *Theory and Society* 47: 113–131.

Jasper, James M., Michael P. Young, and Elke Zuern. 2020. *Public Characters: The Politics of Reputation and Blame*. New York: Oxford University Press.

Jones, Tod, Ali Mozaffari, and James M. Jasper. 2018. "Heritage Contests: What Can We Learn from Social Movements?" *Heritage & Society* 10: 1–25.

Kagan, Marc. 2016. "Re-Examining New York City's 1980 Transit Strike from the Bottom-Up." Unpublished manuscript.

Kagan, Marc. Interviews. 2014–2016. Transport Workers Union Local 100: Sean Ahern, Stanley Aronowitz, Steve Downs, Marty Goodman, Sonny Hall. New York: Tamiment Labor Library, New York University.

Karni, Annie. 2013. "NY City Council Speaker Candidates Differ on Participatory Budgeting." *NY Daily News: The Daily Politics*. Accessed March 3, 2016. http://www.nydailynews.com/blogs/dailypolitics/ny-city-council-speaker-candidates-differ-participatory-budgeting-blog-entry-1.1697311.

Kasdan, Alexa, and Lindsay Cattell. 2012. *A People's Budget: A Research and Evaluation Report on the Pilot Year of Participatory Budgeting in New York City*. New York: Community Development Project at the Urban Justice Center.

Kasdan, Alexa, Erin Markman, and Pat Convey. 2014. *A People's Budget: A Research and Evaluation Report on Participatory Budgeting in New York City, Cycle 3*. New York: Community Development Project at the Urban Justice Center.

Katz, Maksim. 2013. "Organizatsiya shtaba Navalnogo—Pervaya nedelya" [Organizing Navalny's Headquarters—The First Week]. *LiveJournal*. November 6. http://maxkatz.livejournal.com/200574.html.

Katz, Maksim. 2014. "Organizatsiya shtaba Navalnogo—Otdel vstrech kandidata s izbiratelyami" [Organizing Navalny's Headquarters—The Department of Candidate's Meetings with Voters]. April 14. http://maxkatz.livejournal.com/251325.html.

Katz, Richard. 2014. "Political Parties." In *Comparative Politics*. Edited by Daniele Caramani. Oxford: Oxford University Press.

Katz, Richard, and Peter Mair. 1995. "Changing Models of Party Organization and Party Democracy. The Emergence of the Cartel Party." *Party Politics* 1: 5–28.

Katznelson, Ira. 1981. *City Trenches: Urban Politics and the Patterning of Class in the United States*. New York: Random House.

Keck, Margaret, and Kathryn Sikkink. 1998. *Activists beyond Borders. Advocacy Networks in International Politics*. Ithaca, NY: Cornell University Press.

King, Brayden G. 2008. "A Political Mediation Model of Corporate Response to Social Movement Activism." *Administrative Science Quarterly* 53: 395–421.

King, Brayden G., Keith G. Bentele, and Sarah A. Soule. 2007. "Protest and Policymaking." *Social Forces* 86: 137–164.

King, Brayden G., Marie Cornwall, and Eric C. Dahlin. 2005. "Winning Woman Suffrage One Step at a Time." *Social Forces* 83: 1211–1234.

Kitschelt, Herbert P. 1986. "Political Opportunity Structures and Political Protest." *British Journal of Political Science* 16: 57–85.

Kitschelt, Herbert P. 1989. *The Logics of Party Formation*. Ithaca, NY: Cornell University Press.

Kolb, Felix. 2007. *Protest and Opportunities: The Political Outcomes of Social Movements*. Frankfurt, Germany: Campus Verlag.

Kong, Tsung-gan. 2019. "In Full: The Testimony of Protest Organiser Chan Kin-man at the Trial of the Umbrella Movement 9." *Hong Kong Free Press*. January 12. https://hongkongfp.com/2019/01/12/full-transcript-umbrella-movement-convener-chan-kin-mans-testimony-trial-occupy-9/.

KPÖ Steiermark. 2012. Landesprogramm: Analysen und programmatische Vorschläge der KPÖ Steiermark. https://www.kpoe-steiermark.at/dl/59a0b5b7aa721c376e894133c6bae09b/Landesprogramm%202012.pdf?target=1&target=0.

KPÖ Steiermark. 2020. "167.750 Euro für 1.577 SteierInnen: Warum KPÖ-PolitikerInnen zwei Drittel ihrer Gehälter spenden. Das war der Tag der offenen Konten 2020." https://www.kpoe-steiermark.at/tag-der-offenen-konten-2020.phtml.

Kriesi, Hanspeter, Ruud Koopmans, Jan Willem Duyvendak, and Marco G. Giugni. 1995. *New Social Movements in Western Europe*. Minneapolis: University of Minnesota Press.

Krinsky, John, and Colin Barker. 2009. "Movement Strategizing as Developmental Learning." In *Culture, Social Movements and Protest*. Edited by Hank Johnston. Cambridge. UK: Ashgate.

Kurzman, Charles. 2004. *The Unthinkable Revolution in Iran*. Cambridge, MA: Harvard University Press.

Kurzman, Charles. 2012. "The Arab Spring Uncoiled." *Mobilization* 17: 377–390.

La Botz, Dan. 2010. "The Tumultuous Teamsters of the 1970s." In *Rebel Rank and File: Labor Militancy and Revolt from below in the Long 1970s*. Edited by Aaron Brenner, Robert Brenner, and Calvin Winslow. London: Verso.

Laclau, Ernesto, and Chantal Mouffe. 1985. *Hegemony and Socialist Strategy*. London: Verso.

Lam, Jeffie. 2014. "Beijing's White Paper Makes Passing Reform Tougher, Carrie Lam Says." *South China Morning Post*, June 20. http://www.scmp.com/news/hong-kong/article/1536448/beijings-white-paper-makes-passing-reforms-tougher-carrie-lam-says.

Lam, Jeffie, and Keith Zhai. 2014. "Cyberattacks against Occupy Central Poll Traced to Mainland Firms' Computers in Hong Kong." *South China Morning Post*, June 24. cmp.com/news/hong-kong/article/1538965/cyberattacks-against-occupy-poll-traced-mainland-firms-computers-hong.

Lander, Brad. 2016. "Bob Hardt Doesn't Want to Participate . . . but We Hope You Will." *Medium.com*. https://medium.com/@bradlander/bob-hardt-doesn-t-want-to-part icipate-but-we-hope-you-will-e2a8c374b374#.b9kzs4gk1.

Lander, Brad, and Michael Freedman-Schnapp. 2012. "Making—and Governing—Places for Democracy." In *Beyond Zuccotti Park: Freedom of Assembly and the Occupation of Public Space*. Edited by Ron Shiffman, Rick Bell, Lance J. Brown, and Lynne Elizabeth. Oakland, CA: New Village Press.

Latour, Bruno. 2005. *Reassembling the Social*. Oxford: Oxford University Press.

Lerner, Josh, and Donata Secondo. 2012. "By the People, for the People: Participatory Budgeting from the Bottom Up in North America." *Journal of Public Deliberation* 8: article 2.

Leung, Priscilla. 2013. "Implementing Dual Universal Suffrage." Speech presented at *Business and Professionals Alliance for Hong Kong*. http://bpahk.org/eng/speech-imple menting-dual-universal-suffrage-priscilla-leung/.

Levada Center. 2013. "Kandidatam Kapayut Procenty." [Candidates' Percentages Grow]. September 2. http://www.levada.ru/2013/09/02/kandidatam-kapayut-protsenty/.

Levi, Margaret, David Olson, Jon Agnone, and Devin Kelly. 2009. "Union Democracy Reexamined." *Politics & Society* 37: 203–228.

Lichbach, Mark I. 1995. *The Rebel's Dilemma*. Ann Arbor: University of Michigan Press.

Lichtenstein, Nelson. 2002. *The State of the Union*. Princeton, NJ: Princeton University Press.

Lipman, Maria. 2016. "How Putin Silences Dissent: Inside the Kremlin's Crackdown." *Foreign Affairs* 95: 38–46.

Lipset, Seymour Martin, Martin A. Trow, and James S. Coleman. 1956. *Union Democracy; the Internal Politics of the International Typographical Union*. Garden City, NY: Doubleday.

Lipsky, Michael. 1980. *Street-Level Bureaucracy: Dilemmas of the Individual in Public Services*. New York: Russell Sage.

Luders, Joseph E. 2010. *The Civil Rights Movement and the Logic of Social Change*. New York: Cambridge University Press.

Luders, Joseph E. 2016. "Feminist Mobilization and the Politics of Rights." In *The Consequences of Social Movements*. Edited by Lorenzo Bosi, Marco Giugni, and Katrin Uba. Cambridge: Cambridge University Press.

Magun, Artemy, and Svetlana Yerpylyova, eds. 2014. *Politika Apolitichnykh* (The Politics of the Apolitical). Moscow: Novoe Literaturnoe Obozrenie.

Mallard, Grégoire. 2014. *Fallout: Nuclear Diplomacy in an Age of Global Fracture*. Chicago: University of Chicago Press.

Mansbridge, Jane J. 1986. *Why We Lost the ERA*. Chicago: University of Chicago Press.

Markoff, John. 1997. "Peasants Help Destroy an Old Regime and Defy a New One." *American Journal of Sociology* 102: 1113–1142.

Martin, John Levi. 2011. *The Explanation of Social Action*. New York: Oxford University Press.

Martin, Nick, Sarah de Lange, and Wouter van der Brug. 2020. "Holding on to Voters in Volatile Times: Bonding Voters through Party Links with Civil Society." *Party Politics*. Advance Online publication.

McAdam, Doug. 1982. *Political Process and the Development of Black Insurgency 1930–1970*. Chicago: University of Chicago Press.

McAdam, Doug, and Hilary Schaffer Boudet. 2012. *Putting Social Movements in Their Place*. New York: Cambridge University Press.

McAdam, Doug, Sidney Tarrow, and Charles Tilly. 2001. *Dynamics of Contention*. New York: Cambridge University Press.

McCammon, Holly J. 2012. *The US Women's Jury Movements and Strategic Adaptation: A More Just Verdict*. New York: Cambridge University Press.

McCarthy, Irving Lee, Tim Schermerhorn. Tamiment Labor Library, New York University.

McCarthy, John, and Mayer Zald. 1977. "Resource Mobilization and Social Movements: A Partial Theory." *American Journal of Sociology* 82: 1212–1241.

McDonnell, Mary-Hunter, Brayden G. King, and Sarah A. Soule. 2015. "A Dynamic Process Model of Private Politics: Activist Targeting and Corporate Receptivity to Social Challenges." *American Sociological Review* 80: 654–678.

McGarry, Aidan, and James M. Jasper, eds. 2015. *The Identity Dilemma: Social Movements and Collective Identity*. Philadelphia: Temple University Press.

McVeigh, Rory, David Cunningham, and Justin Farrell. 2014. "Political Polarization as a Social Movement Outcome." *American Sociological Review* 79: 1144–1171.

Melgar, Teresa R. 2014. "A Time of Closure? Participatory Budgeting in Porto Alegre, Brazil, after the Workers' Party Era." *Journal of Latin American Studies* 46: 121–149.

Melucci, Alberto. 1989. *Nomads of the Present*. Philadelphia: Temple University Press.

Meyer, David. 1990. *A Winter of Discontent*. New York: Praeger.

Meyer, David. 2006. "Claiming Credit: Stories of Movement Influence as Outcomes." *Mobilization* 11: 201–229.

Meyer, David S., and Suzanne Staggenborg. 1996. "Movements, Countermovements, and the Structure of Political Opportunity." *American Journal of Sociology* 101: 1628–1660.

Meyer, Rachel, and Howard Kimeldorf. 2015. "Eventful Subjectivity: The Experiential Sources of Solidarity." *Journal of Historical Sociology* 28: 429–457.

Mische, Ann. 2015. "Fractal Arenas. Dilemmas of Style and Strategy in a Brazilian Student Congress." In *Players and Arenas*. Edited by James M. Jasper and Jan Willem Duyvendak. Amsterdam: Amsterdam University Press.

Morris, Aldon D., and Suzanne Staggenborg. 2004. "Leadership in Social Movements." In *Blackwell Companion to Social Movements*. Edited by David A. Snow, Sarah A. Soule, and Hanspeter Kriesi. Malden, MA: Blackwell.

Moses, Joel C. 2015. "Putin and Russian Subnational Politics in 2014." *Demokratizatsiya: The Journal of Post-Soviet Democratization* 23: 181–203.

New York City Council. 2014. "Participatory Budgeting: Proposal for 2014–15 Cycle." New York. Unpublished memo.

Ngo, Emily. 2016. "Melissa Mark-Viverito Eyes Political Options in NYC, Puerto Rico." *Newsday*, July 31. http://www.newsday.com/news/new-york/melissa-mark-viverito-eyes-political-options-in-nyc-puerto-rico-1.12116704.

Ninth Meeting of the Coordinating Board of the Russian Opposition. 2013. June 15. https://www.youtube.com/watch?v=yM7HhEY_wxo.

O'Connor, Meg. 2016. "City Council Raises Provoke Questions About Staff Pay." *Gotham Gazette*, March 8. http://www.gothamgazette.com/index.php/city/6211-city-council-pay-raises-provoke-questions-about-staff-pay.

Pagis, Julie. 2018. *May '68*. Amsterdam: Amsterdam University Press.

Parteder, Franz Stephan. 2013. "Die Wohnungsfrage in der Politik der KPÖ Graz." Referat von Franz Parteder in Berlin-Spandau. Accessed February 19, 2017. www.

kpoe-steiermark.at/der-stellenwert-der-wohnungsfrage-in-der-politik-der-kpoe-graz.phtml.

Participatory Budgeting Project. 2013a. "Best of 2013 and Happy Holidays." Accessed September 15, 2016. http://www.participatorybudgeting.org/blog/best-of-2013-happy-holidays/.

Participatory Budgeting Project. 2013b. "New York Election Results: Participatory Budgeting Wins Big." Accessed March 3, 2016. http://www.participatorybudgeting.org/blog/new-york-election-results-participatory-budgeting-wins-big/.

Payne, Charles M. 1995. *I've Seen the Light of Freedom*. Berkeley: University of California Press.

Perlman, Selig. 1949. *A Theory of the Labor Movement*. New York: A.M. Kelley.

Peterson, Abby. 2016. "The Institutionalization Process of a Neo-Nazi Movement Party." In *The Consequences of Social Movements*. Edited by Lorenzo Bosi, Marco Giugni, and Katrin Uba. Cambridge: Cambridge University Press.

Petrocik, John. 1996. "Issue Ownership in Presidential Elections, with a 1980 Case Study." *American Journal of Political Science* 40: 825–850.

Piccio, Daniela R. 2016. "The Impact of Social Movements on Political Parties." In *The Consequences of Social Movements*. Edited by Lorenzo Bosi, Marco Giugni, and Katrin Uba. Cambridge: Cambridge University Press.

Pierson, Paul. 1993. "Review: When Effect Becomes Cause: Policy Feedback and Political Change." *World Politics* 45: 595–628.

Piven, Frances Fox. 2006. *Challenging Authority*. Lanham, MD: Rowman and Littlefield.

Piven, Frances Fox, and Richard A. Cloward. 1977. *Poor People's Movements*. New York: Random House.

Polletta, Francesca. 2006. *It Was Like a Fever*. Chicago: University of Chicago Press.

Pratt Institute. 2010. *From Budget Cuts to a People's Budget? Connecting Participatory Planning and Public Budgets in New York*. New York. Accessed January 13, 2015. http://vimeo.com/16545673.

Pratt Institute. 2012. *International Participatory Budgeting Conference*. New York. Accessed April 16, 2017. http://vimeo.com/40615971.

Pressman, Jeffrey L., and Aaron Wildavsky. 1973. *Implementation*. Berkeley: University of California Press.

Progressive Caucus. 2010. "Statement of Principles." Accessed April 16, 2017. http://graphics8.nytimes.com/packages/pdf/nyregion/2010/20100323_NYCCPCprincip les.pdf.

Public Opinion Programme, University of Hong Kong. 2014. "Results of the 6.22 Civil Referendum." June. https://www.hkupop.hku.hk/english/release/release1164.html.

Report. 2013. Alexey Navalny. Kandidat v mery Moskwy 2013. Otchet o predvybornoy kampanii. http://report.navalny.ru/media/navalny_report.pdf.

Right to the City NYC. 2009. *Right to the City–New York City: Policy Platform, 2009*. New York. Accessed February 20, 2015. http://fiercenyc.org/sites/default/files/resour ces/0944_RTTCNYCPlatform.pdf.

Robinson, Jo Ann. 1987. *The Montgomery Bus Boycott and the Women Who Started It*. Knoxville: University of Tennessee Press.

Roxborough, Ian. 2015. "The Military: The Mutual Determination of Strategy in Ireland, 1912–1921." In *Breaking Down the State*. Edited by Jan Willem Duyvendak and James M. Jasper. Amsterdam: Amsterdam University Press.

Saunders, Clare. 2013. *Environmental Networks and Social Movement Theory*. New York: Bloomsbury Academic.

Schwartz, Michael. 1976. *Radical Protest and Social Structure*. New York: Academic Press.

Schwedler, Jillian. 2018. "Routines and Ruptures in Anti-Israeli Protests in Jordan." In *Microfoundations of the Arab Uprisings*. Edited by Frédéric Volpi and James M. Jasper. Amsterdam: Amsterdam University Press.

Seiß, Reinhard. 2011. "Zwischen Anspruch und Wirklichkeit. Die Entwicklung der Wiener Wohnbaupolitik." In *Ökosystem Wien. Die Naturgeschichte einer Stadt*. Edited by Roland Berger, and Friedrich Ehrendorfer. Vienna: Böhlau Verlag.

Semenov, Andrei. 2017. "Against the Stream: Political Opposition in the Russian Regions During the 2012–2016 Electoral Cycle." *Demokratizatsiya: The Journal of Post-Soviet Democratization* 25: 481–502.

Shorter, Edward, and Charles Tilly. 1971. "The Shape of Strikes in France 1830–1960." *Comparative Studies in Society and History* 13: 60–86.

Silent Majority for Hong Kong. 2014. *They Can Kill This City*. People's Republic of China. https://www.youtube.com/watch?v=QEH_TdDwXjo.

Skocpol, Theda. 1979. *States and Social Revolutions*. Cambridge: Cambridge University Press.

Smyth, Regina, and Irina V. Soboleva. 2016. "Navalny's Gamesters: Protest, Opposition Innovation, and Authoritarian Stability in Russia." *Russian Politics* 1: 347–371.

Snyder, David, and William R. Kelly. 1976. "Industrial Violence in Italy, 1878–1903." *American Journal of Sociology* 82: 131–162.

Soule, Sarah A., and Brayden G. King. 2006. "The Stages of the Policy Process and the Equal Rights Amendment, 1972–1982." *American Journal of Sociology* 111: 1871–1909.

Sørensen, Majken Jul, and Brian Martin. 2014. "The Dilemma Action: Analysis of an Activist Technique." *Peace & Change* 39: 73–100.

Stinchcombe, Arthur. 1991. "The Conditions of Fruitfulness of Theorizing about Mechanisms in Social-Science." *Philosophy of the Social Sciences* 21: 367–388.

Stoddart, Mark C. J., Alice Mattoni, and Elahe Nezhadhossein. 2021. "Environmental Movement Interventions in Tourism and Energy Development in the North Atlantic." *Contention* 8: 74–98.

Su, Celina. 2015. "Redemocratizing Democracy, or Affirmative Governmentality? New York's Recent Experiences with Participatory Budgeting." Paper presented at the Annual Interpretive Policy Analysis Conference, Policies and Their Publics: Discourses, Actors, and Power, Lille, France.

Su, Celina. 2018. "Managed Participation: City Agencies and Micropolitics in Participatory Budgeting." *Nonprofit and Voluntary Sector Quarterly* 47(4S): 76S–96S.

Summers-Effler, Erika. 2010. *Laughing Saints and Righteous Heroes*. Chicago: University of Chicago Press.

Swerdlow, Marian. 1998. *Underground Woman: My Four Years as a NYC Subway Conductor*. Philadelphia: Temple University Press.

Tai, Benny Yiu-ting. 2013. "公民抗命的最大殺傷力武器." *Hong Kong Economic Journal* (January 16). http://www1.hkej.com//dailynews/article/id/654855/公民抗命的最大殺傷力武器.

Tattersall, Amanda. 2013. *Power in Coalition: Strategies for Strong Unions and Social Change*. Ithaca, NY: Cornell University Press.

Tausch, Nicole, and Julia C. Becker. 2012. "Emotional Reactions to Success and Failure of Collective Action as Predictors of Future Action Intentions." *British Journal of Social Psychology* 52: 525–542.

Taylor, Kate. 2014. "An Unassuming Liberal Makes a Rapid Ascent to Power Broker." *New York Times* (January 23). http://www.nytimes.com/2014/01/24/nyregion/una ssuming-liberal-suddenly-becomes-council-kingmaker.html.

Taylor, Verta. 1989. "The Women's Movement in Abeyance." *American Sociological Review* 54: 761–775.

Thompson, AK. 2010. *Black Bloc, White Riot*. Oakland, CA: AK Press.

Tilly, Charles. 1978. *From Mobilization to Revolution*. Reading, MA: Addison-Wesley.

Tilly, Charles. 1999. "From Interactions to Outcomes." In *How Social Movements Matter*. Edited by Marco Giugni et al. Minneapolis: University of Minnesota Press.

Touraine, Alain, Francois Dubet, Michel Wieviorka, and Jan Strzelecki. 1983. *Solidarity*. Cambridge: Cambridge University Press.

Trevizo, Dolores. 2006. "Between Zapata and Che: A Comparison of Social Movement Success and Failure in Mexico." *Social Science History* 30: 197–229.

Uba, Katrin, and Eduardo Romanos. 2016. "Introduction: Rethinking the Consequences of Social Movements and Cycles of Protest." *Revista Internacional de Sociologia* 74: e-044. https://www.academia.edu/29402436/Introduction_Rethinking_the_ Consequences_of_Social_Movements_and_Cycles_of_Protest.

Van Dyke, Nella, and Marc Dixon. 2013. "Activist Human Capital." *Mobilization* 18: 197–212.

Verhoeven, Imrat, and Jan Willem Duyvendak. 2017. "Understanding Governmental Activism." *Social Movement Studies* 16: 564–577.

Viterna, Jocelyn. 2013. *Women in War*. New York: Oxford University Press.

Volkov, Denis. 2012. "The Protesters and the Public." *Journal of Democracy* 23: 55–62.

Volkov, Leonid. n.d. Upravleniye politicheskoy kampaniyey ["Managing a political campaign"] [Online course]. https://www.eduson.tv/courses/65.

Volpi, Frédéric, and Janine A. Clark. 2019. "Activism in the Middle East and North Africa in Times of Upheaval: Social Networks' Actions and Interactions." *Social Movement Studies* 18: 1–16.

Volpi, Frédéric, and James M. Jasper, eds. 2018. *Microfoundations of the Arab Uprisings*. Amsterdam: Amsterdam University Press.

Voss, Kim. 1993. *The Making of American Exceptionalism*. Ithaca, NY: Cornell University Press.

Wagner-Pacifici, Robin. 2000. *Theorizing the Standoff*. New York: Cambridge University Press.

Walker, Edward T., and Lina Stepick. 2013. "Strength in Diversity? Group Heterogeneity in the Mobilization of Grassroots Organizations." *Sociology Compass* 8: 959–975.

Wallerstein, Immanuel. 2002. "New Revolts against the System." *New Left Review* 18: 29–39.

Walzer, Michael. 1983. *Spheres of Justice*. New York: Basic Books.

Weber, Max. 1978. *Economy and Society*. Berkeley: University of California Press.

Weisskircher, Manès. 2019. "The Electoral Success of the Radical Left. Explaining the Least Likely Case of the Communist Party in Graz, Austria." *Government and Opposition* 54: 145–166.

Wiwa, Ken. 2000. *In the Shadow of a Saint*. New York: Alfred Knopf.

Wong, Joshua. 2015. "Scholarism on the March." *New Left Review* 92: 43–52.

Wong, Stan Hok-Wui. 2015. *Electoral Politics in Post-1997 Hong Kong.* Singapore: Springer Press.

Wood, Alex J. 2021. *Despotism on Demand: How Power Operates in the Flexible Workplace.* Ithaca, NY: ILR Press.

Yakovlev, Alexey. 2013. "Alexey Navalny—Kandidat v mery Moskvy" ["Alexey Navalny—Moscow's Mayoral Candidate"] [Video file]. July 10 https://youtu.be/T3N9Ug1vvY8.

Yamasaki, Sakura. 2009. "A Boolean Analysis of Movement Impact on Nuclear Energy Policy." *Mobilization* 14: 485–504.

Young, Kevin, and Michael Schwartz. 2014. "A Neglected Mechanism of Social Movement Political Influence." *Mobilization* 19: 239–260.

Young, Lauren. 2016. "The Psychology of Political Risk: The Effect of Fear on Participation in Collective Dissent." Paper presented to the Politics and Protest Workshop, New York.

# Index

*For the benefit of digital users, indexed terms that span two pages (e.g., 52–53) may, on occasion, appear on only one of those pages.*
Tables are indicated by *t* following the page number